THE THOUSAND FACES OF VIRTUAL REALITY

Edited by **Cecília Sík Lányi**

The Thousand Faces of Virtual Reality
http://dx.doi.org/10.5772/58637
Edited by Cecília Sík Lányi

Contributors

Florin Graur, Igor Belič, Zahari Taha, Hwa Jen Yap, Hui Kang Choo, Chee Khean Kok, Haruhisa Kawasaki, Tetsuya Mouri, Stephane . Bouchard, Alcínia Zita Almeida Sampaio, Luis Viana, Dong Zhao, Cecília Sík Lányi, Veronika Szucs, Silvia Paxian

Published by InTech

Janeza Trdine 9, 51000 Rijeka, Croatia

Publishing Process Manager Iva Lipovic

Technical Editor InTech DTP team

Cover InTech Design team

First published December, 2014

Printed in Croatia

Additional hard copies can be obtained from orders@intechopen.com

The Thousand Faces of Virtual Reality, Edited by Cecília Sík Lányi

p. cm.

ISBN 978-953-51-1733-9

For EU product safety concerns:
IN TECH d.o.o., Prolaz Marije Krucifikse Kozulić 3, 51000 Rijeka, Croatia,
info@intechopen.com or visit our website at intechopen.com.

Meet the editor

Dr. Cecília Sik Lányi studied Mathematics and Computer Science (M.S.) – József Attila University (1984), and Teacher of Mathematics - Berzsenyi Dániel Teacher Training College in 1988. She obtained the degree of Dr. Univ. at the University of Veszprém, Hungary in Physical-chemistry (1993), and PhD at the University of Veszprém, Hungary in Computer Science (2000). She has worked as a software engineer and as an associate professor for program languages at the University of Pannonia. Currently she is teaching: Virtual Reality and its application, user interface design, and computer graphics for informatics engineering students. PhD and Masters' supervision has an emphasis on Virtual Reality for the rehabilitation of children with disabilities and patients with mental health issues. She got the "Master teacher" award of the Hungarian Ministry of Education in 2001. She has published more than 300 refereed articles and conference papers, and worked as guest editor for many renowned journals and books. Her research area is Virtual Reality, Human Computer Interaction, Design for All.

Contents

Preface

Virtual Reality (VR) has thousand faces. Why? Because from the moment of VR's birth we use it in every field of our life. VR is based on the development of information technology, computer graphics, and strong high speed hardware. Virtual Reality has emerged as a major new technology in the mid 1990s. It became commonplace in our increasingly technological world in recent years. These Virtual Reality Applications comprise almost all fields of the real life activities. VR has high impact not only on research, but on our daily living as well. In this book we have chosen certain areas to cover, which we believe to have potential significant impact on VR and its applications. This book has an aim to present applications, trends and newest development in three main disciplines: health sector, education and industry. In this book several new applications are presented in three sections. The first part of the book deals with health care applications. It is followed by a literature review of Augmented Reality (AR). The second section contains industry field education disciplines. The last part shows several industry applications and research.

The main features of the book can be summarised as follows:

• The book describes and evaluates the current state of the art in the field of VR.

• It also presents several applications of VR in the fields of learning environments, simulations, industry applications and healthcare applications.

• Contributors to the book are the leading researchers from academia and practitioners from the industry.

This book provides a definitive resource for wide variety of people including academicians, designers, developers, educators, engineers, practitioners, researchers and graduate students.

We would like to thank the authors for their contributions. Without their expertise and effort, this book would have never been born. InTech editors and staff also deserve our sincere recognition for their support throughout the project.

Finally, the editor would like to thank her family for their patience, Professor Janos Schanda, the head of the Virtual Environments and Imaging Technologies Research Laboratory, for giving her the freedom of research, for the help of all her co-workers at the Laboratory and, last but not least, the work for her students.

Cecília Sik Lányi
Associate professor at the University of Pannonia
Veszprém, Hungary

Section 1

Health Care Applications and AR

Chapter 1

Using Virtual Reality to Provide a Naturalistic Setting for the Treatment of Pathological Gambling

Stéphane Bouchard, Claudie Loranger,
Isabelle Giroux, Christian Jacques and
Geneviève Robillard

Additional information is available at the end of the chapter

http://dx.doi.org/10.5772/59240

1. Introduction

Recent studies reveal psychotherapy is effective in reducing gambling behaviours [1, 2]. However, an important issue in treating pathological gambling is that, despite understanding the negative consequences of continued gambling, problem gamblers at times experience an overwhelming craving to gamble [3]. Furthermore, the therapeutic work carried out when patients are emotionally distant from the gambling situation, such as in a therapist's office, is hard to transfer to real-life tempting situations.

Previous researches have studied the efficacy of imaginal [4, 5]; and *in vivo* exposure to gambling-related cues in order to reduce gamblers' cravings [6-9] either in cue exposure therapy or as part of a broader Cognitive-Behaviour Therapy (CBT) package where skills are developed or strengthened while confronted to the addictive stimuli [10, 11]. In imaginal exposure, patients are asked to imagine different stimuli, while *in vivo* exposure requires the physical presentation of the stimuli. Results from these studies indicate that these two forms of exposure therapy can help reduce cravings among pathological gamblers [4, 9] and generate broader therapeutic impact such as significant improvements on other gambling variables and psychopathological symptoms [4, 8].

Since the 90s, a new kind of exposure tool has appeared in clinical psychology: Virtual Reality (VR) or *in virtuo* exposure [12, 13, 14]. VR can be defined as "an application that makes it possible for the user to navigate and to interact in real time with an environment in three dimensions generated by a computer" [15]. *In virtuo* exposure is usually conducted using a Head Mounted Display (HMD or helmet) which is a pair of goggles allowing the presentation of images in stereoscopy, combined with audio stimuli and a motion tracker that follows the user's head movements [13,14]. Both for cue exposure and broader CBT package, VR presents the same advantages as imaginal exposure since it offers great control over different stimuli and the rhythm of exposure in a context that assures patients' confidentiality and eliminates many ethical problems unlike *in vivo* exposure. However, VR also presents some advantages over imaginal exposure because it reduces problems related to lack of memory, difficulties inducing emotions solely with thoughts or patients' refusal to fully access their memories [13,14]. Finally, VR allows therapists to control the impact of stimuli related to patients' other addictions on the course of therapy. For example, alcohol, cigarettes or drugs could also be found in a virtual environment to provide specific cues for a patient. VR also offers the possibility to conduct exposure and relapse prevention in various locations (for example, a bar or casino) that could provoke different reactions in the same person. The fact that VR is interactive and very similar to real-life situations could also positively influence gamblers' perceptions about therapy and encourage them to seek treatment. But they key argument in favor of using VR is its potential to replicate an environment where addictive behavior is usually taking place, thereby allowing to witness pathological gamblers' emotions and dysfunctional behaviors, and accessing their mental state as it is operating in gambling situations. Replicating gambling situations with a naturalistic setting in the safety of the therapist's office should be quite an advantage to treatment efficacy.

A significant number of outcome studies have been conducted where CBT is combined with VR to treat anxiety disorders [16]. Indeed, VR exposure has shown its efficacy in the treatment of acrophobia, claustrophobia, arachnophobia, fear of driving, fear of flying, social anxiety disorder (fear of speaking in public) and posttraumatic stress disorder [17]. Less work has been done with addictions, but researchers have shown that VR can be used with pathological gamblers, either for experimental research, to induce cravings or in single-case trials.

In 2008, a study using VR by Young and colleagues [3] revealed that for pathological gamblers, the desire to gamble was influenced by wins, losses and the different amounts won which was not the case for non-gamblers. This research is interesting because it shows VR can induce a desire to gamble, but it didn't use VR as a treatment tool. The first study using VR in a CBT program for pathological gambling was realized in Spain [18]. Unfortunately, results from this research were never officially published.

In the current chapter, two virtual environments and their clinical applications for pathological gambling and co-occurring problems will be detailed. First, data from a validation study and a pilot clinical trial with gamblers will be presented. Then, a presentation of a CBT manual for using VR will follow. The two virtual environments described in this chapter, a bar and a casino, were the first in North America designed for the treatment of pathological gambling to be empirically tested [19, 20]. Note that the choice of Video Lottery Terminals (VLT) in bars and slot machines in casinos was based on epidemiological data on gambler's playing habits [21].

Before using these two environments in treatment (see section 2.1.2 for a detailed description), a validation study was conducted in order to determine if they could induce a desire to gamble [19,20]. First, a training immersion in VR was performed to allow participants learning how to navigate in VR and manipulate the equipment. All immersions were performed on a PC computer with an nVisor SX HMD, a pair of computer loudspeakers, an Intersence Cube2 motion tracker for measuring head rotations, a wireless mouse for translations / navigation in the virtual environments, and a box with push-buttons allowing the user to physically interface and play with the VLT and slot machines. Second, participants removed the HMD and had to physically play a game of Scrabble™ (a control condition where the game is not significantly based on chance) with the experimenter for a period of 7 minutes. Then, participants were randomly assigned to 7 minutes of playing on: a real VLT (gold standard control condition), playing VLT in a virtual bar (VR bar condition), and playing slot machines in a virtual casino (VR casino condition). Subjects' desire to gamble was assessed after each game with the Gambling Craving Scale (GACS) [22] and physiological reactions (skin conductance and heart rate) were measured throughout the experiment. It is noteworthy that participants recruited for this validation study (n=67) had prior experience with games of chance and VLTs but were not pathological gamblers. Participants presenting a potential gambling problem according to the South Oaks Gambling Screen (SOGS) [23] were excluded from the project and referred to proper resources. Accepted participants were divided in two categories according to self-reported frequency of gambling: frequent gamblers (played at least once a month with VLT or slot machines) or non-gamblers (played a maximum of twice a year). Results show that physiological arousal (according to the skin conductance), desire to gamble, and anticipation of positive mood while gambling were statistically higher in the frequent gamblers group than in the non-gamblers group for the real VLT and the two virtual environments. The Time by Condition interaction was significant [$F_{(3,186)}=11.53$, $p<.001$] and revealed that, compared to playing Scrabble™, the craving to gamble was increased as significantly in the two virtual conditions than with the real VLT for the gamblers group. In sum, the two virtual environments seemed to provoke among gamblers the same desire to gamble than a real machine, even if no real money was involved [19,20].

A pilot clinical trial was then conducted with 28 pathological gamblers participating in a 28-day residential CBT program with group and individual interventions [20]. A more affordable HMD was used and the treatment was adapted from an already validated CBT program developed by Ladouceur [24]. Only two sessions of the CBT program were modified to include VR (the first and last sessions described further in this chapter), allowing to compare the use of imaginal exposure (standard technique) with immersions in virtual reality in the bar. Participants were randomly assigned either to the virtual reality condition or the imaginal exposure condition. Results revealed that the first VR immersion allowed finding significantly more high risk situations and more dysfunctional thoughts than the standard imaginal exposure exercise [20]. In the second experimental therapy session, devoted to relapse prevention, immersion in the virtual bar was associated with stronger changes in urges to gamble compared with the imaginal exposure condition. Furthermore, a multiple regression predicting pre to post-treatment improvements revealed that the strength of changes in urges to gamble induced during the relapse prevention session significantly predicted patients' improvements [$F_{(1,19)}=5.13$, $p<.025$]. Finally, another interesting finding from this clinical trial is that no ethical issue or adverse events were reported following the use of VR [20] (e.g., inducing cravings that would be too intense).

2. Description of a treatment manual using VR

Following the pilot clinical trial described above [19,20], a randomized control trial was launched, this time using four sessions devoted to immersions in VR. Two additional sessions devoted to conducting cognitive restructuring were added. These sessions were not included in the pilot studies due to logistical constraints and were positively anticipated by the therapists. Their advantage is to allow conducting cognitive restructuring while patients are emotionally aroused and operate on an "emotional mode" instead of a "cold logical mode" that translates poorly to what happens in potential gambling situations. The treatment illustrated in this chapter refers to the virtual bar in the examples, but details about using the virtual casino in therapy are also mentioned. Detailing how to effectively treat pathological gambling is outside the scope of this book and, therefore, using our program requires professionals to become familiar with traditional CBT programs (e.g., such as the one developed by Ladouceur et al [24]) and this clinical population. The following sections will: (a) briefly introduce the equipment required and different features of the virtual environments; (b) suggest sessions when to use immersion in virtual reality; (c) describe in details the four therapy sessions where virtual reality can be exploited (identifying high risk situations, conducting cognitive restructuring and practicing relapse prevention techniques); and (d) address potential problems during immersion and related solutions.

2.1. Description of the equipment and of the virtual environments

2.1.1. Equipment

In the pilot [20] and current clinical trials, immersion in VR is conducted with an immersive version of the virtual bar with the help of a HMD (iWear VR920 from Vuzix), head-tracking system (Cube2 from Intersence), speakers, a wireless mouse, and a box with pushbuttons replicating the interface panel of a real VLT. Visual and audio stimuli from the virtual environment were controlled by the user's movements and external stimuli were essentially blocked when wearing the HMD. This immersive version allowed the user to feel completely present in the virtual environment and make him forget that he or she is actually in his therapist's office[1]. The pushbutton control box does not have to be used if therapists do not feel comfortable allowing their patients to actually play at a game of chance.

This immersive equipment provides a visual field of view of 32-degrees and a reliable 3 degrees-of-freedom head tracking, allowing the user to explore with the mouse a rather large area and interacting with virtual objects and virtual characters in the environments. Sound files are triggered and their loudness modulated by the proximity of various stimuli (e.g., music starts when entering the bar, sounds from the reels of the slot machines in the casino become louder as you approach the machines) or by the therapist (i.e., to have the barman talk with

1 A less immersive version of the system is also available but it has not been tested with patients yet. In the non-immersive version, the virtual environments are simply presented on a computer screen, without the need of a HMD and motion tracking. However, there is no data documenting that a non-immersive VR system could be effective in the treatment.

the user), and the pushbutton box allows selecting how many lines to bet on, how much credits to bet, and to start / stop the VLT machines.

2.1.2. Virtual environments

The virtual bar (named *Chez Fortune / At Fortunes*) and the virtual casino (named *Les 3Dés / The 3Dices*) were created at the Cyberpsychology Lab of UQO with the intention of simulating a gambling situation without the use of real money (see Figure 1 and 2). Any resemblance with real locations and these fictive locations is fortuitous.

Figure 1. Screenshots of the virtual bar Chez Fortune / At Fortune

Figure 2. Screenshots of the virtual casino Les 3Dés / The 3Dices

A hierarchy has been constructed in the virtual bar to guide interventions, with users progressively approaching the machines where they can gamble (see steps 1 to 7 on Figure 3) and, in the last two steps of the hierarchy, actually sitting and playing. Users are invited to walk to each step of the hierarchy and apply various CBT techniques described later in the chapter: (1) at the starting point outside of the bar, in front of the ATM machine; (2) at the entrance doors of the bar, with two people smoking outside; (3) at the bar, in front of the waitress; (4) further inside the bar, in front of the barman; (5) even further inside the bar and closer to the VLTs; (6) close to the washroom, very near of the VLTs; (7) right in front of two available VLTs (one VLT becomes available after the therapist activates an animation where a frustrated player leaves his seat); (8) the user is now allowed to sit and gamble 20 virtual dollars; (9) the user continues gambling more money and keeps playing as long as desired.

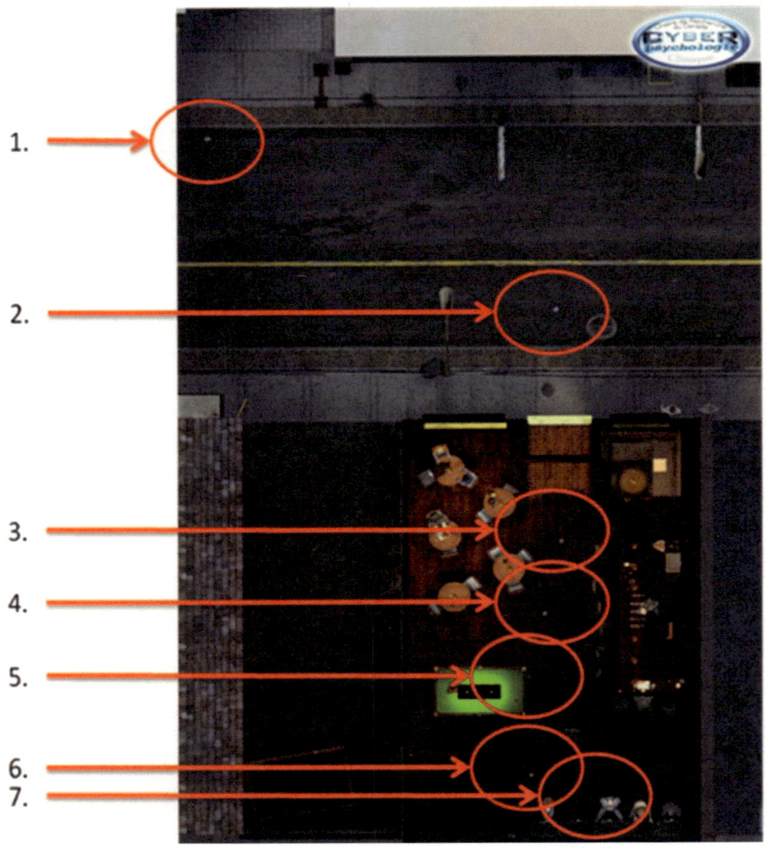

Figure 3. Birds-eye view of the virtual bar and first seven steps of the hierarchy

The objective with the hierarchy of pre-identified steps is to allow the user to progress gradually in the environment. During the immersion, the therapist can invite the user to stop at each step and observe the environment. Users can also be encouraged to share their thoughts and feelings at different steps. Users should always be told they can end their progression or the immersion whenever they want. It is noteworthy that the two last steps of the hierarchy were not used in the pilot clinical trial because gambling was not permitted in the treatment centers [20], but they are used in one center involved in the current randomized clinical trial. Therapists should use their clinical judgement when assessing gambler's urges to gamble, emotional stability and readiness to move to the next steps, as they always remain accountable for the safety of their patients.

2.2. Before using VR with pathological gamblers

Before introducing patients to VR, therapists should always assess the presence of any health conditions that could provoke or aggravate VR-induced unwanted side-effects, often called cybersickness [25,26]. Cybersickness is not a disease but a reaction which could occurs during or after an immersion in a virtual environment. It is similar to motion sickness and essentially includes three categories of symptoms: (1) visual symptoms (eyestrains, blurred vision, headaches), (2) disorientation (vertigo, imbalance) and (3) nausea (vomiting, dizziness) [25]. These symptoms are normal, temporary and can be prevented to some extent. For example, people under the influence of alcohol or other psychoactive drugs should not be immersed in a virtual environment. Also, VR shouldn't be used with patients presenting medical conditions such as serious cardiac problems, epilepsy, vestibular problems, and migraines (see [26] for a more exhaustive list). People suffering from comorbid psychotic disorders should probably not be immersed in VR because of their difficulties with reality testing.

Even in users in good health condition, cybersickness have to be assessed throughout the immersions. Different questionnaires, such as the Simulator Sickness Questionnaire [25], allow clinicians to monitor these symptoms when they use VR. In sum, the therapist's evaluation of his patient's health and his clinical judgement are always necessary before conducting immersion in VR and to pursue the immersions. In research settings, in order to prepare the patient to *in virtuo* exposure to gambling-related cues and control for the effect of novelty, it is common to start with an immersion in a training environment. The purpose of a training environment is to allow the user to learn how to use the equipment in a context devoid of stimuli eliciting strong emotions or cravings. It also offers a good opportunity for clinicians to assess the presence of cybersickness, as some symptoms may be confounded with physiological symptoms of arousal and cravings (e.g., sweating).

Since the virtual environments induce real cravings to gamble [19], it is very important for the clinician to determine if the patient is ready for such an exercise and implement strategies to cope with strong urges if they occur. The immersion in a gambling situation has to be conducted by trained therapists. Gamblers who's cravings have been stimulated during a therapy session should be followed closely by the staff to ensure that this experience is positively integrated emotionally, is not destabilizing the patient too much, and is leading to a positive therapeutic outcome instead of a worsening of the situation. Because it is more difficult to check on gamblers after an immersion session that elicited urges to gamble in an outpatient setting, clinical wisdom suggest using this technique in inpatients settings until its safety has been documented. In addition to urges induced by the immersion, other factors could put the gambler at risk for discomfort or relapse. These risks are usually implicitly controlled in a residential treatment facility, where access to cues associated with gambling and other addictions are absent. However, although VLT are not available on the premises of a residential facility, they are in the virtual environments, and this environment may be accessible if it is stored in an unlocked room of the residence. Seeing alcoholic beverages during an immersion in VR could elicit emotional reactions in a gambler who also has issues with alcohol. Witnessing people enjoying gambling in a virtual casino can trigger sadness in a person who must accept to become abstinent. Again, the take home message is that VR is a clinical tool that must be used by mental health professional using their clinical judgment.

As mentioned earlier, in the context of the treatment of pathological gambling, three specific moments are suggested for the use of VR immersion: (a) at the beginning of treatment, to identify high risk situations and erroneous perceptions about gambling, (b) at mid treatment, to implement cognitive restructuring of dysfunctional beliefs, and (c) at the end of therapy, to practice relapse prevention techniques.

2.3. Illustration of the four sessions of VR immersion in the virtual bar

2.3.1. First immersion: Identifying high risk situations

Before the identification of high risk situations with the help of the virtual environment, it is important to prepare the patient for the immersion. As mentioned previously, an evaluation of the user's health condition should be done before using VR. Cybersickness should also be discussed with patients and it is recommended to use a training environment to allow users to feel more comfortable with the equipment. Since the virtual environments induce a desire to gamble, therapists have to inform their patients of this possible consequence. It is also important to discuss the objective of the session with the patient before starting the immersion. Users should be encouraged to express out loud their feelings and thoughts during the immersion. Communication with the user is always possible during immersion in VR and is important to pace the progression of the immersion. However, constant verbal interventions from therapist could make some users feel less present in the virtual environment since it could be a continuous reminder that the situation is not real. Clinicians can use brief questions or 0-10 scales to measure users' desire to gamble, self-efficacy or cybersickness for example. Since the patient in the virtual environment doesn't have a visual contact with his therapist, every questionnaire or scale used should be presented in detail before the immersion.

For this first immersion in VR, 20 minutes should be enough to go through the identified steps in the virtual environment. It is also possible to repeat the user's progression through the environment multiple times. The goal of the session is to detect as many stimuli, behaviors and dysfunctional thoughts associated with situations that represent a high risk of gambling. During the immersion, the therapist says: "*Please behave naturally and say openly what comes through your mind during this visit in the bar. You can describe what you see that triggers the desire to gamble, your thoughts and ideas, your observations, what you would do in such a situation, or it you think of situations you would avoid because you could lose control of your desire to gamble.*" The therapist is encouraged to explore the situation with the patient, ask if some elements could trigger urges (e.g., walking pass an ATM located close to a place where it is possible to gamble, on a payday). The therapist must pay attention to patient's behaviors that would be representative of gambling patterns (e.g., a patient once checked both his left and right pocket for money, revealing his habit of putting some money in his right pocket to increase his winning chances). When the therapist has gathered enough information, or if the patient asks to end the immersion, the patient should be asked to walk out of the bar before actually taking off the HMD. In some case, it has been revealing to ask patient to go back to the ATM and return the money they didn't use. Since the first session of immersion takes place at the beginning of therapy, it is normal for most gamblers to feel an urge to gamble during or after exposure to gambling related cues. Thus, therapists can decide to discuss more thoroughly the identified high risk situations with their patients, and it is wise to dedicate the last minutes of the session to try to reduce the gambler's craving. Some patients are shocked by the strength of their reactions; despite the fact this is a simulation. This can be explored as a motivation for the therapy (e.g., starting the discussion with *"If this makes you react so strongly, imagine how it would be in a real life situation. What conclusion can we draw from this regarding your own situation?"*). Table 1 summarizes the essential instructions for the first session of immersion.

Before the immersion	During the immersion	After the immersion
• Prepare your VR session (e.g., launch program) • Assess patient's health condition. • Explain cybersickness. • Practice with a training environment. • Inform about inducing and managing cravings. • Explain the objectives of the session.	• Guide the patient through the different steps. • Encourage the patient to openly share all feelings and thoughts. • Ask about high risk situations and perceptions about gambling. • Use your creativity to gather as much relevant information as possible. • Observe the presence of cybersickness. • Write down all information relevant to high risk situations (stimuli, thoughts, emotions, behaviors, etc.).	• Verify the actual desire to gamble. • Reduce patient's urge to gamble, if any. • Observe a reduction in cybersickness, if any. • Discuss the identified high risk situations and perceptions about gambling. • Assess perceived self-efficacy to control gambling. • Use other therapeutic techniques if needed (e.g., motivational interviewing).

Table 1. Key points for therapists to remember for the first immersion in VR

2.3.2. Second and third immersions: Conducting cognitive restructuring

It is now time for therapists to exploit VR to challenges patients' dysfunctional beliefs while emotionally aroused. Dysfunctional thoughts contributing to the pathological gambling [2,6,21] fall into two large categories: (a) those about specific maintaining factors underlying pathological gambling and, (b) those about perceived control toward one's own gambling behavior. The second category plays a significant role to maintain pathological gambling but is addressed more thoroughly in the session devoted to relapse prevention [21] and should not be targeted before enough therapy time has been allocated to other maintaining factors. Several erroneous and dysfunctional beliefs are involved in the treatment of gambling addiction [21], including illusory perception of control[2] regarding games of chance (e.g., "I have a trick to beat the odds and make money"), gambling as a positive source of pleasure (e.g., "I feel good when I'm playing"), gambling as an effective solution to avoid negative mood (e.g., "Gambling allows me to forget my problems"), facilitating / permissive beliefs (e.g., "It's all right to play today and I'll bet only 20$"), going to a gambling place to socialize with other gamblers (e.g., "I have fun with other people sharing my passion"), superstitions (e.g., "If I press the button quickly three times I have more chances to win because 3 is a lucky number"), and beliefs specific each game (e.g., for VLT, "This machine is due to pay because it has not been used for a while and the previous player lost a lot of money on it").

The assessment, case conceptualisation and previous therapy sessions, including the first immersion in VR, should have provided the therapist with a good understanding of the specific beliefs that maintain the patients gambling addiction. These beliefs are usually addressed by therapists using traditional cognitive restructuring techniques, which essentially involves helping patients identifying core beliefs and challenging them. Exercises that have been developed for traditional CBT packages [for more information, see 1,6,7,10, 21] can be used during the immersions in the virtual bar. At immersions 2 and 3, the patient is invited to wear the HMD and walk through the nine steps previously explored, until he or she reaches a desire to gamble that is sufficiently strong yet manageable. The therapists can then ask about thoughts that give the urge to gamble, challenge them, and help the patient come with thoughts that give control over the urge to gamble. Dysfunctional thoughts occurring before, during and after typical gambling sessions should be questioned. Because these thoughts are strongly believed in, it will probably take more than one session to counteract all of them, which explains why two sessions are devoted to this step. Exercises to conduct after the immersion are important to continue master the skills of cognitive restructuring and gain confidence in the more adaptive and functional beliefs. Moreover, having the patient emotionally aroused makes it even more difficult to create doubt, revise erroneous beliefs and reframe the situation. Presenting the technique of cognitive restructuring, detailing the key role of dysfunctional thoughts and initiating cognitive restructuring should either be introduce before the immersion, or *in virtuo* at the first step of the hierarchy, before emotional arousal influences objectivity. Finally, it is important to underline that cognitive restructuring is not a heated logical debate between the patient and the therapist; it is a set of tool where the therapist constructively guide the patient to develop thoughts reflecting more accurately the realities of gambling and that are in line with their goal of putting an end to pathological gambling. When the session is over, we again encourage the patient to exit the bar and go to the ATM to put back the money in his or her bank account. This is another interesting moment to observe dysfunctional thoughts and behaviors and to foster motivation.

These two immersions are good opportunities for therapists to: (a) have access to emotions in patients that appear very rational; (b) work on potential situations of denial (e.g., when patients are describing reactions that do not correspond to what is observed *in virtuo*);

---

2 Note the distinction between illusion of control towards the possibility to win at a game of chance, which is targeted during immersions 2 and 3, and the illusion of control toward oneself that is addressed during the immersion devoted to relapse prevention.

http://dx.doi.org/10.5772/59240

(c) observe physiological reactions associated with cravings, (d) catch dysfunctional beliefs and behaviors associated with expectations to win; (e) increase perceived self-efficacy to challenges strongly held beliefs when emotions are blurring logical thinking, and (f) tests the believability and strength of alternative more functional beliefs. More than two sessions may be necessary and future research will show what are the most efficient ways to use VR for cognitive restructuring.

2.3.3. Fourth immersion: Practicing relapse prevention techniques

This session occurs toward the end of the treatment and by then gamblers should already have learned different skills to build their self-efficacy about refraining from gambling. Before this last immersion in VR, the therapist should always verify with their patients if they wants to proceed with the immersion since it will confront them with gambling situations and could induce cravings. The main goal of this immersion is to increase patients' feeling of control over the desire to gamble. Relapse prevention exercises can be practiced in multiple contexts with the virtual environments. In the virtual bar, the user can rate his self-efficacy at any of the nine hierarchy steps in order to determine which situations to choose for the exercise. It is recommended to pick an easier situation to start with (i.e. where the gambler thinks he could easily resist temptation to engage in the behavioral chain of excessive gambling) and to follow with a more difficult situation (i.e. the gambler believes he would have a hard time resisting urges to gamble). For example, one relapse prevention technique could be to replace thoughts that increase the user's desire to gamble with thoughts that increase his feeling of control over himself in situation [10, 11, 21, 24]. The last session of immersion could also be very helpful for gamblers who believe they still can gamble small amounts of money without losing control. The therapist could allow the patient to virtually gamble 20$ and encourage him to observe his reactions in this situation. An important arousal or an overwhelming urge to gamble more money could be good indicators for the patient that he can't allow himself to gamble even small amounts without relapsing. The ability of the patient to resist his desire to gamble should be strongly reinforced by the therapist during and after the VR immersion. As it was the case for all other immersions, the immersion should end with the patient walking out of the bar. At this moment, if the user's desire to gamble is still high, more CBT interventions should be proposed. In this context, the virtual environment could also be considered as an assessment tool to verify gambler's readiness to end the treatment. The patient and the therapist can use the last immersion to identify the most appropriate behavioral techniques in different contexts and discuss the gambler's preferred exercises. The advantage of VR is to offer a naturalistic environment to test the skills acquired during the treatment, without actually having to leave the office and go in a place where it is possible to play at games of chance.

A few potential difficulties have been identified from experience with pathological gamblers or *in virtuo* exposure for other disorders. The next section describes these problems and proposes clinical strategies to facilitate the intervention.

2.4. Potential problems during immersion and possible solutions

2.4.1. The patient presents an intense desire to gamble after the immersion

If the gambler feels an important craving to gamble after leaving the virtual environment, many strategies are available. First, therapists should anticipate this situation and plan their sessions to have enough time after the immersion to complete other interventions (e.g., at least 20 minutes). Sometimes, reviewing previous exercises or discussing other matters less related to gambling is enough to significantly reduce the desire to gamble. During the session, the therapist can also discuss with the patient his motivation to stop gambling and write down the negative consequences of this behaviour in his life. It can also be interesting for the therapist to ask his patient what he usually does when he has an urge to gamble (talking to someone, sports, breathing exercises, reading therapy notes). Finally, if the desire to gamble is still present at the end of the session it might be important to involve other experienced professionals (e.g. in a residential facility) or a patient's relative or members of support group (with his permission) to refrain engaging in gambling behaviors.

2.4.2. The patient doesn't want to stop at the different steps and consistently asks to gamble on the VLT

First, the therapist can disable the possibility to use the VLT by simply unpluging the pushbutton playing interface. Thus, the immersion in the virtual environment can be pursued and if the user sits in front of a VLT to gamble it will not be possible to activate the VLT. Since this strong desire to gamble is very similar to what the patient might face in real-life situations, it is a powerful context for interventions. Thus, it is important that the therapist helps the gambler realize that his craving to gamble and his loss of control over the situation are not virtual. Finally, the emotional arousal of the gambler can be helpful in the identification of high risk situations and erroneous perceptions about gambling. Once the automatic thoughts are identified, the therapist can apply cognitive restructuring to reduce the desire to gamble.

2.4.3. The patient doesn't feel any desire to gamble and is indifferent to the environment

Some patients have negative appraisals about the use of VR. For example, if the patient keeps telling himself that "it is not real" during the immersion, the possibility to practice *in virtuo* effective interventions is unlikely. Some gamblers might also think that the immersion is a "trap" or a "test". Thus, it is important for the therapist to verify the presence of these automatic thoughts and apply cognitive restructuring if necessary. If the patient is indifferent despite the absence of such automatic thoughts, it can also be helpful to ask the patient to narrate a previous session of gambling before the immersion or while he is in the virtual environment. The therapist can try to induce a desire to gamble with specific questions about favourite games, previous wins, etc... This last strategy should only be used with the patient's permission. If the gambler does not want or is not ready to face his desire to gamble, the therapist should respect his decision and focus on other interventions that do not involve VR.

2.4.4. The patient is uncomfortable with VR technology

If the patient is worried by the use of the virtual environment, more time could be needed to answer questions about the equipment or cybersickness, for example. The immersion in the training environment could also last longer to allow the user to navigate comfortably with the equipment.

2.4.5. Patient's high risk situations are not reproducible in VR

Even if the patient's high risk situations are not similar to what is occurring in the virtual environments, an immersion in VR can still be useful. The therapist can encourage the patient to at least try the immersion to verify his feelings in this context. The immersion in the virtual environment could then be presented as a new situation the patient might face one day (e.g. "An old friend asks you to go out at the bar even if you don't usually like going there"). However, in some cases, the relevant gambling stimuli are simply not there in the virtual environment (e.g., for a patient addicted to Poker or other games of cards). In these cases, the immersion may be irrelevant and the therapist has to rely on traditional tools such as imaginal exposure.

2.4.6. The therapist can't help the patient to verbalize his thoughts

The verbalization of high risk situations and perceptions about gambling is essential in the treatment of pathological gamblers. Therapists who feel less competent with this strategy should consult classical CBT treatment manuals [10, 21, 24] or seek clinical supervision with more experienced professionals.

2.4.7. The patient is hesitant to try the immersion

Multiple studies have shown that exposure with pathological gamblers can have positive effects. A research by Echeburúa, Báez and Fernández-Montalvo [6] has indicated that an individualized intervention focused on stimulus control with graded *in vivo* exposure was better than cognitive restructuring or the combined use of these two treatment modalities. Two single case studies presented by Symes and Nicki [9] have resulted in considerable reductions in gambling behaviours after a treatment with exposure and response prevention. Therefore, if the patient is hesitant, the therapist must assess his fears, see if they are justified, and either not use VR or reassure the gambler and reframe his worries.

3. Using VR with gambling and co-occuring disorders

The validation study [19] and the pilot clinical trial [20] have indicated that the two virtual environments developed for the treatment of pathological gambling have a therapeutic potential for this specific addiction. Because a significant proportion of gamblers also suffer from substance abuse or dependence problems, the impact of other addictions on gambling behaviours and patients' reaction to stimuli in the environment need to be considered in VR sessions.

The possibility of immersion in VR to induce cravings has been demonstrated for different substances. Virtual environments including specific stimuli have been shown to produce strong cue responses to cigarette [27], alcohol [28], cannabis [29], methamphetamine [30], and crack cocaine [31]. Recent studies have explored the possibility to use VR in the treatment of addictions as well. A research by Bordnick and colleagues [32] assessed the feasibility of VR skills training in a CBT smoking cessation program. Their results show that smokers who completed a VR skills training treatment (in addition of a nicotine replacement therapy) had lower cravings and self-reported smoking than participants who received nicotine replacement therapy only. Their self-efficacy ratings were also higher after treatment and at follow-up [32]. These results are promising, but more research is clearly needed to measure VR's efficacy as a tool in the treatment of addictions.

Nevertheless, this study and others show that VR can induce cravings for other addictions, which has two implications for the treatment of gambling: (a) the possibility of gamblers reacting emotionally to cues that are irrelevant to games of chances while in the virtual environment due to co-occurring disorders (e.g., co-occurring alcoholism and seeing an open bottle of beer on a table); and (b) the possibility for skilled therapist to use stimuli irrelevant to games of chance to conduct treatment that either target both gambling and the co-occurring disorder (e.g., practicing relapse prevention skills for gambling while close to a table with an open bottle of beer) or target the treatment of gambling in the context of emotions elicited by a co-occurring disorder.

Because virtual situations are designed to replicate the complex nature of day to day stressors, learning and practicing CBT skills in VR may be more representative of real life situations than in the therapist's office. Naturalistic settings like the virtual bar and casino described in this chapter include various stimuli that are associated with other addictions and could trigger unexpected reactions that are irrelevant to games of chances, such as cravings in people addicted to tobacco (e.g., two people are smoking at the entrance of bar), to alcohol (e.g. there are many open bottles of beer on tables and people drinking), to sex (e.g., the sexy waitress), etc. People suffering from co-occurring disorders unrelated to addictions can also react to cues in the virtual environments, as the virtual bar and casino include people from a variety of ages, skin tone, gender and revenues (which could trigger reactions in people suffering from social phobia or schizophrenia), a cat (e.g., for people suffering from cat phobia), food and people with various body shape (e.g., for people who are dissatisfied with their body image), a dark city atmosphere (e.g., for people suffering from agoraphobia), and an aggressive man hitting his VLT and leaving (e.g., for people suffering from posttraumatic stress disorder). Although these stimuli were not meant to be salient and strong enough to elicit reactions in the user, it is important for therapists to be aware of their existence. Actually, some therapist may even use these environments with people who suffer from a primary disorder other than gambling (e.g., practicing relapse prevention skills for alcohol using the open bottle of beer in the virtual bar, or using the virtual bar for *in virtuo* exposure with a phobic). It is important to recognize the existence of these contextual stimuli. It can help therapists preventing some unexpected reactions in gamblers, but most of all it gives the opportunity to practice CBT skills in settings that resemble complex real life situations.

For the skilled therapist, the existence of stimuli related to other substances or to other mental disorders offer opportunities to practice CBT skills and reinforce gamblers' self-efficacy in more challenging situations. The virtual casino and bar [19,20] offer multiple possibilities for working on multiple targets at the same time. For example, seeing the smokers at the door could provoke a nicotine craving in some patients, or a desire to drink could be induced by the multiple bottles of alcohol and people drinking at the bar. Therapists may have access to more dysfunctional beliefs and observe interactions between the two addictions when people with comorbid pathological gambling and alcoholism are in certain areas of the bar. Being in a virtual bar can facilitate the therapist's task of transferring skills learned with gambling with VLTs to addiction to alcohol. Practicing cognitive restructuring may become more difficult in the presence of several emotional triggers, but also richer in clinical material. Second, pathological gamblers with comorbid social phobia can work on interpersonal issues by using the virtual characters discussing in the casino. They can also use the proximity and attitude of virtual characters to make relapse prevention exercises more challenging. In these naturalistic contexts, VR presents the advantage of offering standardized environments in multiple declinations to conduct research or tailor exposure to patients' needs. Finally, a better understanding of contextual elements in situations leading to cravings (e.g., seeing signs indicating the presence of a VLT, accessibility of an ATM, seeing other people drinking) could lead to develop stronger CBT skills in pathological gambling and co-occurring disorders.

4. Conclusion

In sum, early experiments with two virtual environments have not only allowed our research team to measure the potential of an intervention tool that can induce cravings to gamble, but have also helped therapists discover new possibilities in the treatment of pathological gamblers. Multiple advantages of using immersion in VR have been identified by the therapists after the pilot clinical trial [20]. For example, therapists believed they could access more spontaneous reactions in more "rational" patients. It was also easier for them to access gamblers' emotional reactions and dysfunctional thoughts. Furthermore, the use of VR allowed them to reveal contradictions between patients' expressed ideas and their reactions or behaviours in the virtual environment. According to the therapists, the immersions in VR offered a great opportunity to assess patients' comprehension of new techniques, observe the integration of learned skills and reinforce self-efficacy. In addition, therapists believed immersion in VR allowed gamblers to acknowledge the physiological reactions associated with cravings and to properly evaluate their ability to control their cravings. Finally, therapists believed the use of VR could also eventually facilitate the identification of possible interventions for co-occurring disorders.

Taken altogether, results of the validation study, the clinical trial and clinicians' observations reveal that the integration of virtual reality in the treatment of pathological gamblers may leads to significant therapeutic improvements. In addition, the available data suggest this modality is innocuous, at least in the context of a residential treatment facility.

More research still needs to be done to assess the true potential of immersion in VR for pathological gamblers. Future studies should measure the efficacy of virtual reality as a treatment tool in different contexts of intervention, such as: (a) in a complete CBT package, which includes cognitive restructuring, (b) physiological assessment of gamblers' reactions in high risk situations to identify risk of relapse and the need to pursue treatment, (c) patients allowed to gamble on the virtual VLTs or slot machines to observe their emotions, thoughts and behaviours, (d) increasing or optimizing the number of immersions, and (e) exploiting more efficiently the assets of the virtual casino. Future investigation could also address questions such as: (a) the difference between the immersive and less immersive version of the virtual environments, (b) the distinction between cybersickness and physiological signs of craving or withdrawal, (c) the influence of virtual reality-related variables such as presence, and (d) the systematic integration of cues associated to other addictions. It is important for researchers to understand that virtual reality is not only a treatment tool, but it also offers a standardized and controlled context to conduct research. For example, virtual environments could be used to observe the neurophysiology of gamblers during cravings while using an fMRI scan or measure the impact of alcohol consumption on gambling behaviours.

Finally, the dissemination of virtual environments for psychological intervention is another important concern. First, the costs of the equipment required for the immersive version of the virtual environments need to be considered. Second, proper training is prerequisite to use VR adequately and insure patients' safety. However, the benefits of such technology seem to outweigh its downsides. The control over the stimuli, interest of patients for this new kind of treatment, ease to access emotions, and possibility to work in a context similar to real-life while staying in a safe situation, are all great advantages of using VR with people suffering from pathological gambling.

Acknowledgements

This chapter was made possible thanks to: (a) a grant awarded from the Fondation Mise Sur Toi to the Fondation de l'UQO to support the work from the Cyberpsychology Lab; (b) financial support from the Canada Research Chair in clinical cyberpsychology; (c) from an internal grant from the Centre de réadaptation en dependence de Montréal – IUD; and (d) a scholarship from the Fond de Recherche du Québec en Santé awarded to the second author. The authors wish to thank J. Boulanger, L. Brisson, A.C. Charrette, R. Fraser, L. Laniel, L. Poirier, A. Goulet, P.-M. Fournier, É. Fortin-Gagnon, and M. Beaulieu for their contribution in the development of the virtual environments and the original version of the treatment manual.

Author details

Stéphane Bouchard[1*], Claudie Loranger[1], Isabelle Giroux[2], Christian Jacques[2] and Geneviève Robillard[1]

*Address all correspondence to: stephane.bouchard@uqo.ca

1 Université du Québec en Outaouais, Gatineau, Canada

2 Université Laval, Québec, Canada

References

[1] Pallesen SL, Mitsem M, Kvale G, Johnsen BRH, Molde H (2005). Outcome of psychological treatments of pathological gambling: a review and meta-analysis. Addiction 100: 1412-1422. doi: 10.1111/j.1360-0443.2005.01204

[2] Toneatto T, Ladouceur R (2003). Treatment of pathological gambling: A critical review of the literature. Psychology of Addictive Behaviors 17: 284-292. doi: 10.1037/0893-164X.17.4.284

[3] Young M, Wohl M, Matheson K, Baumann S, Anisman H (2008). The desire to gamble: The influence of outcomes on the priming effects of a gambling episode. Journal of Gambling Studies, 24: 275-293. doi: 10.1007/s10899-008-9093-9

[4] Blaszczynski A, Drobny J, Steel Z (2005). Home-based imaginal desensitisation in pathological gambling: short-term outcomes. Behaviour Change 22: 13-21. doi: 10.1375/bech.22.1.13.66782

[5] McConaghy N, Blaszczynski A, Frankova A (1991). Comparison of imaginal desensitisation with other behavioural treatments of pathological gambling: a two to nine year follow-up. British Journal of Psychiatry 159: 390-393. doi: 10.1192/bjp.159.3.390

[6] Echeburúa E, Báez C, Fernández-Montalvo J (1996). Comparative effectiveness of three therapeutic modalities in the psychological treatment of pathological gambling: Long-term outcome. Behavioural and Cognitive Psychotherapy, 24: 51-72.

[7] Echeburúa E, Fernández-Montalvo J (2002). Psychological treatment of slot machine pathological gambling. Clinical Case Studies 1: 240-253.

[8] Echeburúa E, Fernández-Montalvo J, Baez C (2000). Relapse prevention in the treatment of slot-machine pathological gambling: long-term outcome. Behavior Therapy 31: 351-364. doi: 10.1016/S0005-7894(00)80019-2

[9] Symes BA, Nicki RM (1997). A preliminary consideration of cue-exposure, response-prevention treatment for pathological gambling behaviour: Two case studies. Journal of Gambling Studies 13: 145-157. doi: 10.1023/A:1024951301959

[10] Daley DC, Marlatt GA (1997). Managing Your Drug or Alcohol Problem : Therapist Guide. New York, Oxford University Press.

[11] Marlatt GA, Gordon JR (1985). Relapse prevention. New York, The Guilford Press.

[12] Bouchard S, Côté S, Richard DS (2006). Virtual reality applications of exposure. In DS Richard and D Lauterbach (Eds.) Handbook of exposure (Ch. 16), pp. 347-388. New York, Academic Press.

[13] Simon V, Sik Lányi C, Simon L (2005). Using virtual public transport for treating phobias. *International Journal on Disability and Human Development, Special issue on disability, virtual reality and associated technologies*, 4(3), 211-215.

[14] Sik Lányi C (2006). Virtual Reality in Healthcare. In A Ichalkaranje, A. et al. (Eds.), *Intelligent Paradigms for Assistive and Preventive Healthcare* (pp. 92-121). Springer-Verlag.

[15] Pratt DR., Zyda M, Kelleher K (1995). Virtual reality: In the mind of the beholder. IEEE Computer 28: 17-19. doi:10.1109/MC.1995.10085

[16] David D, Matu SA, David OA (2013). New directions in virtual reality-based therapy for anxiety disorders. International Journal of Cognitive Therapy, 6: 114-137.

[17] Gerardi M, Cukor J, Difede J, Rizzo A, Rothbaum BO (2010). Virtual reality exposure therapy for post-traumatic stress disorder and other anxiety disorders. Current Psychiatry Report 12: 298-305.doi:10.1007/s11920-010-0128-4

[18] Garcia-Palacios A, Lasso de la Vega N, Botella C, Banos R, Quero S (2006). Virtual reality in the treatment of pathological gambling. Oral presentation at the 11th Annual CyberTherapy 2006 Conference, Gatineau (Canada), June 13-15th.

[19] Loranger C, Bouchard S, Boulanger J, Robillard G (2011). Validation of two virtual environments for the prevention and treatment of pathological gambling. Journal of Cybertherapy & Rehabilitation 4 : 233-235.

[20] Bouchard S, Loranger C, Fournier PM, Fortin-Gagnon É, Jacques C, Giroux I, Beaulieu M, Brisson L, Charrette AC, Fraser R, Laniel L, Poirier L (2013). Guide d'utilisation des environnements virtuels pour les problèmes de jeu pathologique (version 1.5). Research Report. Laboratoire de Cyberpsychologie de l'UQO, Gatineau, Qc.

[21] Ladouceur R, Sylvain C, Boutin C, Doucet C (2002). Understanding and treating the pathological gambler. West Sussex, England, Wiley.

[22] Young MM, Wohl MJA (2009). The Gambling Craving Scale: Psychometric validation and behavioral outcomes. Psychology of Addictive Behaviors 23: 512-522. doi: 10.1037/a0015043.

[23] Lesieur HR, Blume SB (1987). The South Oaks Gambling Screen (SOGS): A new instrument for the identification of pathological gamblers. American Journal of Psychiatry 144 : 1184-1188.

[24] Ladouceur R, Boutin C, Doucet C, Lachance S, Sylvain C (2000). Programme d'évaluation et de traitement des joueurs excessifs. Manuel produit dans le cadre du Programme québécois sur le jeu pathologique mis en oeuvre par le Ministère de la Santé et des Services sociaux du Québec.

[25] Kennedy RS, Lane NE, Berbaum KS, Lilienthal MG (1993). Simulator Sickness Questionnaire: An enhanced method for quantifying simulator sickness. International Journal of Aviation Psychology 3: 203-220. doi:10.1207/s15327108ijap0303_3

[26] Lawson BD, Graeber D, Mead AM (2002). Signs and symptoms of human syndromes associated with synthetic experience. In KM Stanney (Ed.) Handbook of virtual environments: Design, implementation, and applications (pp. 589-618) Mahwah, NJ, IEA.

[27] Paris MM, Carter BL, Traylor AC, Bordnick PS, Day SX, et al. (2011). Cue reactivity in virtual reality: The role of context. Addictive Behaviors 36: 696-699. doi: 10.1016/j.addbeh.2011.01.029

[28] Ryan JJ, Kreiner DS, Chapman MD, Stark-Wroblewski K (2010). Virtual Reality Cues for Binge Drinking in College Students. Cyberpsychology, Behavior, and Social Networking 13: 159-162. doi:10.1089=cyber.2009.0211

[29] Bordnick PS, Copp HL, Traylor A, Graap KM, Carter BL, et al. (2009). Reactivity to cannabis cues in virtual reality environments. Journal of Psychoactive Drugs 41 : 105-112. doi:10.1080/02791072.2009.10399903

[30] Culbertson C, Nicolas S, Zaharovits I, London ED, De La Garza II R, et al. (2010). Methamphetamine craving induced in an online virtual reality environment. Pharmacology, Biochemistry and Behavior 96: 454-460. doi: 10.1016/j.pbb.2010.07.005

[31] Saladin ME, Brady KT, Graap K, Rothbaum BO (2006). A preliminary report on the use of virtual reality technology to elicit craving and cue reactivity in cocaine dependent individuals. Addictive Behaviors 31: 1881-1894. doi:10.1016/j.addbeh.2006.01.004

[32] Bordnick PS, Traylor AC, Carter BL, Graap KM (2012). A feasibility study of virtual reality-based coping skills training for nicotine dependence. Research on Social Work Practice 22: 293-300. doi: 10.1177/1049731511426880

Chapter 2

Virtual Reality in Medicine — Going Beyond the Limits

Florin Graur

Additional information is available at the end of the chapter

http://dx.doi.org/10.5772/59277

1. Introduction

In the last years technology had an explosive evolution in the development of new minimal invasive medical instruments and led to a novel need and a brand new field: virtual medicine.

Virtual reality is an "in silico" simulation of a real situation. In particular, in surgery, dimensional modeling of deformable objects with spatial characteristics and specific elastic-dynamic behavior is required. In addition, simulation of tools and their action against the organs in the virtual environment is also required.

The purpose of virtual medicine is to minimize the direct exploration of the human body in order to provide a virtual model for those who want to learn new techniques and to provide advanced treatment options for those who perform delicate maneuvers or in areas inaccessible by conventional methods: in short to minimize the invasiveness of treatment.

Also a number of virtual techniques tend to be held in the virtual environment of the Internet, allowing remote accessibility and an increased number of users.

This chapter is a literature review that explores the current virtual techniques used in research, education, treatment and development trends of these methods in the future.

2. Short history

First virtual system proposed in medicine was developed by Robert Mann in 1965 [1]. It was used to decide what the best procedure for a orthopedic disease would be. Also this system was used for training residents [2].

In the 60s, the first simulators with 3D images appeared. In the 80s the head mounted display (HDM) were developed and the term "virtual reality" was defined. Over a decade later came the application of virtual reality used in medical education (simulator of colonoscopy and upper gastrointestinal endoscopy) and the first simulator for laparoscopy appeared. The simulation systems became more advanced in time, but it was necessary to develop tactile interaction between man and machine. Haptic systems involve the transmission of information from human to computer and vice versa. Virtual reality nowadays is closely linked to haptic devices with force-feedback [2].

3. Research methods using virtualization in medicine

Among research methods using virtual medicine there are a number of examples of software that is used for the three-dimensional reconstruction of protein molecules. Understanding how proteins (whose structure of amino acids is known) are "packed" to reach the three-dimensional structure of the molecule and especially understanding errors of "packing", helps researchers in deciphering the molecular biology of diseases such as: Alzheimer's disease, mad cow disease, Huntington's disease, Parkinson's disease, cystic fibrosis and cancers.

The need for high computing power has led to the creation of online communities such as Rosetta@Home, Human Proteome Folding and Folding@Home. Within these communities an internet user can offer their unused computing capacity of its personal computer to participate in these projects [3-5].

The usefulness of these programs is to understand the physico-chemical properties of different types of proteins and different types of interactions between amino-acids, as well as the evaluation of local energy of short sequences of amino acids. This way the researchers could identify the structures with the lowest energy (i.e., the greatest stability) resulting in the most stable structure of the native protein. Moreover, one can understand the most predictable possibilities of packing for abnormal proteins that can cause diseases. Using computational power of multiple systems generates more structures and several search strategies are tested in order to identify the most effective one.

Foldit game is based on the Rosetta platform. The player or groups of players are able to manipulate the amino acid chain to achieve minimum energy conformations, those that achieve the most favorable energy structure win [6].

Another application helps to identify ways in which a number of drugs bind to a receptor of known 3D structure of a HIV component [7].

4. Methods in medical education that utilizes virtualization

As a method of education, virtual medicine is used in various ways: either to explore the human body, without interacting with the analyzed structures, or by performing maneuvers on simple or complex structures (up to simulate human organs) to quantify gestures.

Satava describes the features of ideal simulator: high fidelity, capacity to simulate the physic-dynamic characteristics of organs, to be interactive and to provide haptic feedback [8].

Some examples of the exploration of the human body for anatomical study are: Visible Human Project [9, 10], The Virtual Body [11]; The Virtual Human Embryo [12]; The Visible Human Server [13]. Most of these resources are online atlases of three-dimensional reconstruction images obtained from computerized tomography or MRI. These sites allow interactive navigation and detailed anatomical study of the structures concerned, including relations with other organs.

Three-dimensional reconstruction of intracellular organelles for a better understanding of physiology is another area in which the research was conducted, allowing visualization of how these structures interact [14].

Rapid development of laparoscopic techniques require the implementation of special training and acquisition of special technical skills. Design and modeling of three-dimensional virtual environments that respect the anatomy and intraoperative conditions require close collaboration between dedicated surgeons and engineers in order to develop such platforms. The virtual environment is connected to a console that allows the surgeon to manipulate the virtual instruments through a dedicated joystick. Also some devices use a system for haptic feedback simulation. Simulation is now an integrated part of medical education. These simulators allow the trainee to make mistakes and to learn how to avoid or to solve them, in order to reduce complications in the real procedures.

Of these simulators the best known are: MIST-VR, The LaparoscopyVR [15]; LapMentor [16]; LapSim [17].

MIST-VR system allows the surgeon's training in a virtual space assimilated to a three dimensional cube where the student can perform different moves with a cylinder and balls and the difficulty can be graded in 6 steps. The time to accomplish the tasks as well as the errors are quantified. The system is used to learn simple gestures in laparoscopic surgery, but does not have force-feedback [18].

The surgical simulator LaparoscopyVR (LapVR™) is a virtual reality simulation system that enables learning and updating skills needed in laparoscopic surgery. The LapVR™ system combines laparoscopic simulation software with haptic hardware, providing a complete unit for the virtual reality training. LapVR™ was designed to help surgeons in acquiring, maintaining, preserving and assessing movement skills and knowledge necessary to perform various laparoscopic surgery procedures. Clinical studies show that novice surgeons trained by laparoscopic simulation have skills that help them in real procedures. LapVR™ system allows both individual and team training and provides a basic technical module composed of five skills steps with increasing levels of difficulty: camera navigation, using the hook electrode, cutting, clipping, suturing and knot tying. The system also contains a module for laparoscopic cholecystectomy with 18 variants of cases and three levels of difficulty as well as one of obstetrics and gynecology that allows simulation of laparoscopic operations performed for ectopic pregnancy, tubal occlusion and adnexa's pathology [12].

Multidisciplinary laparoscopic surgical simulator LapMentor™ provides training opportunities for beginners and experienced surgeons from basic laparoscopic skills to complete laparoscopic operations. LapMentor™ was designed to meet the needs of training and practice of physicians as well as the assessment and management of their instructors. The system is characterized by life-like view of human anatomy and perception of tactile sensations using laparoscopic instruments that mimic reality (haptic system). Application modules provide a relaxing environment outside the operating room to help learning essential skills for a variety of laparoscopic procedures: basic techniques module, suturing module, laparoscopic cholecystectomy module, ventral hernia module, gastric bypass module and gynecology module. The basic techniques module was designed to train surgeons in basic skills in minimally invasive procedures: camera navigation (with 0º and 30º laparoscope), handling of usual instruments, manipulating objects, clipping and cutting. Suture techniques module allows surgeons to learn intracorporeal suturing and knot tying, providing a perfect training environment similar to real-life practice. Laparoscopic cholecystectomy module includes virtual patient reconstructions obtained from CT / MRI images of real patients with multiple anatomical variants and thus training surgeons in recognition of anatomical variants and successful resolution of surgical complications. The Ventral hernias module represents the first opportunity to train surgeons with skills necessary to perform laparoscopic hernia repair procedures and inserting prostheses of different shapes and sizes. The gastric bypass module helps surgeons accustomed with basic laparoscopic surgery in learning, performing and perfecting stages of this bariatric procedure in a safe and monitored environment. The gynecological laparoscopic module trains surgeons in learning different methods applied in the treatment of ectopic pregnancy, tubal sterilization and adnexal disease. Videos of all laparoscopic interventions are available before or during simulation. The skills and knowledge acquired during the virtual training increases surgeon's experience, allowing them to cope with intraoperative complications, such as: bleeding from the implantation site of trocars, organ rupture, flooding the abdominal cavity with blood. LapMentor™ system provides all the elements necessary to validate acquired skills and recorded performances. Detailed information on handling tissue, handling tools, time and movements efficiency are collected during the training session to allow evaluation of the level of skill. Performance indicators are recorded in a file and can be viewed on simulator [19].

LapSim™ system provides a virtual environment very similar to the real one as well as extremely useful simulations for common practice. The skills acquired through this system are directly transferable to the operating room. The interface is easy to use and practical sessions vary in complexity depending on the chosen level. Courses can be modified by an instructor according to specific needs. Functions can be imported and exported to be transferred between instructors and institutions. Standard modules of this system are: the basics skills, anastomosis and suture, laparoscopic cholecystectomy and one dedicated to gynecology [14].

SINERGIA is a new type of simulator for laparoscopic surgery composed of seven teaching modules: eye-hand coordination, handling the camera, grasping, pulling, cutting, dissection and section. It also can achieve differentiation between levels of student skills. Yet, even this simulator does not have an integrated haptic system [20].

Compared to physical simulators (artificial or animal model), virtual simulators stimulate the learner to perform all duties listed and evaluated by software, it does not require the presence of a permanent trainer to verify the correctness of performing the tasks and evaluates more accurate the gestures of the surgeon. Virtual systems for surgical training can be used for assessing the competence of the surgeon. In addition, warm-up concept can bring increased surgical performance. This concept allows the warm-up by making virtual preoperative procedure and later, the surgeon will perform the actual procedure. To improve this concept for preoperative phase in virtual environment, three-dimensional reconstructions created from CT of the patient to be operated can be used, thus simulating more accurately the patient's own anatomical variations in the virtual environment.

The VERT system is a virtual environment used in the training of radiotherapy physician and provides a platform for acquiring the skills necessary for doctors, nurses and auxiliary staff [21, 22].

VirRAD project is an online platform that includes a virtual laboratory where the radiopharmacy community members can experience and learn different aspects of practice [23].

A team from the United States has developed a virtual learning system used for EndoStitch device suture learning and performing laparoscopic nodes. It includes in addition to the virtual environment a working console and a haptic feedback [24].

The usefulness of virtual medicine as a diagnostic method is exemplified through a relatively known example: virtual colonoscopy. This examination allows inspection of virtual colonic lumen obtained using three-dimensional reconstruction based on computed tomography images acquired from a patient. The range of examinations is currently expanded to virtual gastrointestinal exploration, three-dimensional assessment of vascular lumen-especially if coronary obstruction. Also the new geometry of the damaged heart wall after a myocardial infarction could be explored.

For intravenous catheter insertion, CathSim system was developed, that provides the student, besides the virtual environment, with a working console with tactile feedback and a series of simulations of complications that may occur during the real procedure [25].

A large number of simulators were developed for: endoscopic sinus surgery, endoscopic gastrointestinal procedures, bronchoscopy, arthroscopy, cardiac catheterization and ophthalmic surgery [26-29].

By integrating knowledge in the field of acupuncture and three-dimensional reconstruction based on images obtained from computer tomography, Chinese Visible Human was created, which is useful in education and research in Chinese medicine [30].

In dentistry there are 3D models of teeth or of an entire human head simulating the details of anatomy of the teeth or mouth. The trainee could perform drills having a haptic feedback. Also a Virtual Reality Dental Chair system (HapTEL) enables the trainee to test and learn various skills [31].

5. Methods of diagnostic and treatment using virtualization in medicine

There are a number of softwares for three-dimensional reconstruction of organs using 3D ultrasound images or 4D CT or MRI images, acquired for a more accurate evaluation of diseases. Some software even allows a simulation of the proposed intervention thus achieving preoperative planning.

During remote interventions, the surgeon acts on a virtual environment, the operation itself is performed by a surgical robot. This kind of procedure was performed in September 7, 2001 and was called „Lindbergh operation" during which Professor J. Marescaux located in Strasbourg performed a laparoscopic cholecystectomy on a patient who was in New York (at a distance of approx. 15000 km) using a ZEUS robot (Computer Motion), the surgeon's presence being virtual [32].

The utility of this technology is to use the expertise of a specialist at a great distance (i.e. space station) to perform surgery (telemedicine) or to help a less experienced surgeon during interventions with high difficulty (telementoring).

The use of robots in surgery allows more accurate movements, avoiding surgeon's tremor, smaller incisions, decreased blood loss, quicker postoperative recovery, etc.

The new models of modified DaVinci robot uses three-dimensional immersion type image, allowing detailed visualization of the operative field, besides haptic feedback [33].

Virtual reality refers not only to virtualization of visual perception but also to virtualization of tactile perception, the touch feeling being essential in surgery. Haptic systems are designed as a virtual environment for the sense of touch, allowing artificial tactile perception of objects created in the virtual environment or of real objects touched by surgical robot, the sensations being transmitted to the interface with the surgeon.

VerroTouch system is an extension of DaVinci robot proposed by Kuchenbecker et al [34] which makes transfer of vibrations measured by surgical instruments attached to the robot-surgeon interface, allowing haptic sensation to the operator.

Augmented reality facilitates surgical intervention by projecting in the operative field inner images of the organs located in the visual field. These images are obtained by three-dimensional reconstruction from CT or MRI after acquisition and processing. The projected images are adjusted according to the position of organs, instruments and actions of the surgeon in the operating field. For example, large intrahepatic vessels can be projected on the surface of the liver capsule, showing a useful map to the surgeon in order to avoid injuries. This is called also „intraoperative navigation" and it shows the surgeon where he can find important elements and also the anatomic variations.

Navigation systems have been proposed for NOTES (Natural Orifice Transluminal Endoscopic Surgery) surgery [35, 36] which reduce intraoperative accidental injuries. It uses three-dimensional reconstruction from images captured by CT and data of real-time location of the endoscope. The main problem with augmented reality is identifying common reference points of real images and of those obtained by preoperative three-dimensional reconstruction. Augmented reality is very useful during minimally invasive interventions, where the visual field is diminished and thus the orientation of the surgeon in the operating field is hampered.

The current systems of virtual reality and augmented reality fail to perfectly simulate the interaction between surgical instruments and organs. In the future, the researchers aim to

http://dx.doi.org/10.5772/59277

improve the interaction between surgeon and interface with the virtual system, getting feedback for surgeons, synchronization of virtual reality with operative field, etc.

Virtual reality can be very useful in bridging the gap between food and social behavior of patients with diabetes and/or obesity and the rules that they should follow. The software allows interaction with virtual environments that simulate both video and tactile sensations and other sensations (smell, taste). Patients can learn new habits such as the amount of food they should ingest, food choices and given encouragement to perform physical activities. Also in people with heart disease or morbid obesity it may stimulate performing progressive physical activity at home, even by increasing motivation.

Another direction in which virtual medicine interferes with spectacular results is the treatment of phobias. The patient is connected to a virtual environment that simulates situations that produce phobic states, everything being controlled and can be interrupted at any time of the simulation [37]. Phobias treated with such reality simulation programs are: post-traumatic stress, public speaking, arachnophobia, agoraphobia, acrophobia, claustrophobia, panic, social phobia, stress secondary vehicle crush accidents etc. [38]. A number of applications have also been developed, dedicated to various phobias or posttraumatic stress syndromes (Virtual Iraq/ Afghanistan, Virtual Airplane, Virtual Nicotine, Virtual Elevator, Hurricane Katrina Virtual, Virtual World Trade Center and Virtual Vietnam) [39]. Virtual Iraq / Afghanistan is used in more than 60 clinics and has demonstrated efficacy in reducing symptoms of posttraumatic stress [40].

STRIVE (Stress Resilience in Virtual Environments) is an application that is used to adapt future soldiers to fight stress. The body reactions to stress are described to the soldier and also he can learn how to cope with this stress [40].

VirtualPatients is an application used for the clinician involved in the learning process and interaction with the patient [40].

For trypanophobia treatment (fear of needles) a system with two lenses was developed which shows images to the patient. It can project different scenarios such as a visit to a health center where a nurse shall pick a blood sample. The whole system also provides feedback on the mental and emotional reactions [41].

To help patients with disabilities, along with dedicated systems which allow the patients to learn how to use wheelchairs in crowded cities, he can also use Second Life type virtual environments, where through an avatar, these patients can interact with others without the limitations encountered in the real world [42].

To avoid animal experiments there were developed digital models of rats, pigs and humans. For example, a virtual pig head [41] and also a model of a physiological rat [43] was developed, in order to use these models in virtual experiments.

Three-dimensional virtual reality combined with haptic feedback is used for motor recovery of patients with stroke sequelae. This technology is currently used in experimental studies, but it might extend in recovery clinics and even at home recovering. There are commercial systems used for related purposes with the ability to develop complex movements of the hand. These applications provide an assessment of movements and skills acquired in order to follow-up the evolution of these patients [44, 45].

A new area of research with direct implications in the therapy is currently developing: virtual rehabilitation. Also looming as a subdomain, virtual tele-rehabilitation allows the therapist to interact with the patient through a 3D avatar and guide them during therapy sessions. Haptic systems attached to such systems allow the doctor to examine the patient's muscle tone [46, 47].

Another application is the virtual prototyping technology that combines virtual modeling with rapid prototyping in order to be used in biomedical engineering (eg. for the development of prosthetic or medical devices) [48, 49].

6. Ethics in virtual reality medicine and telemedicine

The rapid evolution of virtual reality and telemedicine may result in overcoming limits, more so in this area as yet there are no law or ethics rules. As the interactions between people from different countries become more and more globalized, the implementation of ethical codes should be considered. .

Implementation of very expensive virtual reality and augmented reality systems for use in therapy can create disparities in specialist's presence who will migrate toward the best equipped centers. Also there will be an imbalance in patients addressability, which also would prefer clinics with superior performance [50, 51].

Training therapists in centers with the possibility of using virtual reality will also be more efficient and also preoperative simulations leading to superior results. These issues are already visible in Eastern European countries with subfinanced health systems, where both patients and physicians migrate to Western European states.

Funding the development of such performant systems of virtual reality and telemedicine is not currently covered by health systems or government agencies but more often through projects or private sponsorships. These facts may lead to impairing of projects on long-term [52].

As virtual systems will gain autonomy in different degrees, the responsibility of creators and users of these systems will increase. There is currently no legislation to use autonomous robots or virtual systems. There arises the problem of such systems errors and who will be punished for them.

Some cultural and social problems may occur in telemedicine. Because the distance between doctor and patient, the latter can be reduced to a mere "beneficiary" or, worse, "data source" [53].

Differences between health legislations in different countries may lead to situations such as: doctor without a license in a country may provide remote treatment in another country; some illegal procedures (cloning, abortion) in a country can be remotely performed in another country where they are allowed. These differences can lead to self-limitation of experts

http://dx.doi.org/10.5772/59277

performing remote therapies in countries where laws are not familiar. It is therefore necessary to implement a symmetric legislation.

Storing data in information systems can lead to loss of confidentiality with repercussions on both the patient and the service providers.

Patients are usually informed of these systems by mass-media (stimulated by the industry) and these information is incomplete or insufficient.

7. Future directions

Development of virtual reality in medicine aims in the following directions: increasing fidelity in order to reproduce the reality, haptic systems integration in the usual simulators and surgical robots, identifying new standards for evaluating student performance, expanding the use of simulators in the educational field, research and therapy. Virtual reality is likely to become the most common method of learning and training young surgeons and also for senior surgeons to acquire new skills [2].

The researchers also seek solutions to lower the costs of information systems and especially with force feedback haptic devices, but its price makes them prohibitive for general use.

A new direction is predicted, combining virtual reality with holographic projection which would improve the three-dimensional vision.

The combination of autonomous systems with virtual reality will be able to step into the future for autonomous surgical robots, autonomous systems for rehabilitation of people with disabilities, autonomous educational systems and complex software for virtual research.

8. Conclusion

The spectrum of applications of virtual reality in medicine widens permanently and it is developing in various unexpected directions. The contribution of IT support in the development of medicine is huge but the possibilities and applications that will shape the future of medicine are still unknown.

Virtual reality finds its applications in various fields and its usefulness becomes more predominant in training, preoperative evaluation and preparation of surgeons. Learning with virtual simulators increases the dexterity of the surgeons and reduces the number and severity of intraoperative complications. Also, in computer-assisted research, virtual reality brings benefits that other methods could not reach. Various models are developed for research purposes at different levels, from macro-models to micro-or even nano-levels allowing researchers to perform "in silico" experiments more rapidly and more cheaply.

The combination of virtual reality with the power of multiple computers as in online communities enhances the speed of research to a level otherwise unachievable at this time.

The use of virtual reality in the diagnosis and especially in treatment of certain diseases, widens the range of therapeutic procedures, increases operator safety, patient compliance and reduces the duration of applied treatment. Virtual environments used to treat phobias could not be achieved by any other means, leading to a unique mode of treatment in this field.

Using robot technology as well as telemedicine and telementoring systems will increase surgical accuracy and will reduce hospitalization and complications and on the other hand will increase medical expertise in disadvantaged areas or with difficult access (including inaccessible areas for experts: stations space, underwater).

As in all newly developed fields, the virtual reality domain needs some sound rules to be applied during its use, in order to avoid mistakes and/or injuries, especially in the field of diagnostics and therapeutics.

Author details

Florin Graur[1,2*]

Address all correspondence to: graurf@yahoo.com

1 University of Medicine and Pharmacy "Iuliu Hatieganu" Cluj-Napoca, Romania

2 Regional Institute of Gastroenterology and Hepatology "Octavian Fodor" Cluj-Napoca, Romania

The author has no conflict of interest.

References

[1] Mann, R.W. *The evaluation and simulation of mobility aids for the blind*. in *Rotterdam Mobility Research Conference*. 1965. New York: American Foundation for the Blind.

[2] Custura-Craciun, D., et al., *Surgical virtual reality-highlights in developing a high performance surgical haptic device.* Chirurgia (Bucur), 2013. 108(6): p. 757-63.

[3] *Folding@Home*. 2014 [cited 2014 24 August]; Available from: http://folding.stanford.edu/.

[4] *Rosetta@Home*. 2014 [cited 2014 24 August]; Available from: http://boinc.bakerlab.org/rosetta/.

[5] http://www.worldcommunitygrid.org/. *Human Proteome Folding Project* 2014 [cited 2014 28 August]; Available from: http://www.worldcommunitygrid.org/research/hpf2/overview.do.

[6] Wikipedia. *Rosetta@home*. 2014; Available from: http://en.wikipedia.org/w/index.php?title=Rosetta@home&oldid=616140030.

[7] *FightAIDS@Home*. [cited 2014 24 August]; Available from: http://www.worldcommunitygrid.org/research/faah/overview.do.

[8] Satava, R.M., *Historical review of surgical simulation--a personal perspective.* World J Surg, 2008. 32(2): p. 141-8.

[9] NLM. *The Visible Human Project*. 2014 [cited 2014 24 August]; Available from: http://www.nlm.nih.gov/research/visible/visible_human.html.

[10] NLM. *Visible Human*. 2014 [cited 2014 24 August]; Available from: http://www.madsci.org/~lynn/VH/.

[11] *The Virtual Body*. 2014 [cited 2014 24 August]; Available from: http://medtropolis.com/virtual-body/.

[12] LSUHSC. *Virtual Human Embryo Project*. 2011 [cited 2014 24 August]; Available from: http://virtualhumanembryo.lsuhsc.edu/.

[13] visiblehuman.epfl.ch. *Visible Human*. 2014 [cited 2014 24 August]; Available from: http://visiblehuman.epfl.ch/index.php.

[14] *Organelle View*. 2014 [cited 2014 24 August]; Available from: http://www.nformation-design.com/portfolio/portfolio01.php.

[15] caehealthcare.com. *LapVR Surgical Simulator*. 2014 [cited 2014 24 August]; Available from: http://www.medsimlab.com/brochuras/lap.pdf.

[16] Simbionix. *LAP Mentor*. 2014 [cited 2014 24 August]; Available from: http://simbionix.com/simulators/lap-mentor/.

[17] SurgicalScience. *http://www.surgical-science.com*. 2014 [cited 2014 24 August]; Available from: http://www.surgical-science.com.

[18] Tarcoveanu, E., R. Moldovanu, and A. Vasilescu, *ÎNVĂȚĂMÂNTUL VIRTUAL ÎN CHIRURGIA MINIM INVAZIVĂ.* Jurnalul de Chirurgie, 2010. 6(3): p. 230-236.

[19] Saunders, N.R., *The Celestin tube in the palliation of carcinoma of the oesophagus and cardia.* Br J Surg, 1979. 66(6): p. 419-21.

[20] Lamata, P., et al., *SINERGIA laparoscopic virtual reality simulator: didactic design and technical development.* Comput Methods Programs Biomed, 2007. 85(3): p. 273-83.

[21] www.virtalis.com. *VERT: Virtual Environment Radiotherapy Training*. 2014 [cited 2014 24 August]; Available from: http://www.virtalis.com/files/articles/flier_whatisvert.pdf.

[22] www.vertual.co.uk. *VERT*. 2014 [cited 2014 24 August]; Available from: http://www.vertual.co.uk/.

[23] VirRAD. *VirRAD*. 2014 [cited 2014 24 August]; Available from: http://www.virrad.org/.

[24] Kurenov, S.N., et al., *Simulation for training with the Autosuture Endo Stitch device.* Surg Innov, 2006. 13(4): p. 283-7.

[25] *CathSim Intravenous Simulator*. 2014 [cited 2014 24 August]; Available from: http://www.pennstatehershey.org/web/simulation/equipment/cathsim.

[26] Bro-Nielsen, M., et al., *PreOp endoscopic simulator: a PC-based immersive training system for bronchoscopy.* Stud Health Technol Inform, 1999. 62: p. 76-82.

[27] Cotin, S., et al., *ICTS, an interventional cardiology training system.* Stud Health Technol Inform, 2000. 70: p. 59-65.

[28] Mabrey, J.D., et al., *Development of a virtual reality arthroscopic knee simulator.* Stud Health Technol Inform, 2000. 70: p. 192-4.

[29] Rudman, D.T., et al., *Functional endoscopic sinus surgery training simulator.* Laryngoscope, 1998. 108(11 Pt 1): p. 1643-7.

[30] Heng, P.A., et al., *Virtual acupuncture human based on chinese visible human dataset.* Stud Health Technol Inform, 2006. 119: p. 194-7.

[31] *THE Awards: Virtual reality chair helps drill trainee dentists*. 2013 [cited 2014 25 August]; Available from: http://www.reading.ac.uk/sse/news/sse-newsarticle-2013-11-25.aspx.

[32] Marescaux, J., *OPERATION LINDBERGH-A World First in TeleSurgery: The Surgical Act Crosses the Atlantic!* September 19, 2001: New York-Strasbourg.

[33] Okamura, A.M., *Haptic feedback in robot-assisted minimally invasive surgery.* Curr Opin Urol, 2009. 19(1): p. 102-7.

[34] Kuchenbecker, K.J., et al. *VerroTouch: High-Frequency Acceleration Feedback for Telerobotic Surgery*. in *EuroHaptics'10 Proceedings of the 2010 International Conference on Haptics: Generating and Perceiving Tangible Sensations*. 2010.

[35] Vosburgh, K.G. and R. San Jose Estepar, *Natural Orifice Transluminal Endoscopic Surgery (NOTES): an opportunity for augmented reality guidance.* Stud Health Technol Inform, 2007. 125: p. 485-90.

[36] Fernandez-Esparrach, G., et al., *The role of a computed tomography-based image registered navigation system for natural orifice transluminal endoscopic surgery: a comparative study in a porcine model.* Endoscopy, 2010. 42(12): p. 1096-103.

[37] VBI. *Virtual Reality Software Programs for Phobias, Substance Use Disorders, Skills Development, PTSD, & Stress/Pain Management*. [cited 2014 24 August]; Available from: http://www.virtuallybetter.com/.

[38] VRMC. *Virtual Reality Phobia*. [cited 2014 24 August]; Available from: http://www.vrphobia.com.

[39] *Virtual Reality Therapy for Phobias*. 2014 [cited 2014 24 August]; Available from: http://psychiatry.duke.edu/divisions/general-psychiatry/virtual-reality-therapy-phobias.

[40] USC-ICT. *Medical Virtual Reality*. [cited 2014 24 August]; Available from: http://medvr.ict.usc.edu/projects/.

[41] VRS.ORG.UK. *Virtual reality and trypanophobia (fear of needles)*. [cited 2014 18 Aug]; Available from: http://www.vrs.org.uk/virtual-reality-healthcare/trypanophobia.html.

[42] VRS.ORG.UK. *Virtual reality for the disabled*. [cited 2014 18 Aug]; Available from: http://www.vrs.org.uk/virtual-reality-healthcare/disabled.html.

[43] *The Virtual Physiological Rat Project*. 2014 [cited 2014 25 August]; Available from: http://virtualrat.org/.

[44] Broeren, J., et al., *Assessment and training in a 3-dimensional virtual environment with haptics: a report on 5 cases of motor rehabilitation in the chronic stage after stroke.* Neurorehabil Neural Repair, 2007. 21(2): p. 180-9.

[45] Merians, A.S., et al., *Sensorimotor training in a virtual reality environment: does it improve functional recovery poststroke?* Neurorehabil Neural Repair, 2006. 20(2): p. 252-67.

[46] Sandlund, M., S. McDonough, and C. Hager-Ross, *Interactive computer play in rehabilitation of children with sensorimotor disorders: a systematic review.* Dev Med Child Neurol, 2009. 51(3): p. 173-9.

[47] ScienceDaily. *Pushing boundaries of virtual reality*. 2013 [cited 2014 24 August]; Available from: www.sciencedaily.com/releases/2013/02/130205143336.htm.

[48] Choi, S.H. and H.H. Cheung, *Multi-material virtual prototyping for product development and biomedical engineering.* Computers in industry archive, 2007. 58(5): p. 438-452.

[49] Clin, J., C.E. Aubin, and H. Labelle, *Virtual prototyping of a brace design for the correction of scoliotic deformities.* Med Biol Eng Comput, 2007. 45(5): p. 467-73.

[50] Chen, L.C. and J.I. Boufford, *Fatal flows--doctors on the move.* N Engl J Med, 2005. 353(17): p. 1850-2.

[51] Dickens, B.M. and R.J. Cook, *Legal and ethical issues in telemedicine and robotics.* Int J Gynaecol Obstet, 2006. 94(1): p. 73-8.

[52] Silverman, R.D., *Current legal and ethical concerns in telemedicine and e-medicine.* J Telemed Telecare, 2003. 9 Suppl 1: p. S67-9.

[53] Irvine, R., Mediating telemedicine: ethics at a distance. Intern Med J, 2005. 35(1): p. 56-8.

Chapter 3

Augmented Reality – Where it Started from and Where It's Going

Veronika Szucs, Silvia Paxian and Cecília Sik Lanyi

Additional information is available at the end of the chapter

http://dx.doi.org/10.5772/59796

1. Introduction

This study provides an overview of augmented reality (Augmented Reality, AR) and some of its important and popular areas of application. Augmented reality technology integrates 3D virtual objects into a real 3D environment, in real time. This book chapter presents the areas of everyday life where AR can be used (including, but not limited to): medical informatics, production repair, visualization, route planning, entertainment and military applications, marketing tasks and education. The basic characteristics of AR systems, the need for compromise in their applicability, and optical and video mixing approaches are presented in the chapter. The chapter introduces the two main areas of sensor errors, which are considered as a basic problem during the design of efficient augmented reality systems. We summarize how the current devices are able to solve these problems. The expected future direction of AR technology developments and the areas where further research is needed are simultaneously introduced.

1.1. Aims

In the course of preparing the study, the actualities of augmented reality technologies have been reviewed. Questions associated with differing scope of application, design and implementation problems of augmented reality systems, and possible solutions have been delineated during the writing process. The book chapter concludes with possible compromises for questions and approaches, which have arisen during the problem-solving process, and possible directions for future developments are presented, which are suitable for further researches.

The present study does not provide new research results. The information from different sources is supported by different journals, periodicals, Internet media, printed books, articles, conference presentations and essays. Thus, the chapter is an up-to-date literature review.

Several expositive articles have been written on the topic [5, 11, 13, 16, 18, 19, 40, 54].This literature sample is comprehensive and up-to-date as far as possible. The study serves as an appropriate starting point for the selection and design of model-creating opportunities, and for potentially applicable technologies in the field of AR (before application development), with the help of which unique AR applications can be developed, based on an independent methodology.

In the "Definitions" section, we clarify what AR is, and summarize what is motivating AR technology developments.

Most of the AR systems that are currently available on the market are affecting various parts of our everyday life. Out of these, the most distinctive, popular and interesting applications have been selected for presentation within the confines of the chapter.

Questions of the feasibility of augmented reality based systems have been emphasized, with a focus on the most important aspects that are responsible for the success and applicability of the AR system.

Finally, a brief overview has been created, in order to know what other areas need further analyses and examination, and which specific points of AR technologies need further research and development, in order to ensure that the area will remain a priority for developers. As a result of this, the developers of entertainment and business applications will geta complex, efficient, fail-safe, highly customizable toolbar, with the help of which a system appropriate for all target groups can be developed.

The first AR interface was developed by Sutherland in the 1960s [60]; however, the first AR conference was organized much later, in 1998. This conference was the International Workshop on Augmented Reality '98 (IWAR 98), in San Francisco. Since then, research results have been continuously presented at the conferences of the International Symposium on Mixed Reality (ISMR) and the International Symposium on Augmented Reality (ISAR). Obviously, these conferences are not the only locations for presenting results, but these are the most renowned events, the premier conferences in the field of AR. Thus, the research tendencies reviewed through these conferences show an interesting historical development. The search for potential applications, the development of AR researches and the formation of tendencies help to identify the research and development points that can be necessary in the future.

Azuma et al. summarized the research results about AR environments in a very broad way, as can be found in their work [2], and a summary of new results can be found in a 2001 article [3].

Since that time, several new research results have been published worldwide on this topic, and new improvements, innovations and developments have been presented at conferences.

http://dx.doi.org/10.5772/59796

To introduce the obtained results, the chapter will deal with some of these publications to show the most important topics, e.g., tracking, interaction and display technologies, as the main problems of development.

1.2. Definitions

Augmented reality (AR) is a technology which makes it possible to put computer-generated virtual pictures and objects in real time, in a three-dimension real space, as if they were the parts of an actual space.

By contrast, in virtual reality (VR) environments, the users are completely immersed in the virtual environment.

AR makes it possible for the user to interact with the real environment through the virtual object. The definition of AR, which is still used today as a definition of the technology, was described by Azuma [2]:

AR as a technology

1. combines real and virtual objects,
2. is real-time and interactive, and
3. registers the virtual objects in the real world.

The abilities of AR, as a technology appropriate to the above described aims, can be used in many areas: from engineering tasks through entertainment and education, to marketing, advertising and multimedia content.

Augmented reality (AR) is a variation on the virtual environment (VE), or virtual reality as it is often misnamed. With the use of VE technologies, the user is placed in a completely artificial environment. While he/she senses this environment, he/she cannot see, hear or sense the real world surrounding him/her.

On the other hand, AR technologies make it possible for the user to be surrounded by virtual objects in a real world; to be incorporated in the real environment. Hereby, AR technologies expand the reality, and do not completely exchange it for virtual elements.

Ideally, it seems that virtual and real objects placed in the same space can achieve the same effects for the users. The differences between AR, as a 'middle-of-the-roader', the VE (completely synthetic) and telepresence (completely real) were adequately defined in two of Milgram's studies in 1994 [39, 40].

Some of the researchers describe AR in such a way that its application requires the use of HMD (head-mounted display) displays. In order to avoid the future limitations of concrete AR technologies, Milgram et al. [40] defined the three characteristics that AR systems need to possess by a survey.

According to the results of Milgram's survey, the necessary characteristics of AR technologies are the same as the characteristics previously defined by Azuma [2].

This definition makes it possible for AR to keep its most essential elements without other technologies, e.g., not applying HMD displays.

No part of Azuma's or Milgram's definition which makes a difference or offers reservations in connection with display interface: the combination of monitor-based displays, monocular system, transparent HMD systems and other technologies can all be applied.

1.3. Motivation

Why is augmented reality such an interesting field? Why is it beneficial to combine real and 3D objects?

The usage of augmented reality extends the user's sense, perception and interaction in real life. Virtual objects mediate information that the user cannot perceive directly with his/her own senses. With the application of virtual environments, the perception of such events that are not directly able to be experienced physically can be accessed, or they might be dangerous. The information given via virtual objects helps the user to accomplish the tasks in the real world.

AR is a specific example of what Fred Brooks calls IA, intelligence amplification: the computer is a device for making the solution to people's tasks much easier [12].

1.4. AR research areas

According to the research experience, studies and the assessment of existing technologies [2, 3] show that AR systems are effective at corresponding to expectations when there are developments available at appropriate levels for the following components:

a. Graphic rendering hardware and software, able to create an overlap of virtual context with real context

b. Adequate tracking techniques, to appropriately mirror the changes from the user's viewpoint to the rendered graphic

c. Accurate synchronizing of tracker calibration and registering

d. Synchronizing of real and virtual view, when the user's view is fixed

e. Display should sufficiently combine the pictures of virtual objects with the appearance of real components

f. Computer processing: supporting AR simulation running on hardware of input and output devices

g. Interaction techniques describe how the users can manipulate the virtual contents of AR.

Several secondary topics are important, depending on which concrete AR application is being examined. Applicability, adaptability of mobile/portable devices, visualization techniques, authorization devices, the multi-modality of AR inputs, rendering methods, software architecture, etc., must be evaluated. The questions of hardware integration and software realization are taken into consideration during the development of complete AR applications.

http://dx.doi.org/10.5772/59796

1.5. Review of AR research results

The growing demands for AR technologies, and the development of the technology, have appeared in several related research topics recently.

The published results can be divided into two groups. The first group includes the five current main research areas:

1. Tracking techniques
2. User interaction techniques
3. Calibration
4. AR applications
5. Display techniques.

These process the questions of AR applications needed for realization in the basic AR fields.

The second category reflects future research plans:

6. Evaluation/investigation
7. Mobile/portable AR
8. AR authorization
9. Visualization
10. AR multimodality
11. Rendering

2. Aspects of AR development

2.1. Tracking techniques

2.1.1. Sensor-based tracking:

The sensor-based tracking techniques are based on sensors, like magnetic, acoustic, inertial, optical and/or mechanical sensors.

Each of the sensor types has its own pros and cons. For example, the magnetic sensors have a high update frequency and are light. However, the presence of any kind of metal, which can disrupt the magnetic field, can distort the signal [53]; this has been discussed by Rolland in his article about sensor-based tracking techniques.

Sensor techniques have developed substantially recently.

Only a few of publications touched on the topic of tracking at the first IWAR 98 conference in reference to non-camera based systems. One exception is the work of Newman et al. [44], which examines how ultrasound sensors can be used for interior tracking on a large area.

The researchers also investigated how they could combine different types of sensors, so that difficult tasks can be solved by dynamic sensor handling. Klinker et al. [35] described how the use of body sensors can be combined with the usage of fixed, global sensors.

In their further researches, Newman et al. [43] have extended this definition for the bigger sensor networks, which support transparent tracking and dynamic data-fusion.

2.1.2. Vision-based tracking

Vision-based tracking techniques use different picture-processing methods to estimate the relative positioning of the camera and the real world [6]. This is the most active field of research into tracking techniques. More than 80% of the publications analyse possible methods of computer vision.

Stricker et al. [59] introduced a method for detecting 3D coordinates according to the four angles of the quadrant marker, while Park et al. [47] presented an algorithm which estimates the camera position according to the known environment.

Since 2002, extensive investigations have been making progress in the field of marker-based tracking, so that Zhang et al. [64] produced a publication where they compared the more advanced approaches. Following this, no generally new marker-based tracking system has been presented; however, some researchers have been investigating the LED-based tracking techniques [42].

Others have been studying the non-quadrant visual marker-based tracking techniques. Vogt et al. [61] designed circle-shaped marker groups with different parameters, where, e.g., the number of markers, the height and radius of the marker field can be customized, and only one camera is used.

This was the most active area of computer vision-based tracking researches.

The most recent trend amongst computer vision-based tracking techniques is the examination of model-based tracking methods. In these techniques, a model is used with the characteristics of a trackable object, which can be a CAD model, or even a 2D model that possesses the characteristics of the object.

The results of the first model-based tracking were introduced by Comport [14] in 2003. Since then, model-based tracking has become a determinant for vision-based tracking techniques [23, 14].

Wuest et al. [63] presented a real-time model-based tracking technique, an adaptive system, in which the robustness and efficiency was considerably improved.

During the creation of the models, pattern recognition is another beneficial function. Reitmayr and Drummond [51] have introduced a textured 3D model-based hybrid tracking system.

http://dx.doi.org/10.5772/59796

Along the same lines, Pressigout and Marchand [50] suggested a model-based hybrid monocular picture processing system that combined edge enhancement and pattern analysis to achieve more robust and accurate setting estimations.

2.1.3. Hybrid tracking technologies

In some of the AR applications, the use of computer vision-based technique cannot provide in itself a robust tracking key; thus, hybrid methods needed to be created, which combine more sensor technologies. As an example, Azuma et al. [4] suggested that developers use GPS-based tracking systems combined with computer vision-based sensors or inertial sensors for the development of outdoor AR systems.

Aside from a few exceptions (e.g., [20]), initial hybrid methods used markers [1] [32]. Afterwards, the increasing importance of compliance and the developing consensus led to the creation of a "closed-loop" type tracking method, with the combination of inertial and computer vision-based technologies. In the case of vision-based tracking [37], the synchronization is usually satisfactory, there is no skew, but it requires evaluation and extremely bad results may appear. Besides this, the abrupt movements can frequently cause tracking errors, the processing is time-consuming and the error correction may temporarily cause the loss of the real-time aspect of processing.

Lang et al. [37, 49] have achieved a well-endowed complementary method through the combination of vision-based tracking methods and inertial sensors.

This system is quick and robust; it can be used for the estimation of quick movements and changes. Moreover, the position of objects can be retrospectively evaluated according to the metric result data of acceleration and rotation, although some distortion can appear because of the agglomerated noise in the inertial systems.

Foxlin [22] used such an optical and inertial hybrid tracker, where a miniature MEMS (micro-electro-mechanical systems) sensor was used in the cockpit to track the movement of the helmet. The differences of inertial sensors were corrected by inclinable sensors and a compass.

Two other studies [55, 56] describe a hybrid head tracking method using a bird's-eye perspective viewpoint and a gyroscope, with the help of which the number of parameters to be evaluated could be reduced.

2.2. Interaction techniques and user interface

It may take some more time until AR technology becomes a 'mature' technology; until then, lots of technical and social questions (e.g., about the handling of possible limitations of users) are waiting to be answered. One of the important aspects is to create appropriate interaction techniques for the AR applications, which can make it possible for users to interact with the virtual contents in an intuitive way.

2.2.1. *Tangible AR*

AR joins the real and the virtual world; thus, besides real objects, there is an opportunity to use virtual objects. These objects are the building blocks of AR, and the physical manipulation of them enables a strongly intuitive connection, interaction with the virtual environment and virtual contents.

Previously, Ishii elaborated a conception for tangible user interfaces (TUIs), through which the user is able to manipulate the digital information through the physical object [31]. The tangible interfaces are significant, because physical contact can be formed with them; the objects used have familiar physical characteristics, limits and possibilities; they are easily applicable. (The possibilities refer to the used device's physical characteristics, shape, surface, deformability and how the object can be applied [24, 45].)

The same TUI aspect can be used for the AR interfaces, in which the intuitive usability of the physical input devices can be combined with the opportunity for a virtual display provided by the augmented display techniques. This new type of interaction received (in a metaphoric way) the name of tangible augmented reality, and became the most frequently used AR input method among the developments of the last 15 years [33].

An adequate example that presents the efficiency of the tangible AR interface is the application named VOMAR, developed by Kato et al. [33]. In the application, the user uses a bench supplied with markers, chooses the appropriate furniture, then organizes them in a virtual dining-room.

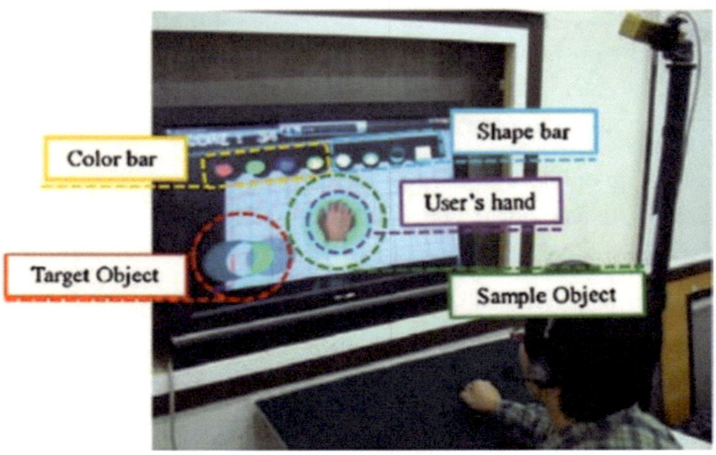

Figure 1. Tangible UI

Gupta's universal media book [25] is a mixed reality interface: it offers the opportunity to get access to information through the display surface, which is a real physical book; the other necessary information will be displayed on it. The pages of the book were not marked with grid points; thus, the user's interaction experience remains based on natural vision or touch.

Figure 2. VOMAR interface

Tangible AR interactions normally hold first place in combining real object input with gesture or voice control, usually leading to the usage multimodal interfaces.

The recognition and then the use of hand gestures is the most natural way of creating user interaction with the AR environment [38]. Irawati et al. [30] introduced the upgraded version of Kato's VOMAR interface. The upgraded version combined the speech-based and (on the input surface) the gesture-based input techniques with the help of time-based and semantic techniques.

The universal aim of the development of the new interaction techniques is to make the manipulation of AR contents as simple as the handling of real-world objects.

2.2.2. *Collaborative AR*

Although, for decades, single-user AR applications had been investigated and developed, the first collaborative AR applications started to be developed during the middle of the 1990s.

The Studiersube [57] and the Shared Space project [8] verified that AR is able to support remote and multi-location activities, even in cases where it would be not be accomplishable in real life [52].

Under the direction of Billinghurst, a 3D CSCW (computer supported collaborative work) interface has been developed [7]; this was the Shared Space application.

The most recent researches are dealing with how mobile AR platforms might be used for collaboration among people.

The Invisible Train project made possible for up to eight users to play at the same time in the AR train game, on PDAs. Wagner [62] and Henrysson et al. [26] introduced the first personal collaborative AR application on a mobile phone, which was *AR Tennis*. An experimental user study proved that the users preferred the AR game to the non-AR technology games, and the multi-sensor feedback enhanced the game experience.

2.3. Display techniques

According to the examination of display techniques, the display devices can be classified into three main categories:

- Transparent, HMD displays,
- Projection-based displays and
- Manual displays.

2.3.1. Transparent HMD devices

The most frequently used devices are the transparent HMD devices. HMD enables the user to see the virtual objects projected onto the real world, for which different optical and video technical methods are used.

The optical see-through displays (optical see-through - OST) are those which permit the user to see the real world with their own eyes and the virtual objects are projected with graphical interlace-technique, holographic optical elements and reflection.

The video see-through displays (video see-through - VST) are those where the user cannot see the outside world, they can only see the real environment through a videocamera record, on which the pictures of virtual objects are likewise projected with interlaced graphical solutions. As an advantage, in the case of VST-HMD displays, there is a greater concordance between the real and virtual views thanks to the different available picture-processing techniques, which adequately correct the intensity and tint [34].

Bimber and Fröhlich [9] introduced a method where the appearance of the virtual object is made universal with the projection of the right shadows if it is in front of the real object; for this method,a projector-based lighting technique was used.

Olwal et al. [46] presented a new auto-stereoscopic OST system, where a transparent holographic optical element (HOE) was used for the division of views projected from two digital projectors. HOE can be built into different surfaces, and the users do not need to wear glasses. Thus, it provides flexibility with minimal interference.

As a VST-HMD device, State et al. [58] developed and constructed an orthoscopic HMD prototype from components available in commercial trade, and they optimized it with the help of a simulator. This VST-HMD device is suitable for selective medical AR tasks, and this device is likely to be the most refined VST-HMD that has ever been constructed.

The head-mounted projective displays (HMPD) [28] are the alternatives to HMD devices. In these devices, a pair of miniature projectors are equipped on a head-mounted surface. The pictures of the virtual and real objects are projected on a light-reflecting material, and the user senses the reflected picture with his/her own eyes.

The main advantage of HMPD in contrast with HMD is that it can support the wide view angle (max. 90°) of the fields; it facilitates the correction of optical distortions, making it possible for the projector to project unbiased pictures on the bent surface. Its disadvantage is that, in HMPD, the light has to pass optically through the display, which can cause a decline in luminance. The idea of HMDP was first published by Fergason [21], but more information about related works can be found in Hua's [29] article.

2.3.2. Projector-based displays

Projector-based displays are good opportunities for AR applications, because the users do not need extra devices to wear.

Other researchers saw an opportunity in operating projectors and cameras at the same time [10, 15]; however, due to the different, opposing lighting techniques these systems are difficult to actualize. Ehnes et al. [17] have upgraded Pinhanez's [48] previous work, in which the virtual objects were directly projected onto real objects for the display.

2.3.3. Man-portable displays, mobile devices

Man-portable displays are adequate alternatives to HMD and HMPD devices in AR applications, because they are easily accessible and highly mobile. Recently, various manual devices have become available which can be applied for mobile AR platforms: tablet PC, ultra-mobile PC, and phones (mobile phones, smartphones and PDAs). Most of the earlier portable prototypes, like the Touring Machine [20] and MARS [27], are based on tablet PC, notebook or unique PC hardware, but they are usually heavy and hardly portable. Although these provided higher evaluation performance and had better input opportunities than the PDAs and mobile phones, they are much more extensive and expensive.

Möhring et al. [41] have introduced the first independent AR system, which is running on a mobile phone available on the market. The current smartphones (with Android, iOS, Symbian, Windows 8 systems), with their built-in cameras, GPS, fast processors, dedicated graphical hardware and wireless network interface, are much more useful for the actualization of AR applications than their contemporaries some years before.

3. AR applications in practice

3.1. Assembly, product support

The IKEA merchant chain-store[1] made itsuser-manuals more interactive with the use of AR technology for the construction of its do-it-yourself furniture. With the use of marker-based technology, the users get a comprehensive guide for the products and their construction.

1 http://www.youtube.com/watch?feature=player_embedded&v=V4b4ArHZupM

Figure 3. IKEA Do-it-yourself support

3.2. Design

AR technologies are perfectly applicable in several design applications, assisting with the spatial arrangement of future objects and proportional scale design.

3.2.1. IKEA home planner[2] application:

This is an AR application popularizing IKEA's catalogue. This application can help future customers to choose appropriate furniture from the actual offers, then with the webcam and the IKEA marker they can virtually place it in their house. They can check and decide before the actual purchase.

Figure 4. IKEA home planner

2 *http://www.youtube.com/watch?feature=player_embedded&v=s0XxKcYj_IE*

3.3. Repair technique, how-to

BMW, besides car manufacturing, provides comprehensive service for the cars. To improve the professional and punctual completion of tasks, amongst BMW's developments, an AR application has appeared[3], which shows the mechanic the repair process (step-by-step) from dismounting, through repair and up to the last phase of the set-up.

The application uses transparent HMD glasses as a display; the virtual contents are directly projected onto the real object.

Figure 5. BMW step-by-step repaire manual

3.4. Packing technique

Priority Mail'sVirtual Box Simulator[4] helps in the choice of appropriately sized packing in a virtual environment. The application uses marker-based technology. This gives the opportunity to compare the different sized boxes displayed as virtual objects with the things to be packed, thus helping the user with the choice of appropriately sized packing.

3.5. Science (Popular Science)

In the augmented reality application by *Popular Science*[5], with the help of markers, the user is able to access the virtual contents of the magazine.

3 http://www.youtube.com/watch?feature=player_embedded&v=P9KPJlA5yds

4 http://www.youtube.com/watch?feature=player_embedded&v=NKd-zn_hw5g

5*http://www.youtube.com/watch?feature=player_embedded&v=_4D0JPchqDA*

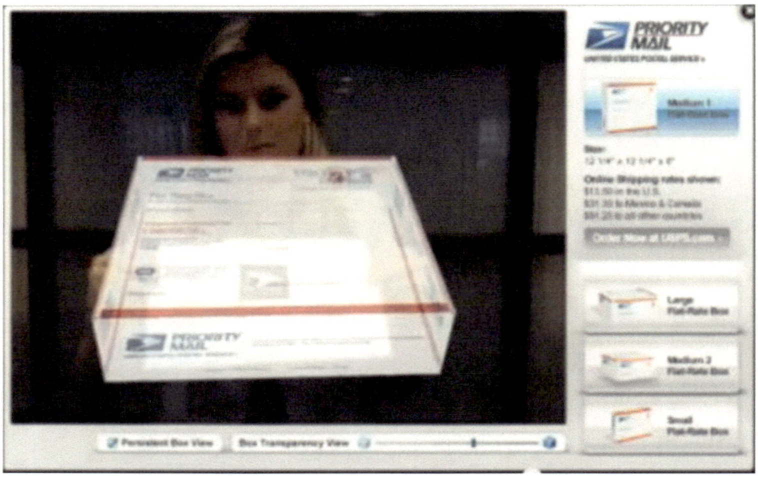

Figure 6. Priority Mail Virtual Box

Figure 7. Popular Science Magazine

3.6. Advertising, marketing

FordKa interactive advertisement

The Ford company has popularized its Ford Ka city car with an interactive AR application[6]. In the advertisement published in local newspapers they have placed a marker and a web contact.

6 http://www.youtube.com/watch?feature=player_embedded&v=s9JT0Fs3JXM

With the use of the marker and the webcam, the user can test how easy parking is with a Ford Ka: the user can drive the car with the arrows on the keyboard, then he/she can park the car and check the results.

Figure 8. Ford Ka advertisment

MAX AR poster by Ogilvy & Mather (Ford advertisement)

In the advertisement campaign for the Ford C Max[7] in Britain, the first 3D image formation technology appeared that used AR environment, but despite using markers, the user interaction was based on natural movements and gestures.

Figure 9. Ford advertisment

7 http://www.youtube.com/watch?feature=player_embedded&v=bl8T9oYO5vY

3.7. Product testing and purchase

RayBan- Virtual mirror

On the sunglasses market, one of the leading manufacturing companies is RayBan[8]. The company provides an opportunity for potential customers, through an AR application, to try on the different types, fashions and coloursof sunglasses, to help them choose the most suitable item for their personalities.

To use the application, a webcam is needed. The program places pilot point pairs, with the help of which it can set the size of the face. After these steps, the customer has to choose from the sunglasses on offer, and the program projects the chosen item as a virtual object onto the face.

Hair simulator, hairstyle probe

The hair simulator byHallNeotech[9] uses AR technology to provide the user with more than 300 previously stored hairstyles and hair colours to choose the most suitable one. The technology is marker-free,so the appropriate points of the face have to be set on the display of the webcam, according to which the program will fit the scale model of the chosen hair.

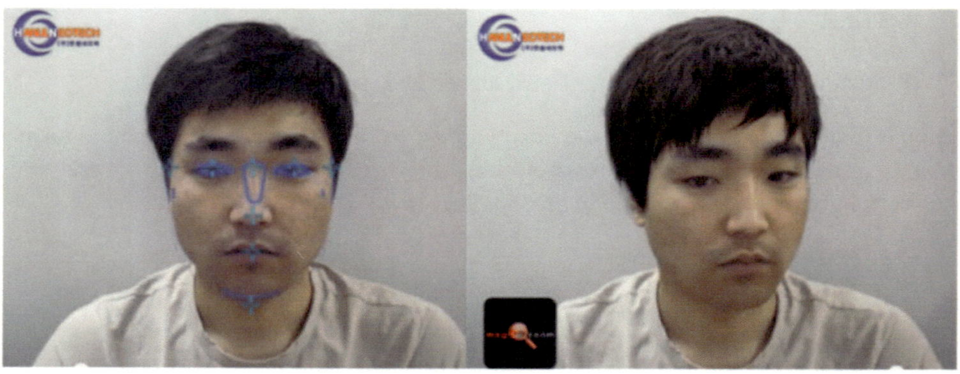

Figure 10. Hair simulator from HallNeoTech

Fashionista

Fashionista[10] is a new device supporting public shopping. This combines the advantages of a fitting room with the possibilities and freedom of online shopping.

The users of the program are able to virtually try on their chosen clothes, and they only need a webcam. They can choose directly from the right price category, and their favourites can immediately be shared on Facebook.

8 http://www.youtube.com/watch?feature=player_embedded&v=Ag7H4YScqZs

9 http://www.youtube.com/watch?feature=player_embedded&v=coqIWj7T6Oo

10 http://www.youtube.com/watch?feature=player_embedded&v=ZnBcqV9POkY

Figure 11. Fashionista - shopping assist

3.8. Language education, e-learning

WordLens

With the help of theWordLensAR[11] (www.questvisual.com) application, the user is able to translate foreign-language titles and text into his/her own mothertongue with the use of a mobile phone with built-in camera and the available built-in dictionaries. The application is availablefor Android-based systems and iOS.

Figure 12. World Lens

11 http://www.youtube.com/watch?feature=player_embedded&v=h2OfQdYrHRs

Augmented reality- the future of education (AraPacis)

The AraPacis webpage[12] graphically introduces the prospect of changing the quality of training and education with the use of AR technologies.

In the presentation, the user can use the digital manipulation of the contents of a book, available at the library, for his/her own needs with the use of a transparent HMD device in the form of glasses. Based on the contents of the recognized book, such extra information will be available (in the form of virtualobjects), which can only be feasible with digital techniques: the interactive enlarging of the seen picture, the storing of the observed picture for later use and the display of other related information projected onto the pages of the book, as if onto a real physical object.

The possibilities of arbitrary interactive operations raise a question regarding digital rights management: how can the aspects of DRM (digital rights management) be kept in mind, and what kind of freedom to create digital copies of the medium is respected in the AR-based world? This question needs further investigation.

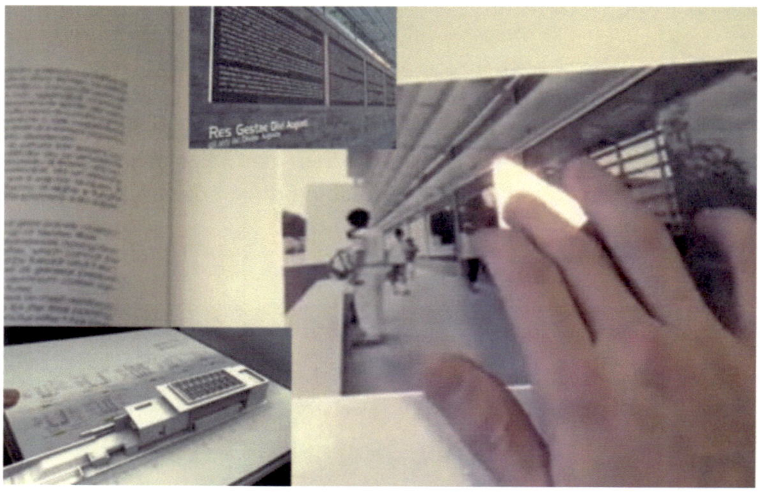

Figure 13. AR book

3.9. Tourism

AR travel guide

This application based on augmented reality technology presents the Wikitude mobile travel guide[13]on a mobile phone. The application displays the information based on the camera

12 http://www.youtube.com/watch?v=hge4eonM8hc

13 http://www.youtube.com/watch?feature=player_embedded&v=tpaJBu4BEuA

picture. It shows the location on the map, or a list of information, or in AR camera view it places the information on objects in the real environment.

Figure 14. AR travel guide

3.10. Virtual games

Red Bull game

A trailer for a game using AR technology, developed for iPhone, can be viewed at http://www.youtube.com/watch?v=PbJCRAgVqYY&feature=related.

The mobile application called *RedBull Augmented Racing* is a car racing game, where the user can create their own fields besides the built-in fields. For advertising purposes, the upper surface of Red Bull energy drink cans needs to be first shown to the application through the mobile device's camera, and after this initiation the next level of development follows: to create a track, the top surfaces of the cans have to be captured by the camera. The application stores the route, and after starting the race, the users have to go through this route with the racing car.

3.11. Company introduction, company presentation

Helge Lund, the director of the London office of oil company Statoil[14], held a 201-minute long presentation about the company's results achieved so far and demonstrated their future plans. For this presentation, he used a high-tech AR application: he illustrated his speech with spectacular, projected virtual objects. His aim was to convince his colleagues to use lifelike graphical models for the design tasks needed for the operation of the company, and to use

14 http://www.youtube.com/watch?feature=player_embedded&v=mBk1l5yARiE

augmented reality technologies during presentations.Thus, he could look forward to the more transparent and more effective synergy of different company units.

Figure 15. Company presentation

3.12. Digital art

The quick spread of PC use has event affected different fields of art. In the area of audio-visual media, digital creations are becoming widespread. Obviously, the penetration of AR technologies has likewise appeared in visual arts. On http://jamesalliban.wordpress.com or http://skive.co.uk, expressive examples can be found.

In the Virtual Ribbons[15] AR application, the user can create virtual ribbons using his or her hands or the mobile's light using a webcam; the movement of these ribbons can be arbitrarily controlled on the display.

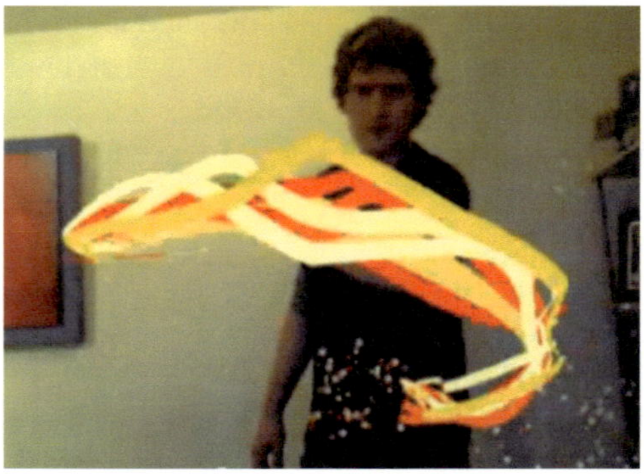

Figure 16. Virtual Ribbons

15 http://www.youtube.com/watch?feature=player_embedded&v=NX746nN62uk

3.13. SixthSense technology

The most interesting AR applications in the near future will be those based on SixthSense technology. During the development of these applications, the developers are searching for probable solutions for how can we use our knowledge about everyday objects to efficiently interact with the digital world. In this field, Indian researchers have made great progress; their work has been presented several times. Their applied devices are simple: as markers they use coloured rings on their fingers; as video input they use any kind of video camera that can be hung on the neck or fixed on a cap; and for display they use a small-size projector, which directly projects the virtual objects onto real-world objects. The advantage of SixthSense technology is that it does not restrain the user's real sight, there is no need to use an extra input device, and it is a mobile technology that can be used anywhere.

As an example, a video is presented at http://www.youtube.com/watch?v=Tq22KBGwMxc, which shows how this technology can be applied for taking photos while walking, and the developer suggest show the system can be controlled based on gesture recognition.

Figure 17. Sixth Sense Technologie

3.14. Healthcare

The usage of AR applications is becoming important too in the field of healthcare. Several healthcare informatics applications are using such visualization techniques, which help in diagnostics, and can even model a planned surgical intervention.

Mirracle – the magic mirror

The Mirracleis an AR technology "magic mirror", which serves for visual display of medical data.

At http://www.youtube.com/watch?feature=player_embedded&v=Oske0c1sOVE, a short presentation can be seen about the application.

Figure 18. Magic Mirror demo

The application uses the Microsoft Kinect sensor for displaying visual information based on the physical parameters of the user standing in front of it, as though it could see through the human body with a real X-ray. The Kinect sensor, based on its camera view, models and shows the skeleton-based construction, or shows photorealistic virtual sectional pictures, which are similar to CT or MR technology tomographies.

The introduction of the application is predominantly planned in the field of healthcare education.

4. Conclusion

The technological development of the last few years has reached a level where it is impossible to avoid running into 3D visual tricks created and displayed by computers. Whether it is the stereoscopic (or other stereo) display at the cinema or real-time computer graphics which are constantly developing, the form of these virtual worlds has become part of our daily life.

The technological development (whether from hardware or software sectors) givesthe opportunity for everyone to access 3D content in available forms. A range of expedient programs are available for the public, but their handling and usage is by no means trivial.

A new and dynamically developing branch of informatics is augmented reality (AR), which, besides the current applications, will prospectively come to play a significant role in the fields of advertising and marketing, education, distributed labour, healthcare and spare-time applications. The developmental direction of AR technologies isbringing mobile platforms to prominence. The applications with primarily descriptive aims are becoming highly interactive, and efficient multimedia devices are appearing in numerous areas of life due to the development of back-end support based on underlying artificial intelligence.

Author details

Veronika Szucs*, Silvia Paxian and Cecília Sik Lanyi

*Address all correspondence to: szucs@virt.uni-pannon.hu

University of Pannonia, Veszprem, Hungary

References

[1] Auer, T., Pinz, A. Building a hybrid tracking system: Integration of optical and magnetic tracking. In *IWAR '99*, pp.13-22, 1999.

[2] Azuma, R., Gary, B. A frequency-domain analysis of head-motion prediction. *Proceedings of SIGGRAPH '95* (Los Angeles, CA, 6-11 August 1995). In *Computer Graphics*, Annual Conference Series, 1995, pp. 401-408.

[3] Azuma, R.T., Baillot, Y., Behringer, R., Feiner, S., Julier, S.,MacIntyre, B.Recent advances in augmented reality. *IEEE Computer Graphics & Applications*, 21:6, 34-47, 2001.

[4] Azuma, R. T., Hoff, B. R., Howard, I.,Neely, E., Sarfaty, R., Daily, M. J., Bishop, G., Vicci, L., Welch, G., Neumann, U., You, S., Nichols, R., Cannon, J. Making augmented reality work outdoors requires hybrid tracking. In *IWAR '98*, pp. 219-224, 1998.

[5] Barfield, W., Craig, R.,Wouter, A.L. Augmented-reality displays. In W. Barfield and T. A. Furness III (Eds),*Virtual Environments and Advanced Interface Design*. Oxford University Press (1995), pp. 542-575. ISBN0-19-507555-2.

[6] Bajura, M., Neumann, U. Dynamic registration correction in video-based augmented reality systems. *IEEE Computer Graphics and Applications* 15, 5 (September 1995), 52-60.

[7] Billinghurst, M., Kato, H. Collaborative augmented reality. *Communications of the ACM*, 45:7, 64-70, 2002.

[8] Billinghurst, M., Weghorst, S., Furness, T. III. Shared Space: An augmented reality interface for computer supported collaborative work. In *CVE '96*, 1996.

[9] Bimber, O., Fröhlich, B. Occlusion shadows: Using projected light to generate realistic occlusion effects for view-dependent optical see-through displays. In *ISMAR '02*, pp. 186-319, 2002.

[10] Bimber, O., Grundhofer, A., Wetzstein, G., Knodel, S. Consistent illumination within optical see-through augmented environments. In *ISMAR '03*, pp. 198-207, 2003.

[11] Bowskill, J., John, D. Extending the capabilities of the human visual system: An introduction to enhanced reality. *Computer Graphics* 29, 2 (May 1995), 61-65.

[12] Brooks, F. P. Jr. The computer scientist as toolsmith II. *CACM* 39, 3 (March 1996), 61-68.

[13] Caudell, T.P. Introduction to augmented reality. *SPIE Proceedings Volume 2351: Telemanipulator and Telepresence Technologies* (Boston, MA, 31 October-4 November 1994), 272- 281.

[14] Comport, A., Marchand, E., Chaumette,F. A real-time tracker for markerless augmented reality. In *ISMAR '03*, pp. 36-45, 2003.

[15] Cotting, D., Naef, M., Gross, M., Fuchs, H. Embedding imperceptible patterns into projected images for simultaneous acquisition and display. In *ISMAR '04*, pp. 100-109, 2004.

[16] Drascic, D. Stereoscopic vision and augmented reality. *Scientific Computing & Automation* 9,7 (June 1993), 31-34.

[17] Ehnes, J., Hirota, K., Hirose, M. Projected augmentation - augmented reality using rotatable video projectors. In *ISMAR '04*, pp. 26-35, 2004.

[18] Feiner, S. Augmented reality. *Course Notes, 2: ACM SIGGRAPH 1994*, 7:1-7:11.

[19] Feiner, S. Redefining the user interface: Augmented reality. *Course Notes, 2: ACM SIGGRAPH 1994*, 18:1-18:7.

[20] Feiner, S., MacIntyre, B., Höllerer, T., Webster, T. A touring machine: Prototyping 3D mobile augmented reality systems for exploring the urban environment. In *ISWC '97*, pp. 74-81, 1997.

[21] Fergason, J. Optical system for head mounted display using retroreflector and method of displaying an image. U.S. patent 5,621,572, 15 April, 1997.

[22] Foxlin, E., Altshuler, Y., Naimark, L., Harrington,M. Flight Tracker: A novel optical/inertial tracker for cockpit enhanced vision. In *ISMAR '04*, pp. 212-221, 2004.

[23] Fua, P., Lepetit, V. Vision based 3D tracking and pose estimation for mixed reality. In M. Haller, M. Billinghurst, B. H. Thomas (Eds), *Emerging Technologies of Augmented Reality Interfaces and Design*. Idea Group: Hershey, PA(2007), pp. 43-63.

[24] Gibson, J. J. The theory of affordances. In R. E. Shaw, J. Bransford(Eds), *Perceiving, Acting, and Knowing*. Hillsdale, NJ: Lawrence Erlbaum Associates, pp. 67-82.1977.

http://dx.doi.org/10.5772/59796

[25] Gupta, S., Jaynes, C. O. The universal media book: Tracking and augmenting moving surfaces with projected information. In *ISMAR '06*, pp. 177-180, 2006.

[26] Henrysson, A., Billinghurst, M., Ollila, M. Face to face collaborative AR on mobile phones. In *ISMAR '05*, pp. 80-89, 2005.

[27] Höllerer, T., Feiner, S., Terauchi, T., Rashid, G., Hallaway,D. Exploring MARS: Developing indoor and outdoor user interfaces to a mobile augmented reality system. *Computers and Graphics* 23:6, 779-785, 1999.

[28] Hua, H., Gao, C., Brown, L. D., Rolland, J. P. Using a head-mounted projective display in interactive augmented environments. In *ISAR '01*, pp. 217-223, 2001.

[29] Hua, H., Girardot, A., Gao, C., Rolland, J. P. Engineering of head-mounted projective displays. *Applied Optics* 39:22, 3814-3824, 2000.

[30] Irawati, S., Green, S., Billinghurst, M., Duenser, A., Heedong, K. "Move the couch where?" Developing an augmented reality multimodal interface. In *ISMAR '06*, pp. 183-186, 2006.

[31] Ishii, H., Ullmer, B. Tangible bits: Towards seamless interfaces between people, bits and atoms. In ACM *CHI'97*, pp. 234-241, 1997.

[32] Kanbara, M., Fujii, H., Takemura, H., Yokoya, N. A stereo visionbased augmented reality system with an inertial sensor. In *ISAR '00*, pp. 97-100, 2000.

[33] Kato, H., Billinghurst, M., Poupyrev, I., Imamoto, K., Tachibana, K. Virtual object manipulation on a table-top AR environment. In *ISAR '00*, pp. 111-119, 2000.

[34] Kiyokawa, K. An introduction to head mounted displays for augmented reality. In M. Haller, M. Billinghurst, B. H. Thomas (Eds), *Emerging Technologies of Augmented Reality Interfaces and Design*. Idea Group: Hershey, PA (2007), pp. 43-63

[35] Klinker, G., Reicher, R., Brugge, B. Distributed user tracking concepts for augmented reality applications. *ISAR'00*, pp. 37-44, 2000.

[36] Krueger, M. W. Simulation versus artificial reality. *Proceedings of IMAGE VI Conference* (Scottsdale, AZ, 14-17 July 1992), pp. 147-155.

[37] Lang, P., Kusej, A., Pinz, A., Brasseur, G. Inertial tracking for mobile augmented reality. In *IEEE IMTC*, Vol.2, pp. 1583-1587, 2002.

[38] Malik, S., McDonald, C., Roth, G. Tracking for interactive pattern- based augmented reality. In *ISMAR '02*, pp. 117-126, 2002.

[39] Milgram, P., Kishino, F. A Taxonomy of mixed reality virtual displays. *IEICE Transactions on Information and Systems E77-D*, 9 (September 1994), 1321-1329.

[40] Milgram, P., Takemura, H., Utsumi, A., Kishino, F. Augmented reality: A class of displays on the reality- virtualitycontinuum. *SPIE Proceedings Volume 2351: Telemanipula-*

tor and Telepresence Technologies (Boston, MA, 31 October-4 November 1994), pp. 282-292.

[41] Möhring, M., Lessig, C., Bimber, O.Video see-through AR on consumer cell-phones. In *ISMAR '04*, pp. 252-253, 2004.

[42] Naimark, L., Foxlin, E. Encoded LED system for optical trackers. In *ISMAR '05*, pp. 150–153, 2005.

[43] Newman, J., Wagner, M., Bauer, M., MacWilliams, A., Pintaric, T., Beyer, D., Pustka, D., Strasser, F., Schmalstieg, D., Klinker, G. Ubiquitous tracking for augmented reality. In *ISMAR '04*, pp. 192-201, 2005.

[44] Newman, J., Ingram, D., Hopper, A. Augmented reality in a wide area sentient environment. In *ISMAR '01*, pp. 77-86, 2001.

[45] Norman, D. A. *The Design of Everyday Things*. New York: Doubleday Business (1988).

[46] Olwal, A., Lindfors, C., Gustafsson, J., Kjellberg, T., Mattsson, L. ASTOR: An autostereoscopic optical see-through augmented reality system. In *ISMAR '05*, pp. 24-27, 2005.

[47] Park, J., Jiang, B., Neumann, U. Vision-based pose computation: Robust and accurate augmented reality tracking. In *IWAR '99*, pp. 3-12, 1999.

[48] Pinhanez, C. The Everywhere Displays projector: A device to create ubiquitous graphical interfaces.*Proc. Ubiquitous Computing 2001* (*Ubicomp '01*), Atlanta, Georgia, September 2001, pp. 315- 331. *Springer Lecture Notes In Computer Science*, v. 2201.

[49] Pinz, A., Brandner, M., Ganster, H., Kusej, A., Lang, P., Ribo, M. Hybrid tracking for augmented reality. *ÖGAI Journal*, 21:1, 17-24, 2002.

[50] Pressigout, M., Marchand, É. Hybrid tracking algorithms for planar and non-planar structures subject to illumination changes. In *ISMAR '06*, pp. 52-55, 2006.

[51] Reitmayr, G., Drummond, T. Going out: Robust model-based tracking for outdoor augmented reality. In *ISMAR '06*, pp. 109-118, 2006.

[52] Rodrigo Silva, L.S. Introduction to augmented reality. http://virtual.lncc.br/~rodrigo/links/AR/node19.html. 2003.

[53] Rolland, J. P., Hopkins, T. *A Method of Computational Correction for Optical Distortion in Head-Mounted Displays*. UNC Chapel Hill Department of Computer Science Technical Report TR93-045 (1993).

[54] Rolland, J. P., Holloway, R., Fuchs, H. A comparison of optical and video see-through head-mounted displays. *SPIE Proceedings Volume 2351: Telemanipulator and Telepresence Technologies* (Boston, MA, 31 October-4 November 1994), pp. 293- 307.

[55] Satoh, K., Uchiyama, S., Yamamoto, H. A head tracking method using bird's-eye view camera and gyroscope. In *ISMAR '04*, pp. 202-211, 2004.

http://dx.doi.org/10.5772/59796

[56] Satoh, K., Uchiyama, S., Yamamoto, H., Tamura, H. Robust vision-based registration utilizing bird's-eye view with user's view. In *ISMAR '03*, pp. 46-55, 2003.

[57] Schmalstieg, D., Fuhrmann, A., Szalavari, Z., Gervautz, M. 1996. Studierstube: An environment for collaboration in augmented reality. In *CVE '96*, 1996.

[58] State, A., Keller, K., Fuchs, H. Simulation-based design and rapid prototyping of a parallax-free, orthoscopic video see-through head-mounted display. In *ISMAR '05*, pp. 28-31, 2005.

[59] Stricker, D., Klinker, G., Reiners, D. A fast and robust line-based optical tracker for augmented reality applications. In *IWAR '98*, pp. 31-46, 1998.

[60] Sutheland, I. The ultimate display. In *IFIP '65*, pp. 506-508, 1965.

[61] Vogt, S., Khamene, A., Sauer, A., Niemann, H. Single camera tracking of marker clusters: Multiparameter cluster optimization and experimental verification. In *ISMAR '02*, pp. 127-136, 2002.

[62] Wagner, D., Pintaric, T., Ledermann, F., Schmalstieg, D. Towards massively multi-user augmented reality on handheld devices. In *Pervasive '05*, pp.208-219, 2005.

[63] Wuest, H., Vial, F., Stricker, D. Adaptive line tracking with multiple hypotheses for augmented reality. In *ISMAR '05*, pp. 62-69,2005.

[64] Zhang, X., Fronz, S., Navab, N. Visual marker detection and decoding in AR systems: A comparative study. In ISMAR '02, pp. 97-106, 2002.

Section 2

Industry Field Education

Chapter 4

Building Bridges Activity within a Virtual Environment

Alcínia Z. Sampaio and Luís Viana

Additional information is available at the end of the chapter

http://dx.doi.org/10.5772/58919

1. Introduction

In the execution of bridge or overpass decks several construction processes are applied. A geometric model 4D (3D+time) in a Virtual Reality (VR) environment which simulates the construction of a bridge deck composed of precast beams was implemented. The model allows viewing and interaction with the various steps and the main elements involved in the construction process. In order to develop the virtual model, the components of the construction, the steps inherent in the process and its follow-up and the type and mode of operation of the required equipment were initially examined, in detail. Based on this study, the 3D geometric modelling of the different elements that make up the site was created and a schedule that would simulate an interactive mode of construction activity was established. As the model is interactive, it allows the user to have access to different stages of the construction process. It allows different points of view in time and in space throughout the development of construction work, and thereby it supports the understanding of this constructive method. Since the model is didactic in character it can be used to support the training of students and professionals in the field of Bridge Construction. The VR application is currently used to support Bridge classes at the Department of Civil Engineering of the University of Lisbon.

In Civil Engineering, there are several construction methods for the execution of bridge decks. This study analyses the constructive method applied to bridge decks using precast beams. In Civil Engineering prefabricated elements are frequently used, because they offer several advantages in urban areas. Namely it is applied in works over railway lines, and in general in areas where the placement of trusses is difficult, as this allows quick and economical construction without generating significant local constraints.

This present work aims to contribute to the dissemination of this methodology of construction through a visual simulation created in a virtual environment. It also draws attention to its usefulness as a teaching tool, supporting, as it does, the in-depth understanding of this process. For the creation of a visual simulation application Virtual Reality (VR) technology was applied. This technology offers advantages in communication allowing the user to interact with the 4D model as it allows access to different modes of viewing the model in space and time (Woksepp, 2007).

2. VR technology in education

In order to create models, which could visually simulate the progressive sequence of the process and allowing interaction with it, techniques of virtual reality were used. When modelling 3D environments there must be a clear idea of what should be shown, since the objects to be displayed and the details of each must be appropriate to the goal the teacher or designer wants to achieve with the model. The use of virtual reality techniques in the development of these didactic applications is, also, generally beneficial to education in that it improves the efficiency of the models in the way it allows interactivity with the simulated environment of each activity. The virtual model can be manipulated interactively allowing the teacher or student to monitor the physical evolution of the work and the construction activities inherent in its progression. This type of model allows the participant to interact in an intuitive manner with 3D space, and to repeat the sequence or task until the desired level of proficiency or skill has been achieved always performing in a safe environment. Therefore, it can be seen that VR technology applied to didactic models brings new perspectives to the teaching of subjects in Civil Engineering education (Sampaio & Henriques, 2008).

Currently, the information related to the construction of buildings is based on the planning of action to be taken and on the log of completed work. It is also applied in education. The capacity to visualize the construction activity can be added through the use of three-dimensional (3D) models which facilitate the interpretation and understanding of process sequence of construction. Furthermore, the possibility of interaction with the geometric models can be provided through the use of Virtual Reality (VR) technology. The developed VR models can be considered as useful computer tool with advanced visualization capacities in the education and construction fields. The interaction with the construction steps visualization allowed by the models turn these applications simple and direct to be used in an educational perspective.

The VR technology is actually used in areas like education as a teaching support tool or in planning processes concerning industry as a collaborative tool. In architectural design studio, Abdelhameed (2013) applies micro-simulation function, inside a virtual reality environment, using the VR Studio program, in order to provide the students with an effective tool to select and visualize a structural system and its construction process. Fillatreau et al. (2013) develop a framework for immersive industry checklist-based project reviews, combining immersive navigation in the checklist, virtual experiments and multimedia update of the checklist. The authors relied on the integration of various VR tools and concepts, in a modular way, and developed a set of learning activities for students, in the Engineering Graphics subjects, in order to acquire, develop and improve their levels of spatial skill. For that purpose; they have structured training with VR and Augmented Reality (AR) technologies. Menck et al. (2013)

uses VR as a tool for collaboration to exchange information and data has increased significantly over time in production-related areas.

The model discussed here follows other didactic VR models applied to the construction of bridge field developed within the University of Lisbon at the Department of Civil Engineering:

- One model presents the cantilever method of bridge deck construction, a frequent construction technique (Figure 1, Sampaio et al. 2005);
- Another model attends the incremental launching method of bridge deck construction (Figure 2, Sampaio & Martins, 2014).

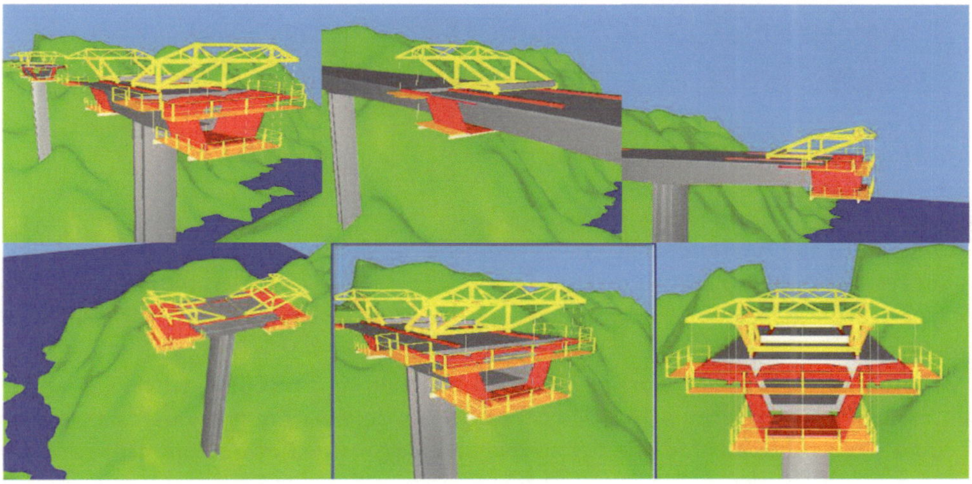

Figure 1. Virtual model of the cantilever process bridge deck construction.

The aim of the practical application of the virtual modes is to provide support in Civil Engineering education. Namely in those disciplines relating to, bridges and construction process both in classroom-based education and in distance learning based on e-learning technology (Birzina et al. 2012). Engineering construction work models were created, from which it was possible to obtain 3D models corresponding to different states of their shape, simulating distinct stages of the carrying out processes. They also assist the study of the type and method of operation of the equipment necessary for these construction methodologies. Furthermore, the possibility of interaction with the geometric models can be provided through the VR technology capacities. The didactic VR models are actually in common use in both face-to-face classes and on an e-learning platform. In a real construction place of a bridge, for security reasons, the student stays far from the local were bridge is under construction, so they cannot observe in detail the way of operation and the progression of the construction. Interacting with the model in class or using their personal computers they better understand what is going on there in the work place.

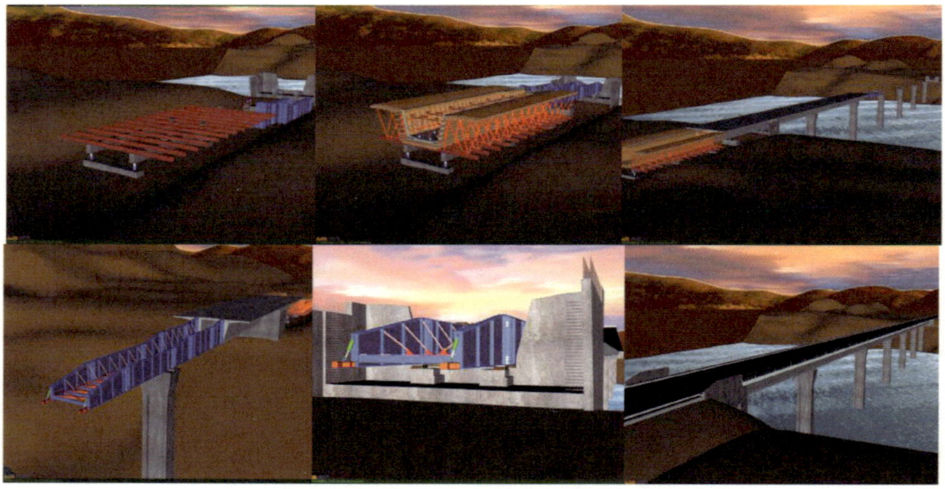

Figure 2. Virtual model of the incremental launching method of bridge deck construction.

The pedagogic aspect and the technical knowledge transmitted by the models are present: in the selection of the quantity and type of elements to show in each virtual model; on the sequence of exhibition to follow; on the relationship established between the components of both type of construction; on the degree of geometric details needed to present; on the technical information that must go with each constructive step. Further details complement, in a positive way, the educational applications bringing to them more utility and efficiency. So when students go to visit real work places, since the essential details were previously presented and explained in class, they are able to better understand the construction operation they are seeing. Specialist in construction processes and bridge design were consulted and implicated in the development of the educational models in order to obtain efficient and accurate didactic applications.

3. VR/4D models in construction

Information technology, namely 4D modelling and VR techniques, is currently in use both in the construction activity and in education (Mohammed, 2007). In construction industry, from the conception to the actual implementation, project designs are presented mostly on successive steps, even though the two dimensional reading is often not enough, as mistakes can be introduced in early stages of conception or elements misunderstood on the construction site. 3D models present an alternative to avoid inaccuracies, as all the information can be included with the necessary detail. Computer systems used in construction for graphic representation have experienced a vast evolution, allowing new ways of creating and presenting projects.

4D models, also labelled as 3D evolutionary models, permit a better comprehension of the project throughout its life, minimizing the information loss through the chain of events. A 4D model combines 3D model with the appropriate scheduling data. Integration of the geometrical representation of the building together with scheduling data has been a topic for many research and development efforts. Different approaches for this integration are the following (contains links to the corresponding approaches) (Kähkönen & Leinonen, 2014). 4D models developed in CIFE (Center for Integrated Facility Engineering, of Stanford University) have shown the benefits and opportunities of visualizing construction information in a 4D (time +space) context. Today, 4D models visually describe how construction progresses. The opportunity, though, is to use the 4D medium to explain planning decisions and impacts of those planning decisions, making 4D models explanative and predictive (4D group, 2014). So, planners can contextually visualize various types of planning information to better support decision making.

In addition VR technology can present a step-by-step guide in assembling complex structures in an interactive way. One of the benefits of VR in construction is the possibility of a virtual scenario being visited by the different specialists, exchanging ideas and correcting mistakes. The models concerning construction needs to be able to produce changes of the project geometry. The integration of geometric representations of a building together with scheduling data related to construction planning information is the bases of 4D models. The use of 4D models just linked with construction planning software or with virtual/interactive capacities, concerns essentially economic and administrative benefits as a way of presenting the visual simulation of the expected situation of the work in several step of its evolution. Therefore in the construction industry, the general use of 3D and 4D models is the visualization of the building design for demonstration purposes to the client, and not as a design support system. The majority of the industry's clients are inexperienced in building design and construction processes. 3D building models are produced to show the client how their building will look like if they decided to procure the proposed project. Provided that the 3D model of the building progress is generated as construction progresses, this data can be used for the calculation of interim payments, schedule control and assessment, conflict management or avoidance purposes.

3D and 4D modelling are being used to improve the production, analysis, and management of design and construction information in many phases and areas of construction projects (Fischer & Kunz, 2004). VTT Building Technology has been developing and implementing applications based on this technique improving a better communication between the partners in a construction project (Leinonen et al. 2013). Note also the contribution of VR in Architecture/ Engineering, to support conception design (Petzold et al. 2007), presenting the plan (Khanzode et al. 2007) or following the progress of construction (Fischer, 2014).

Previous woks in construction field of the author concerns other 4D applications based also on VR technology for use in construction and maintenance planning of buildings (Figure 3.):

- The 4D planning construction application considers the time factor showing the 3D geometry of the different steps of the construction activity, according to the plan established for the construction (Sampaio et al. 2011);

- The maintenance VR models were created in order to help in the maintenance of painted interior walls and facades in a building. It allows the visual and interactive transmission of information related to the physical behaviour of the elements. To this end, the basic knowledge of material most often used in coverings, anomaly surveillance, techniques of rehabilitation, and inspection planning were studied. This information was included in a database that supports the periodic inspection needed in a program of preventive maintenance (Sampaio et al. 2012).

Figure 3. VR models of construction and coating elements of exterior and interior walls.

This work brings an innovative contribution to the field of construction and maintenance supported by emergent technology. The building lifecycle is in constant evolution, so require the study of preventive maintenance, though, for example, the planning of periodic local inspections and corrective maintenance with repair activity analysis. For this reason, the VR models facilitative the visual and interactive access to results, supporting the drawing-up of inspection reports. The focus of the work is on travelling through time, or the ability to view a product or its components at different points in time throughout their life. In maintenance, the time variable is related to the progressive deterioration of the materials throughout the building's lifecycle.

4. Bridge decks composed of prefabricated beams

Using prefabrication in bridges presents several advantages, such as (Câmara, 2001): the good quality of the concrete of the components produced; economic benefits that result from the use

http://dx.doi.org/10.5772/58919

of optimized and standard solutions, which can be used repeatedly throughout the whole process; reduction of congestion on the construction site and the shortening of time-limits for construction, and finally, greater security because it reduces the number of tasks to be carried out on site.

Figure 4. Overpass on A23 performed with prefabrication (Juntas, 2013)

The construction of bridge decks composed of prefabricated beams uses an equidistant distribution of isolated elements placed side by side, complemented by a slab that establishes continuity on the surface of the deck. The prefabricated beams are usually built with a length equal to the bridge spans, each consisting of several beams connected from above by a slab concreted "in situ", and crosswise by transversal beams located on the support.

The slab can be made "in situ" using a false-work or pre-slabs, which can contribute to structural strength or assist only as formwork while the slab of the deck is concreted. The most common cross sections in these types of beams are I-shaped (Figure 5) or, sometimes, U-shaped. The shape of the section is determined by various constraints, such as: the procedure of manufacture; the pre-stressing system used (pre-or post-tensioned); transport and assembly; the construction method of the bridge deck slab.

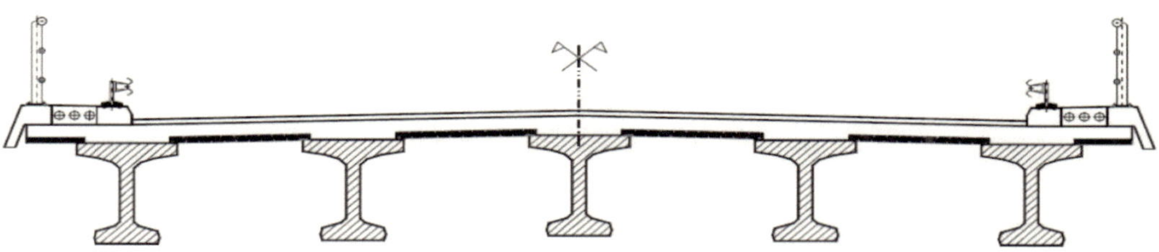

Figure 5. Cross section of a bridge with "I" beams (Sousa, 2004).

The constructive method applied to bridges with prefabricated beams can include differences in placement of prefabricated beams, or the type of connection between elements and execution of slabs. The first step consists of placing the prefabricated beams, which can be carried out by means of cranes a launcher (Figure 6).

a) b)

Figure 6. Placing of precast beams on the pillars (Leonhardt, 1982).

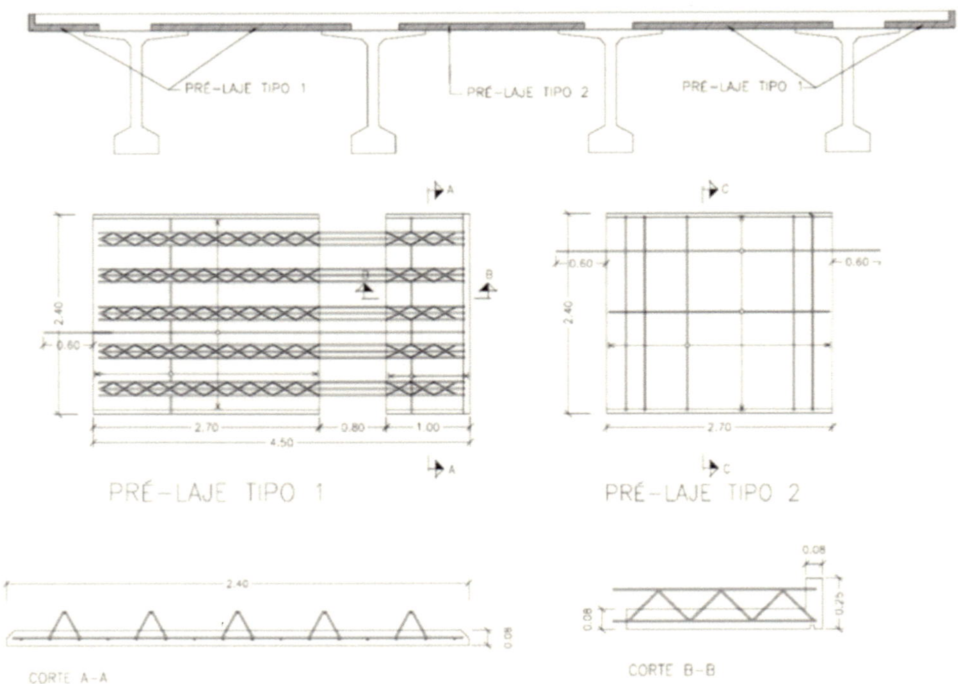

Figure 7. Reinforced pre-slabs used as lost shuttering.

After placing the prefabricated beams in their final position, the connection between these elements is performed using pre-slabs: This method consists of replacing the shuttering and supporting structure of the previous solution for reinforced concrete or pre-stressed slabs with a thickness that usually varies between 6 cm and 10 cm. These pre-slabs can be used as lost shuttering (Figure 7), in construction they can be used only to support the concrete slab or as bi-functional formwork, that is, functioning as formwork during the constructive phase, but as reinforcement during service.

5. 4D didactic model

5.1. Geometric modelling and equipment

After different kinds of bridge deck construction methods had been analysed, a commonly used model was chosen for the implementation of the 4D (3D+time) virtual model (Viana, 2012). The deck is composed of beams with I-shaped cross section, lifted by cranes and supplemented with composite pre-slabs. Initially, three-dimensional (3D) geometric modelling of all elements necessary to the implementation of the desired visual simulation was created. The example modelled corresponds to a bridge with the highway profile composed by five spans with the extension of 30m (central) and 24m (lateral) (Reis, 2006). The cross-section of the bridge deck consists of 4 precast beams (Figure 5).

The 3D modelling process is initiated with the generation of the surroundings of the working place, followed by the pillars, stair towers, worker platforms, provisional and definitive supports and two cranes needed to lift the precast beams (Figure 8).

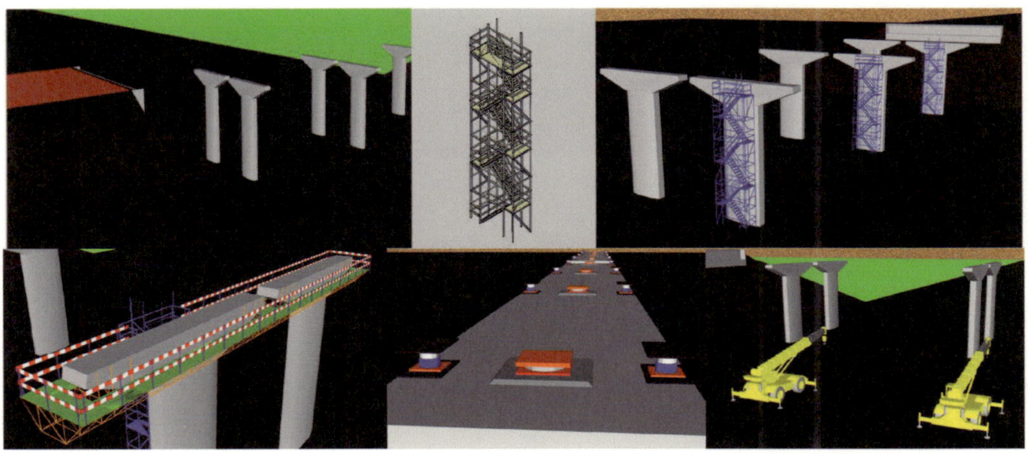

Figure 8. 3D models of the construction environment.

Figure 9. represents the configuration of the cross-section of the prefabricated beam used and the respective 3D model. In the projection it is possible to see: the running boards (red), protruding out of the beam, which serve to provide resistance and support for the connection of concrete of different ages of the deck slab; the reinforcements connecting precast beams (yellow); other reinforcements needed for lifting the beam (blue).

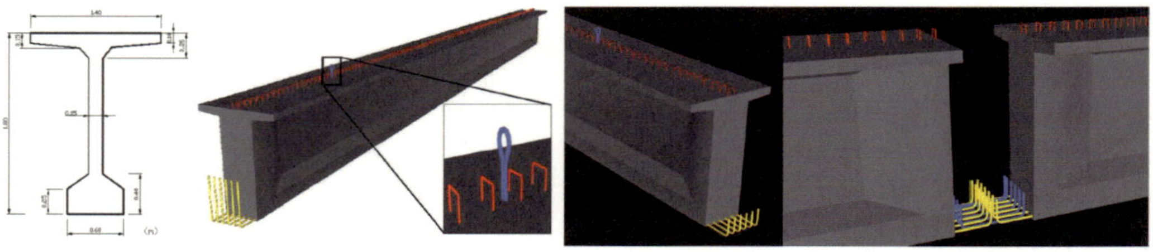

Figure 9. Cross-section and prefabricated beam model.

For the execution of the slab composite pre-slabs were chosen. The dimensions applied in creating the 3D model of the pre-slabs were established based on the drawings of the design of Beira Interior viaducts. Differentiation can be made between pre-slabs, depending on their location on the cross-section: type 1, between beams or type 2, in the console. Figure 10 shows a picture of the placement of both types of pre-slabs. The virtual model includes two types of pre-slabs: central and cantilever. Figure 10 illustrates the geometric model of two kinds of pre-slabs used in the virtual model. The pre-slab in the console is placed in the side of the deck cross-section and the central pre-slab is placed between beams.

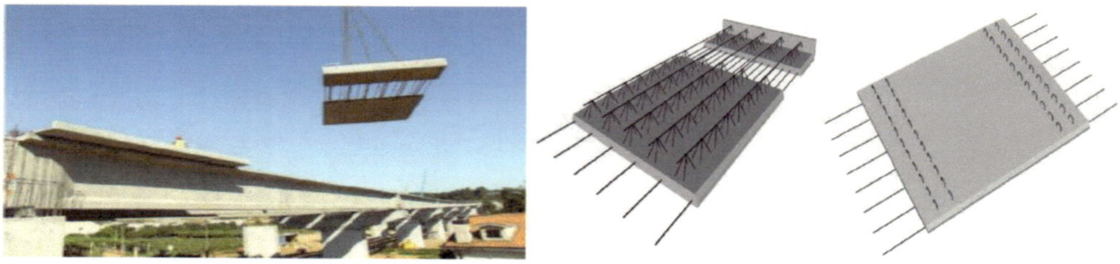

Figure 10. 3D models and placement of pre-slabs on the deck.

5.2. The constructive process activity

The visual simulation of the construction was accomplished using software based on the Virtual Reality (VR) technology, the Eon Studio (EON, 2013). In the application, the geometric model of the building is presented in a sequence simulating the construction activity. For that, each modelled component of the bridge is connected to the programming instruction: hidden and unhidden (Figure 11).

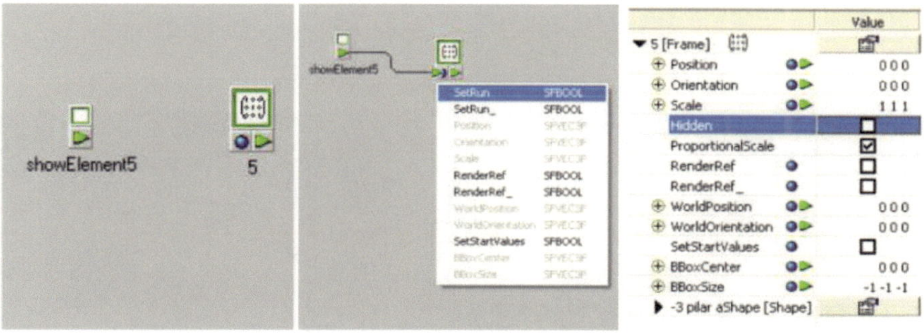

Figure 11. Hidden and unhidden instruction in the interface of the EON software.

This is one of the capacities allowed by the EON software. The command of unhide is first linked to each geometric model. An action will begin when the user click over an unhidden object and then the next object is visualized in the virtual environment, in accordance with the established sequence of the construction:

- The virtual simulation starts with the presentation of the work place environment;
- The simulation of the construction activity continues with the insertion of additional elements, such as the stair towers (for access to the top of the pillars) and the work platforms (which allow the workers to move around and complete their tasks) (Figure 12).

Figure 12. Display stair towers, work platforms and definitive and provisional supports.

- In the virtual space the placing of the definitive support device is simulated, followed by the placement of the temporary support, on the top of the pillars (Figure 12);
- Each beam is raised by two cranes and placed on the temporary support devices (Figure 13);

Figure 13. Prefabricated beams raised by two cranes.

- The simulation of construction process proceeds with the placement of the pre-slabs over the prefabricated beams (Figure 14). At this stage, it was found that due to the large amount of reinforcements set in the pre-slabs, the movement of the camera (from the point of view of the user) through the virtual environment was very slow because the drawing file was already too heavy. It was, therefore, decided not to display 3D model of the pre-slab reinforcements and also the brackets from prefabricated beams;

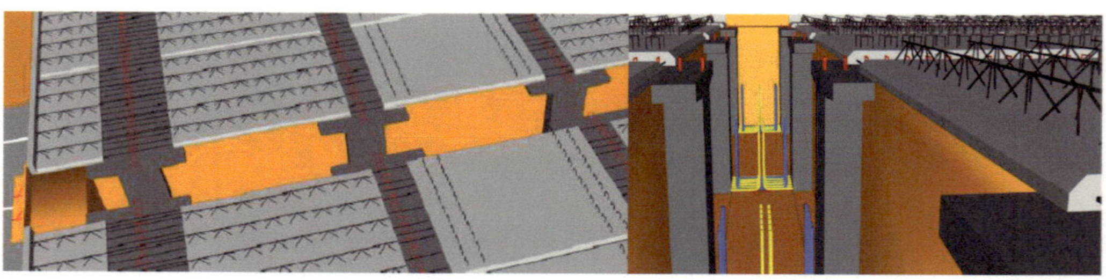

Figure 14. Placement of pre-slabs over the prefabricated beams.

- Then, the reinforcement of the slab is placed over the pre slabs and the deck slab is concreted (Figure 15);

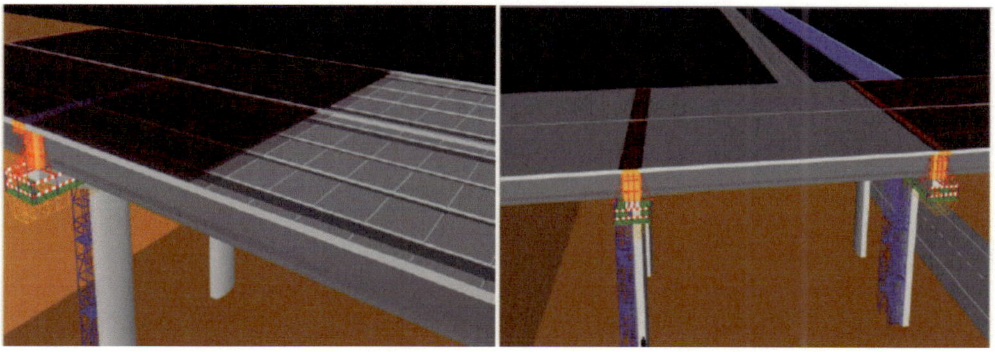

Figure 15. Placing reinforcement and concreting the deck slab.

- Next, the transversal beams are concreted. Figure 15 illustrates the placement of the formwork and reinforcement of one of the transversal beam;

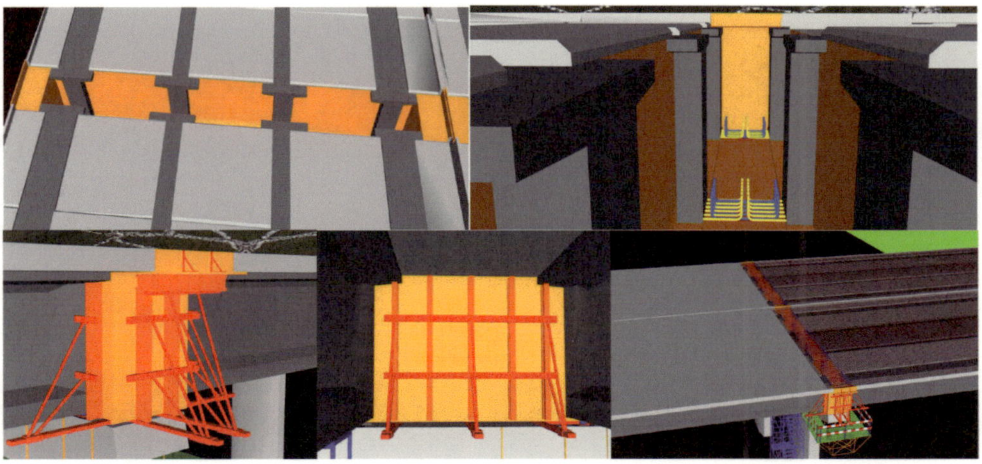

Figure 16. Removing the provisional support devices.

- After the completion of the construction of the deck the provisional support devices are removed (Figure 17);

- Finally all complementary elements necessary for the road traffic were inserted into the top of the deck (Figure 18).

The complete bridge can now be observed from any point of view (Figure 18). The model allows the user to use the zoom sufficiently well in order to understand the final configuration of the bridge. The animation of the VR application can be visualized in the a web site (Luiis, 2013).

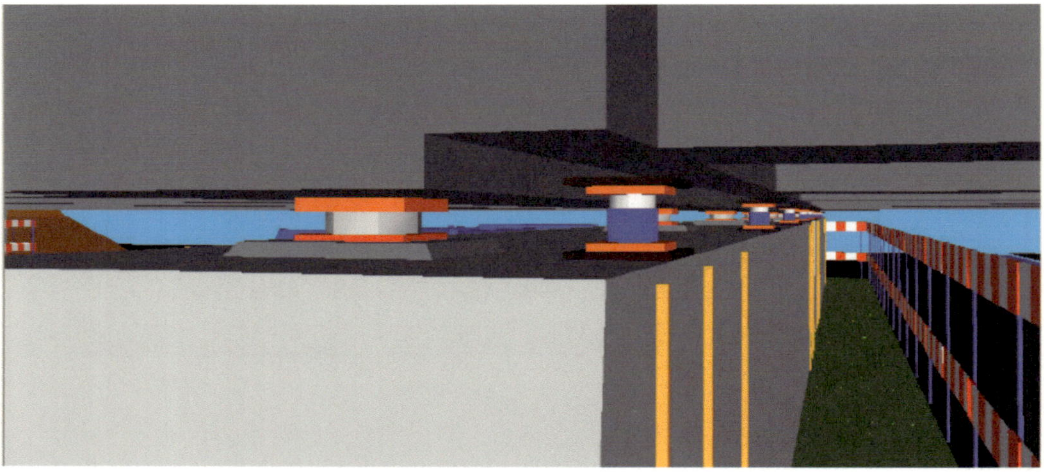

Figure 17. Removing the provisional support devices.

Figure 18. Placing the complementary elements off the deck

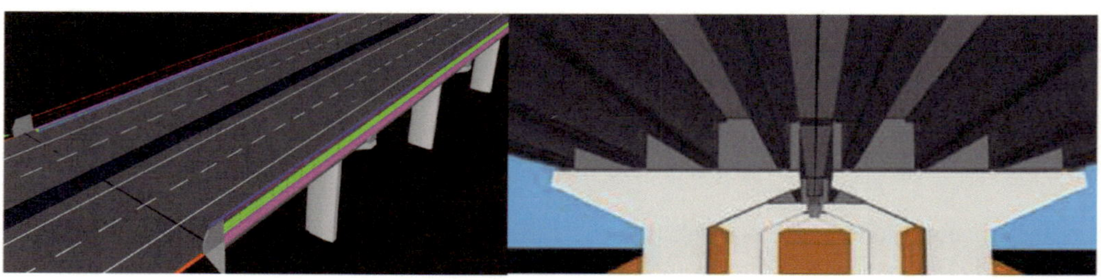

Figure 19. Views of the complete deck

6. Didactic aspects

The main objective of the practical application of this didactic model concerning a bridge construction process is to support class-based learning and in distance learning using e-learning technology. A didactic application to be used as an e-learning tool must meet the following requirements: reusability, accessibility, durability and interoperability (Birzina et al. 2012). Thus, it seeks the same educational database for be used by the international community through different learning software. Furthermore, it is necessary employ an accepted format with the aim of facilitate communication between different databases of several areas of knowledge. Also another important point to be considered is those models in e-learning institutions should be independent of country, language or any other regional circumstances in the process of creation the didactic models.

The bridge model is currently being used in face-to-face classes of disciplines of Civil Engineering curriculum: Construction Process (4th year) and Bridges (5th year). They were placed on the webpage for each discipline thus being available for students to manipulate. The student should download the EON Viewer application available at the EON web site. The traditional way to present the curricular subjects involved in those virtual models are 2D layouts or pictures. Now, the teacher interacts with the 3D models showing the sequence construction and the constitution of the modelled type of work. Through direct interaction with the models, it is possible to monitor the progress of the construction process of the bridge. The objective is not to replace current training methods but to position accurate as an additional teaching method. To do so, there were developed immersive 3D models that were based on an actual method of teaching.

The deck bridges model shows the complexity associated to the construction work of the deck. The model also illustrates in detail the movement of the equipment. In class, the teacher must explain way the process must follow both sequence of steps and the way the equipment devices operates. When the student, of the 5th year, goes to a real work place he can observe the complexity of the work and better understand the progression of construction previously explained. It provides an immersive capacity inherent to virtual world and it allows the students and teachers to go to a specific construction step. The camera movement shows the model in a consistent way to present all sequences of events allowing the user to perceive correctly the most important details of this construction method;

The discipline of Bridges, offered to 5th year students of Integrated Master Degree in Civil Engineering, has a weight of 4.5 curricular credits. The general objectives of the Bridges discipline concerns an introductory course on bridge design and construction, the basic concepts for prestressed concrete bridges and steel-concrete composite bridges, the basic models for the analysis and design of bridge superstructures and substructures. The curricular program of the Bridges discipline contains the specific topic "Design concept and execution methods: superstructure concept; concrete bridge decks-slab, beam-slab and box girder decks; composite (steel-concrete) bridge decks; piers, abutments and foundations; construction methods", along 9 hour, (program, 2014). And the assessment process is based in a final examination (70%) and a work report (30%). The recommended bibliographies are essentially the didactic text of Reis (2006) and two main books concerning construction of bridges (Leonhartd, 1982) and (Calgaro & Virlogeux, 1987). The different construction methodologies that are available must be well known by the future designers, as it influences significantly the choice of most suitable solution of the deck typology, for each particular situation. So the subject concerning bridge construction is of great importance in the discipline. The VR models became useful to teachers when they are presenting the distinct methodologies of constructing deck bridges. The interactive models are also an important support to students when writing the report of the discipline, as some students chose the construction processes topic to study. In these reports there are evident references to constructive details, to the sequence of activities and to the equipment needed to construct the bridges, aspects which are clearly presented in the virtual models. So the VR models have been contributing to a better understanding of the issue concerning bridge construction and also to motivate students to this specific topic.

The model was worked out attending both the technical knowledge and didactic aspects namely in how and what to show. It also attend that the model is going to be manipulated by undergraduate students of Civil Engineering. So, the model could be an important support to teachers to illustrate bridges construction issues in class and after, by themselves, using their own PCs. The animation of the construction process can then be visualized.

The didactic application of deck bridge construction was developed by the co-author L. Viana, as an engineering student, and supervised by the first author. This work complemented the author's skill concerning the use of the AutoCAD software. Along the course the engineering students learn how to use AutoCAD, mainly applied on the execution of 2D drawing and basic 3D models. L. Viana when generating the presented VR model increased their knowledge relating to the use of AutoCAD and learned how to use a new tool based on VR technology. Sik & Sik L. (2013) points that the knowledge of the 3D design and engineering software are indispensable for all kind of engineering activity (civil engineer, mechanical engineer, architecture and transportation engineering) and ask, among the students, about the necessity of learning AutoCAD in the faculty. The answer is naturally positive. The VR application presented in this chapter, complementing the AutoCAD training introduced at the 1st year, is in line with the point of view of those authors.

7. Conclusions

This paper analyses some constructive processes concerning bridge deck formed of precast beams and describes the implementation of an interactive model that simulates the construction work activity. The virtual application shows one of the methods most often applied in the construction of this type of bridge.

In the creation of the model software based on the Virtual Reality (RV) technology was used. VR allows, through interaction with 3D models of the environment, representing building components and equipment, the creation of the constructive sequence in time and space by simulating the progression of the construction of the deck, which allows a good understanding of the whole process.

The model 4D (3D+time) offers several advantages, allowing a deeper awareness of the relationship of the components of the building and the phasing of the work, leading to a better understanding of the spatial movement of equipment and of the component placement in

http://dx.doi.org/10.5772/58919

work. Since the traditional designs of graphic documentation of the construction project are sometimes more difficult to understand, it can be seen that this model is clearly didactic in character and as such can be used to support the training of students and professionals in the field of Bridges.

Author details

Alcínia Z. Sampaio and Luís Viana

University of Lisbon, Dep. Civil Engineering, Lisbon, Portugal

References

[1] 4D group (2014). 4D annotator: A visual decision support tool for construction planners, CIFE-Center for Integrated Facility Engineering, of Stanford University, http://web.stanford.edu/group/4D/workspace/papers/cife-98prop2.pdf, accessed: July, 2014.

[2] Abdelhameed, W.A. (2013).*Virtual reality used in architectural design studios: A case of studying structure and construction,* Procedia Computer Science, Vol. 25, 2013, pp. 220-230.

[3] Birzina, R.; Fernate, A.; Luka, I.; Maslo, I.; & Surikova, S. (2012) E-learning as a challenge for widening of opportunities for improvement of students' generic competences, journal E-Learning and Digital Media, ISSN 2042-7530, 01/2012, vol. 9 (2), pp 130-142.

[4] Calgaro, J.; & Virlogeux, M. (1987) Project et construction des ponts, Presses de l'École Nationale des Pontes et Chaussées, Vol I

[5] Câmara, J.N. (2001). Prefabrication of bridges and viaducts, didactic text, Lisbon, Portugal. http://www.civil.ist.utl.pt/~cristina/EBAP/PreFabricacaoEstruturas/Pontes%20e%20viadutos.pdf, accessed: July, 2014

[6] EON (2013). Introduction to working in EON Studio, EON Reality, Inc., http://www.eonreality.com/. accessed: July, 2014.

[7] Fillatreau, P.; Fourquet, J.-Y.; Cailhol, R.M.; Le Bolloc'h, S.; Datas, A.; & Puel, B. (2013). Using virtual reality and 3D industrial numerical models for immersive interactive checklists, Computers in Industry, Volume 64, Issue 9, Dec. 2013, pp. 1253-1262.

[8] Fischer, M. (2000) 4D CAD-3D Models incorporated with time schedule, CIFE-Centre for Integrated Facility Engineering in Finland, VTT-TEKES, CIFE technical report, Helsinki, Finland.

[9] Fischer, M.; & Kunz, J. (2004) The scope and role of information technology in construction, in: CIFE Centre for Integrated Facility Engineering in Finland, technical report #156, Stanford University.

[10] Juntas, P. (2013). Picture CC-BY-SA-2.5, http://creativecommons.org/licenses/by-sa/2.5), accessed: June, 2014.

[11] Kähkönen, K.; & Leinonen, J. (2014) VTT Building and Transport VTT, Finland, http://cic.vtt.fi/4d/4d.htm, accessed: July, 2014.

[12] Khanzode, A.; Fisher, M.; & Reed, D. (2007). Challenges and benefits of implementing virtual design and construction technologies for coordination of mechanical, electrical, and plumbing systems on large healthcare project, in: CIB 24th W78 Conference, Maribor, Slovenia, pp. 205-212.

[13] Leinonen, J.; Kähkönen, K.; & Retik, A. (2013) New construction management practice based on the virtual reality technology. In Raja R.A., Flood I, William J, O'Brien (Ed.), 4D CAD and Visualization in Construction: Developments and Applications, A.A. Balkema Publishers, pp. 75-100.

[14] Leonhardt, F. (1982) Concrete constructions – basic principles of construction of concrete bridges, Vol 6, Ed. Interciência Rio de Janeiro, Basil.

[15] Luiis (2013) http://www.youtube.com/watch?v=zSIRXL64HnQ&feature=youtu.be, accessed: July, 2014

[16] Menck, N.; Weidig, C.; & Aurich, J.-C. (2013). Virtual reality as a collaboration tool for factory planning based on scenario technique, Forty Sixth CIRP Conference on Manufacturing Systems 201, Procedia CIRP, Vol. 7, 2013, pp. 133-138.

[17] Mohammed, E.H. (2007). n-D Virtual Environment in Construction Education, Proc. the 2nd International Conference on Virtual Learning, ICVL 2007, pp. 1-6.

[18] Petzold, F.; Bimber, O.; & Tonn, O. (2007). CAVE without CAVE: on-site visualization and Design Support in and within existing building, in: eCAADe 07, 25th Conference of Education and Research in Computer Aided Architectural Design in Europe, Frankfurt, Germany, pp. 161-168.

[19] Program (2014), https://fenix.tecnico.ulisboa.pt/disciplinas/Pon25/2014-2015/1-semestre/program, accessed: July, 2014

[20] Reis, A.J. (2006). Bridges, Didactic text, Technical University of Lisbon, Lisbon, Portugal.

[21] Sampaio A.Z., Santos J.P., Gomes A.R., Rosário D.P. (2012). Construction and maintenance planning supported on virtual environments, Book: Virtual Reality-Human

Computer Interaction, Ed. Xin-Xing Tang, Publisher: InTech, Published: September 05, 2012, ISBN 978-953-51-0721-7, DOI: 10.5772/46409, ch. 07, pp. 125 – 152. http://www.intechopen.com/articles/show/title/construction-and-maintenance-planning-supported-on-virtual-environments, accessed: July, 2014.

[22] Sampaio A.Z.; Cruz C.O.; & Martins, O.P. (2011). Didactic models in Civil Engineering education: Virtual simulation of construction works, Book: Virtual Reality, Ed. Jae-Jin Kim, ISBN: 978-953-307-518-1, Publisher: InTech, Copyright: Janeiro 2011, ch. 28, pp. 579 – 598, http://www.intechopen.com/articles/show/title/didactic-models-in-civil-engineering-education-virtual-simulation-of-construction-works, accessed: July, 2014.

[23] Sampaio, A.Z.; & Henriques, P.G. (2008). Virtual reality technology applied to the visual simulation of construction activities, The Open Construction & Building Technology Journal, Mathew Honan, Editorial Director, Bentham Science Publishers Ltd., vol. 2, pp. 7-14.

[24] Sampaio, A.Z.; & Martins, O.P. (2014). The application of virtual reality technology in the construction of bridge: The cantilever and incremental launching methods, Automation in Construction, Vol. 37, January 2014, pp. 58-67. http://www.youtube.com/watch?v=S3Kf9e6JgF4, accessed: July, 2014.

[25] Sampaio, A.Z.; Henriques, P.G.; Studer, P.; & Luizi, R. (2005). Interaction with virtual 3D models in order to access the construction processes of a wall and a bridge, in B.H.V. Topping, (Editor), Proceedings of the Tenth International Conference on Civil, Structural and Environmental Engineering Computing – CC 2005, Rome, Italy, Civil-Comp Press, Stirlingshire, UK, Paper 79, abstract pp. 185-186, 2005. doi:10.4203/ccp.81.79, accessed: July, 2014.

[26] Sik G.; & Sik Lanyi C. (2013) Is necessary to teach 3D design and engineering software for engineering students or the knowledge of these software are required skills?, Journal of Applied Multimedia 1(8), pp. 17-24, http://www.jampaper.eu/Jampaper_H-ARC/2013._VIII._1.sz._files/JAMPAPER130103e.pdf, accessed: July, 2014

[27] Sousa, C.F.F. (2004). Structural continuity in bridge decks built with prefabricated beams. Solutions with reinforced concrete connection. MSc thesis in Civil Engineering Structures, FEUP, Porto, Portugal.

[28] Viana, L.F. (2012). Simulation of the construction of the bridge deck composed of prefabricated beams based on Virtual Reality technology. MSc thesis in Civil Engineering Structures, IST, Lisbon, Portugal.

[29] Woksepp, S. (2007). Virtual Reality in Construction. Tools, Methods and Processes, PhD thesis in Civil Engineering, Luleå University of Technology, Sweden.

Chapter 5

Virtual Reality-based Training System for Metal Active Gas Welding

Hwa Jen Yap, Zahari Taha, Hui Kang Choo and
Chee Khean Kok

Additional information is available at the end of the chapter

http://dx.doi.org/10.5772/59279

1. Introduction

Metal Active Gas (MAG) welding is defined as a joining process where the metal electrode is fed continuously to contact the base metal. It is widely used in many industries. A decreased in skilled welders have seriously affect the manufacturing and construction industries. This scenario is due to high cost of training, material and maintenance. Complex geometry trajectory and welding path is difficult to weld and can only be done either by an experienced welder or a welding robot due to differences in surface profiles. With a virtual reality based welding simulator, learning MAG welding can be made easier and faster.

Virtual Reality (VR) is an artificial environment or computer-generated virtual environment with the association of hardware to give the impression of real world situation to the user [1]. It gives a person a sense of reality and its utilization has increased in many fields [2, 3]. The sensorial modalities are visual, auditory, tactile, smell, taste and others. With the aids of interactive devices such as goggles, head-mounted display (HMD), headsets, gloves fitted with sensors, haptic input devices and external audio system which are able to send and receive information, this enable people to manipulate the virtual object. The created virtual environment is accomplished by motion sensors for movement tracking purpose and the output displayed is adjusted accordingly, usually done in real time to enhance the realism. The output is usually displayed through a computer screen or through special stereoscopic displays. The illustration of the physical presence in the environment provides the welder an insight of the welding techniques and proper postures. The word 'haptics' is defined as the sense of touch which includes both tactile and kinesthetic sensory information [4]. SensAble Technologies claimed that haptic is the science of incorporating the sense of torch and control into computer applications through force (kinesthetic) or tactile feedback [5]. Haptic is also defined as the touch-based interface construction techniques [6]. In order to achieve realistic haptic rendering, a minimum update rate of 1 kHz and 5 kHz – 10 kHz for a rigid surface and a textured surface are required. Whereas for haptic rendering, 1 kHz for haptics is recommended in contrast to 30 Hz for graphics.

Previous work on weld training system such as CS WAVE, ARC+and SIMWelder of VRSim support either single pass or multi-pass welding process with some graphical metaphors to teach welding motions. In Wang's studies, he developed a manual arc welding training system that uses Phantom haptic device to provide force feedback [7]. Using the method of co-location combined with multi-modal input and sensory modes have led to better performance of the system [8]. In 2012, Kenneth developed a low cost virtual reality welder training system [9]. The virtual welding simulator gave the position and the orientation of the torch while the graphics engine of the simulator manages the virtual scenes with the input data [10]. According to [11], the problem of skill transmission faced is as shown in Figure 1. Researchers believed that the trainees can learn welding easily and effectively through visualization [12].

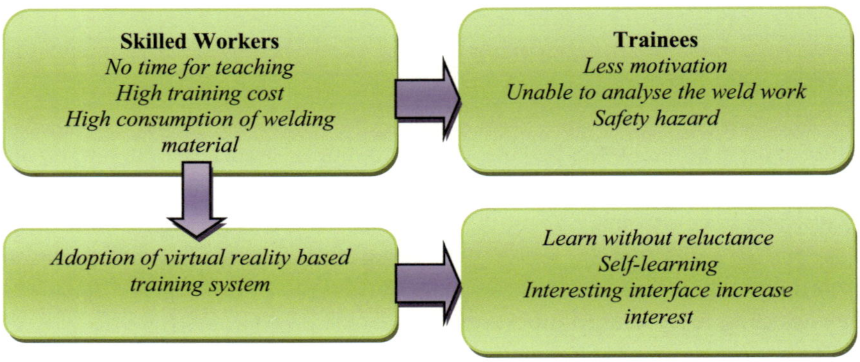

Figure 1. Problems and countermeasures for training

From the economic aspect, virtual welding training program brings potential savings from the materials and resources. In addition, it brings significant reduction in the usage of energy by reducing the use of regular welding machines as well as reducing the maintenance cost of the conventional welding machine. From the environmental aspect, this training program helps in decreasing the carbon offsets and carbon emission. With the virtual welding simulator, it can be used to supplement existing welding curriculum which provides a gateway to the user involved in modern learning spaces to build up their interest with the initial approach of fun besides aligning with the strategic objective of the curriculum under true-to-life condition without any safety risks and free from the hazardous working environment.

The importance of study can be summarized as follow:

- Optimum welding speed, the contact tip-to-work distance (CTWD) and welding torch orientation is shown to the welder candidate by the system. It helps the welder candidate in learning the correct welding posture.

- Visibility of results and error analysis can be provided immediately or subsequently to the welder candidates.
- A better educational monitoring can be implemented for self-learning which consists of full guidance in defining various conditions and standardized training can be pre-programmed.

2. Background of study

Recent years, with the improvement in high speed computing especially of high resolution graphics and the user interaction devices, the technology of virtual reality (VR) has been widely used. VR has emerged as a useful and important tool in today's society. A VR system creates an environment which enables human to interact with anything or anyone on a virtual level. In fact, this technology has emerged twenty years ago. Now, VR has been widely applied in the medical field, manufacturing, education, military, gaming, entertainment, commerce, and architecture.

One of the major applications of VR is in the manufacturing field. Virtual manufacturing (VM) and virtual assembly (VA) have played an important role today. Furthermore, many VR systems have been widely applied in today's industry especially as a training simulator. One of the most popular VR systems is the co-location stereoscopic visualization system. The term co-location refers to the existence of the display and the input in the same location at the same time. The advantages of using the co-location VR system is to increase immersion, allow easy interaction between the user and the object as well as enable the user to directly manipulate the virtual object. In addition, this system can help the user to eliminate the need to model the whole working environment.

In the manufacturing and construction industries, joining plays a vital role in mechanical strength of the structure as well as the aesthetic value. Thus welding method is commonly used to eliminate the screw and nut in the joining. There are several different ways to weld, such as: Shielded Metal Arc Welding (SMAW), Gas Tungsten Arc Welding (GTAW), Tungsten Inert Gas (TIG), Metal Active Gas (MAG) and Metallic Inert Gas Welding (MIG). SMAW has an electrode that has flux, the protectant for the puddle around it. The electrode holder holds the electrode as it slowly melts away. The slag protects the weld puddle. GTAW or TIG involves a much smaller hand-held gun that has a tungsten rod inside of it. Gas Metal Arc Welding (GMAW) involves a wire fed "gun" that feeds wire at an adjustable speed and sprays a shielding gas over the weld puddle to protect it. GMAW can be divided into two categories based on the types of shielding gas used which are Metal Inert Gas (MIG) welding and the Metal Active Gas (MAG) welding. If the shielding gas used is inert gas or noble gas such as argon and helium, it is known as MIG welding. MAG welding uses active gas such as carbon dioxide and oxygen. This is because most gasses or gas mixtures used are not only the inert gas, but in many welding cases they are actually active gasses such as carbon dioxide. The purpose of these shielding gasses is to prevent the molten weld pool from being contaminated by the oxygen or nitrogen present in the atmosphere. Insufficient gas flow may result in "porosity" of the weld bead while excessive gas flows creates turbulence and it will reduce weld pool temperature causing decreased penetration.

There are three types of weld transfers that can be perform by GMAW.

a. Short Circuit – When the welding torch is triggered, the electrode wire feeds continuously to the arc, "short circuiting" (touching) to the base metal. It is suitable to be used on thinner metals, which produces a fast, high pitch crackling sound. High percentage of carbon dioxide shielding gas or 100% carbon dioxide need to be used with voltage set on the lower range. The number of short circuits per second will upon inductance settings and the diameter of wire that is being used.

b. Globular – The globs of wire are expelled from the electrode wire to the arc after the electrode wire touched the base metal at the beginning of welding. Basically, it is used on thicker metals, producing a popping sound and more spatters of metal. This process requires higher voltage, amperage and wire feed speed.

c. Spray – A stream of tiny molten droplets is transferred across the arc from the electrode wire to the base metal. This method is used on thicker metals, producing deep, fast crackling sound. A higher percentage of argon gas or pure argon depending on metal welded is used and the process requires high current density hence needing higher voltage and amperage. Usually, it is use for horizontal position and flat position (T-fillet weld).

Based on the facilities available in the Faculty of Engineering, University of Malaya, and Metal Active Gas (MAG) welding is chosen for the virtual reality application. Material is fixed as low carbon mild steel as it is the main material used in the industries. With the technology of virtual reality system, variety of techniques, seam shapes and welding movements can be practise and commercial MAG welding equipment and typical workpiece are used in familiarizing the beginner welder.

3. Problem statement

Currently many industrial fields such as automobiles industry, pipelines industry and construction industry are faced with the shortage of qualified welders due to high training cost in welding. In order to ensure the quality of weld work, the companies have to bear the huge cost in consumption of materials and energy, maintenance of the welding machine and the cost of hiring the expert to teach the beginner. Large amount of waste material will be produced from the conventional welding training program. This causes the serious issues in environmental pollution and carbon emission. In addition, the trend of using the virtual reality technologies in training environments has increased due to several benefits. User can undergoes self-learning process with all the standardizing training without the guidance of expert. Virtual reality based training system is a better choice of supplement tool and lower cost relative to conventional welding program for welder candidates.

Welding robots and robot automatic welding technology are familiar and was widely used in automotive industry and shipping industry. Welding robot control system are improved by

http://dx.doi.org/10.5772/59279

using intelligent control system, welding seam tracking technology and advanced adaptive capability. However, the trajectory of the welding path is yet imperfect. Some 3D paths are difficult determine the location point and hence difficult to be programmed. The inverse kinematics is impossible to determine the end effector's point in the joint space or Cartesian space for the path trajectories. The seam tracking performance is varying from one material to another material due to their different surface reflectivity. Teach and playback technique was used in such situation. Several welding testing was done by welder to ensure the weld quality, suitable parameters and orientations were set before teaching the robot. Thus, many materials and time were wasted in the manual testing stage. Hence, VR technologies have been across as a strategy to solve it.

Besides that, welding is hazardous to our health. Welding health hazards from Occupational Safety & Health Administration (OSHA) can be categorised into chemical agents and physical agents. In the welding process, welding smoke occurred and it is a complex mixture which consists of oxide fumes, condensed solids and harmful gases including ozone and carbon monoxide. Inhalation and long term exposure to theses metal fumes will cause long term effects on lungs such as metal fume fever, respiratory illness, lung irritation and pulmonary oedema. In addition, MAG welding have to be carried out in a close ventilation space to ensure the fully protection from shielding gas and maintain the quality of weld. Thus, it increases the percentage of health hazards. For example, carbon steel, the most common material welded contain of manganese. If overexposure to it, chronic manganese poisoning can cause Parkinson's disease and other neurological effects. On the other hands, physical agents are ultraviolent radiation (UV), infrared radiation (IR) and intense visible light. In the welding process, UV and IR were generated by the electric arc which may cause the skin effects or result in severe burns on the skin surface and cause retinal damage if the welder careless observing the arc without eye protection due to lack of experience. For the beginners, they do not have enough of safety knowledge and welding experience. This could be an adverse impact on health effects as they are exposure to those harmful factors. This is the reason why the virtual reality based welding training program is needed.

4. Objectives of study

The objectives of this study are:

- To simulate the Metal Active Gas (MAG) welding in virtual environment.
- To train the welder to maintain proper arc length, proper welding torch orientation, proper travel speed by using haptic guidance.
- To develop a path planning system for industrial robot in MAG welding.
- To decrease in waste, environment resources and cost in conventional welding training program.

5. Methodology

The hardware set up includes a SensAble PHANTOM Omni™ device (Figure 2), a standard welding torch, computer workstation and speakers. The PHANTOM Omni™ device was chosen in this application as its 6 degree of freedom (DOF) is easily mapped to the movement of welding process. This equipment has a six-axis encoder and three-axial servomotor. Thus, the coordinates of the position in both real and virtual space can be the output for the path planning for robotic welding. PHANTOM Omni and its interfaces are considered affordable electromechanical kinesthetic haptic desktop device. The interaction between the virtual space and the haptic device can be realized through the stylus. In this study, the stylus pen was replaced with the standard welding torch in order to familiarizing beginning welder candidates with the welding equipment. The user's force and motion information are tracked by the Phantom system with its 6 DOF of maneuverability. In addition, it provides feedback to 3 DOF and high performance force effects which can reach 3.3N.

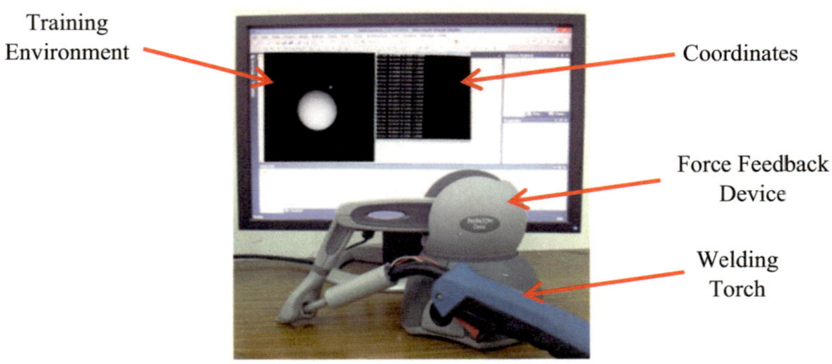

Figure 2. System Setup

The software is designed with multi-threaded application. The graphics, physics engine and haptic run in separate threads (Figure 3). The haptic application requires 1 kHz rendering frequency to reproduce forces convincingly. SensAble OpenHaptics Toolkit is a comprehensive platform which has a large coverage for creating interactive 3D applications. With OpenHaptics, OpenGL and Visual Studio C++ SDK, it is possible to include customized functions and special features based on programmers knowledge.

OpenGL interface consists of about 150 distinct commands that can be used to specify the objects and operations needed to produce interactive three dimensional applications. It is independent of the graphics hardware and windows system and is a state machine. OpenGL has been selected as the Application Programming Interface (API). It is because OpenGL is a free and platform independent API. C++ has been chosen as the language for this program. In OpenGL, the programmer usually provides the steps necessary to achieve a certain appearance or effect. OpenGL is used for a variety of purposes from CAD engineering and architecture applications to modelling programs used to create realistic computer-generated 3D model and

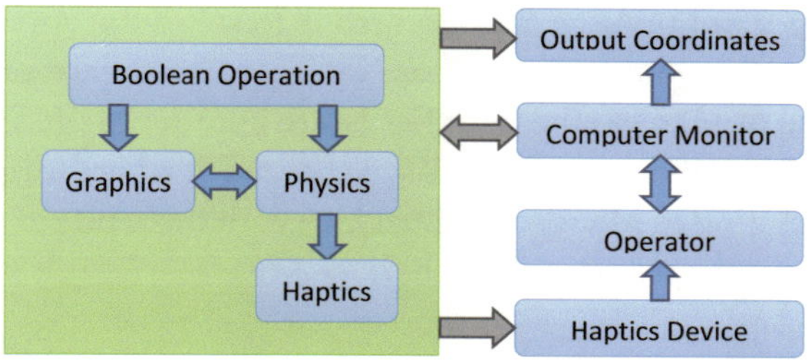

Figure 3. Software Architecture

images. Instead of describing the scene and how it should appear, the programmer actually prescribes the steps necessary to achieve a certain appearance or effect. These 'steps' consists of calls to OpenGL which includes more than 200 commands and functions. These commands are used to draw graphics primitives such as points, lines, and polygon in three dimensions.

OpenHaptics® Toolkit 3.0 is a two layer haptic library. Higher layer library, high-level application programming interface (HLAPI), provides advanced support to haptic rendering in managing the threads model. Haptic display, force feedback and collision detection operate in three separate threads that are updated respectively at 30, 100 and 1 kHz. Features such as impulse and vibration are created to enhance the realism of the VR system. The positions and orientation of the welding torch was further extracted from the virtual space which can be used for path planning in robotic welding.

OpenHaptics 3.0 made programming simpler by encapsulation the basic steps common to all haptics or graphics application. This encapsulation is implemented in the C++ classes of the QuickHaptics micro application programming interface. By anticipating typical use scenarios, a wide range of default parameter settings is put into place that allow the user to code haptically enabled applications very efficiently. The common steps required by haptics or graphics applications include:

- Parsing geometry files from popular animation packages.
- Creating graphics windows and initializing the OpenGL environment.
- Initializing one or multiple haptics devices.
- Scene and camera design.
- Mapping force and stiffness parameters to objects in the scene.
- Setting up callback responses to interactions.

In the second QuickHaptics level are functions that provide custom force effects, more flexible model interactions, and user-defined callback functions. The third level of the pyramid shows that QuickHaptics is built on the foundation provided by the existing OpenHaptics 2.0 Haptic Library (HL) and Haptic Device (HD) functions.

SensAble OpenHaptics® Toolkit is a comprehensive platform which has a large coverage for creating interactive 3D applications. With the OpenHaptics®, OpenGL® and Visual Studio C

++ SDK. The most important thing in this research is to setup the appropriate virtual reality based training system in welding application. Necessary hardware setup for the computer system is crucial as one need to get the right hardware in order to precede the research. After the hardware setup, drivers and software are implemented into hardware and then proceeding step is to start programming in Microsoft Visual C++ with the guide of OpenHaptics Toolkit. The Figure 4 below show the research flow chart.

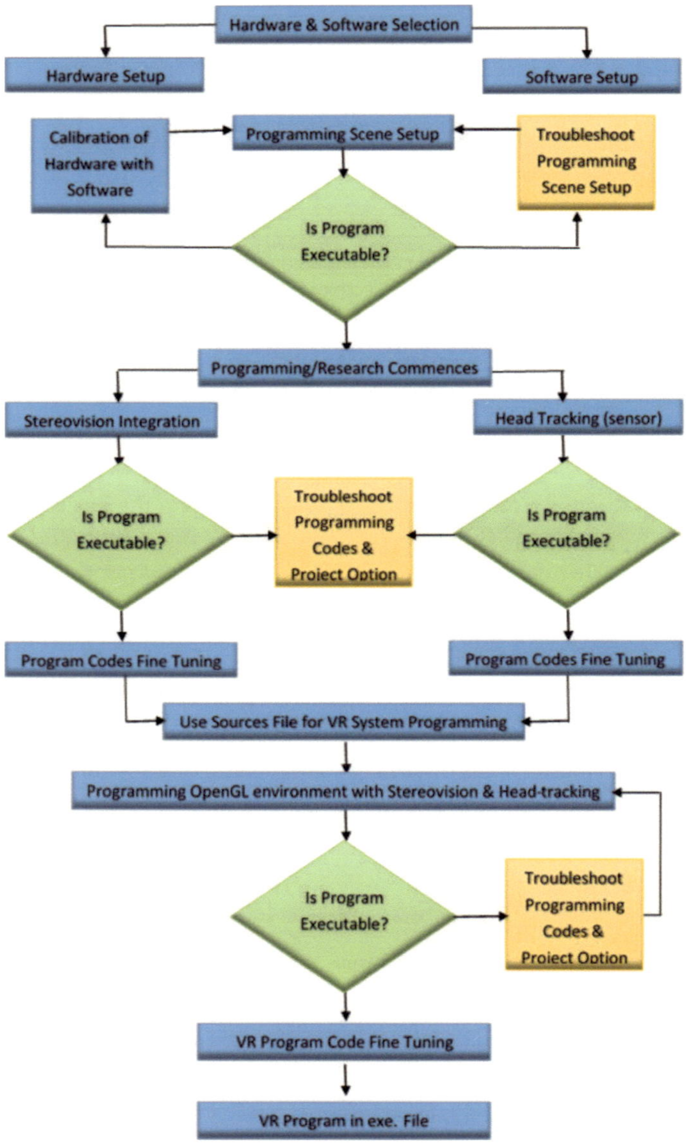

Figure 4. Research Flow Chart

5.1. Haptic feedbacks

The impulse function was included and used as a force that generated due to the creation of plasma at the beginning of the welding process. The provided toolkits are able to configure the magnitude, direction, duration and events (Figure 5). The function is trigged when the distance between the welding torch and virtual object is smaller than pre-defined optimum welding distance. The parameter are tested and simulated to mimic the actual welding process. Besides, the vibration function (Figure 6) is uses to simulate as the generated welding force between workpiece and the electrode. This feedback will be trigged continuously during the whole welding process. Nevertheless, the sound effect is added once the haptic feedback is trigged.

```
/* Trigger an impulse by commanding a force with a
   direction and magnitude for a small duration. */
hlEffectd(HL_EFFECT_PROPERTY_DURATION, duration);
hlEffectd(HL_EFFECT_PROPERTY_MAGNITUDE, 0.8);
hlEffectdv(HL_EFFECT_PROPERTY_DIRECTION, direction);
hlTriggerEffect(HL_EFFECT_CONSTANT);
```

Figure 5. Configuration of impulse feedback

```
/*************************************************************************
 Modifies the vibration frequency being used by the haptic thread.
*************************************************************************/
HDCallbackCode HDCALLBACK SetVibrationFreqCallback(void *pUserData)
{
    HDint *nFrequency = (HDint *) pUserData;
    gVibrationFreq = *nFrequency;
    return HD_CALLBACK_DONE;
}

/*************************************************************************
 Modifies the vibration amplitude being used by the haptic thread.
*************************************************************************/
HDCallbackCode HDCALLBACK SetVibrationAmplitudeCallback(void *pUserData)
{
    HDdouble *amplitude = (HDdouble *) pUserData;
    gVibrationAmplitude = *amplitude;
    return HD_CALLBACK_DONE;
}
```

Figure 6. Configuration of vibration feedback

6. Usability test

In the welding task, the complex geometry three dimensional models and animation were created from the OpenGL in C/C++ languages. During the basic welding training, positional and vibrational guided haptic feedbacks were generated in the program and experienced through the haptic device.

Two groups of subjects with a total of 50 people were included: Group-A and Group-B. The subjects were randomly selected from the students at the Faculty of Engineering, University of Malaya. For the Group-A, the students will be trained by using the VR-based welding system before proceed to workshop for actual MAG welding training. Meanwhile, Group-B will be trained in reverse training process, they will be trained using actual apparatus before proceed to VR-based training system. During the VR-based training process, the subject looks at the scene and starts the welding training. When the trigger of the welding torch is pressed, the feature of impulse and vibration is generated to the torch as in the real welding force in the welding process. Acoustic effect is generated to represent the sound of the welding process. The haptic was demonstrated and they were tried the virtual haptics system before the actual usability query. A questionnaire regarding the experience level and system feedback was then given to the subjects, which cover the following aspects:

a. The easiness of haptic interface

b. User interface is natural

c. The usefulness of the sense of force feedback

d. The usefulness of haptic welding application

e. Adoption of haptic as a training tool

f. Recommendation from users

The questionnaire is in the form of satisfactory levels. The subject can also give free comments and ideas about the VR based training system for MAG welding.

7. Results and discussion

From the questionnaire analysis, 76% of the subjects (38 out of 50 subjects) preferred Head-Mounted Display (HMD) rather than digital video (DV). They suggested that head-mounted display can be modified and inserted in the welding mask as part of the actual welding equipment. It is found that 90% of the subjects agreed with the force feedback feature to be included in the VR based training system to give them more impression about virtual space. They will enable the force feedback function during the virtual training system, which claimed that the haptics feedback provided more realistic and immersive virtual environment. The weakness of this training system is shown in Table 1.

Figure 7 shows the results of section-B from the survey from question 4 to question 9. This section is mainly focused on the level of satisfaction toward the training system after the candidates tested the developed VR-based training system. It is found that majority of the subjects support the VR interface and accept it as the supplement activity in the welding

Reasons	Number (%)
Lack of the sense of reality	42 (84%)
Difficult to handle the device	18 (36%)
Lack of interactive teaching aid	38 (76%)
Lack of auditory feedback	21 (42%)

Table 1. Weakness of this training system

training program. The sense of haptics feedback is the most important components to improve the realism of the VR system and improves the MAG welding training application.

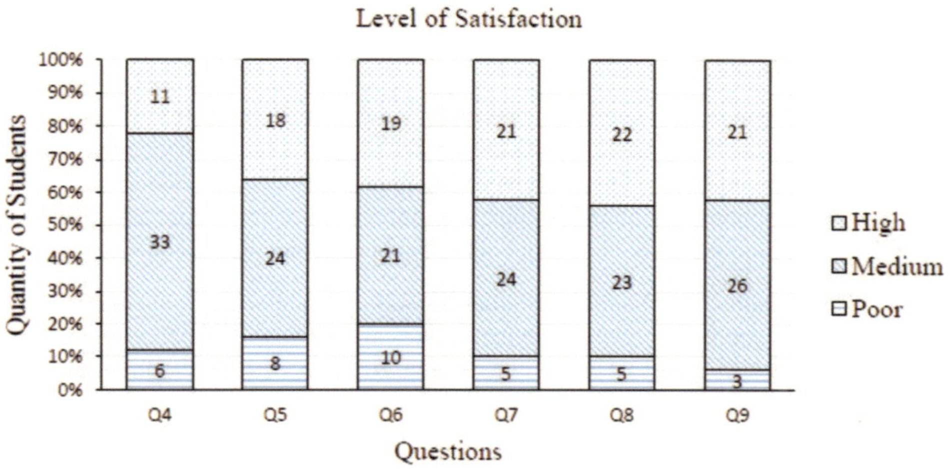

Figure 7. Level of satisfaction for post-experiment questions

Figure 8 shows the feedback from the welder candidates regarding the recommendations and future work in order to improve this training system. Total of 46 subjects agreed that the beginner welder should undergo the virtual reality based training system before expose to the real welding application. Besides, nearly 80% of the subjects agreed that the implementation of the VR based training system (supplement activity) for the existing welding curriculum, the overall training cost can be reduced. This is because the elimination of the hiring fee for expect welder, less maintenance fee for the welding machine as well as the reduction in the material used in welding. More than 80% of the subjects suggested that the playback function should be included to review the training performance. Furthermore, 100% of the candidates think that the instant computer aided instruction with haptic guidance should be included.

From the analysis aspect, a playback video is necessary to review the hand movement and welding performance. Instant Computer Aided Instruction (CAI) with the haptic guidance should be included as well to make the VR based training system practical.

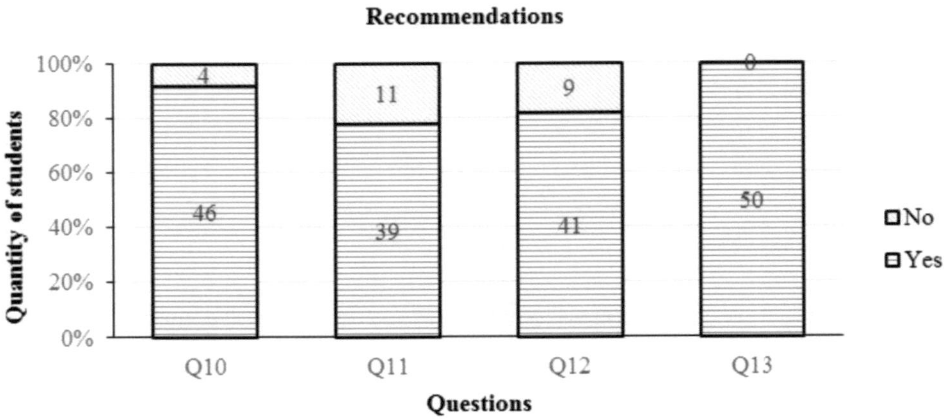

Figure 8. Recommendations from the candidate

Weld penetration has an important role in determining the mechanical strength of welds. The coordinates and the gimbal angles of the welding torch are extracted from its movement in the virtual space and saved into a file for further process which can be used in the trajectory planning of complex geometry model in robotic welding. This is important because the seam detection for autonomous robotic welding was difficult to be programmed.

The use of virtual reality based simulation that display a dynamic 3D environment is seems like playing a video game. All the welder candidates are younger than 25 as they approach this VR system, they will though it was a video game. Although the simulation tools employs game-like behaviours and look alike as a video game, there is a difference between them. For example, visual realism and special effects are focused in video games whereas welding simulation is stressed on reproducing an accurate representation of weld profile.

Scoring for the weld work done in the training system should be implemented. This is because the younger users have the competitive behaviour in their characteristics. The friendly competition being able to have more practice among the welder candidates and it is indirectly provides a good platform for self-learning. With the integrated training system, the consumption on the material used in welding training is zero, no scrap, no limit on test plates and safe to everyone. Through the virtual reality based training system, it should help the welder candidates to gain a better understanding or early exposure to welding process in proper weld postures and techniques. The welding features such as movement angle, work angle, contact tips to workpiece distance, welding speed, feeding speed and the voltage adjustment were the main focus points in the welding simulator.

The system should be built as similar as to the reality welding process either the welding features or the physical features [13]. It can be concluded that the welder candidates' welding skill can be trained efficiently and more competent by using this VR based system. Vora stated that the positive transfer effect exist when dealing a task between virtual condition and actual surroundings [14]. According to the results of the initial user study, the major advantage of

http://dx.doi.org/10.5772/59279

the VR based training system for MAG welding appears to be its efficiency. Virtual space is a controlled environment where distracting elements could be ruled out training for improving efficiency of the training process. In virtual training environment, lesser time can cost needed for preparing and managing the training materials. And by providing safe and convenient environment, training and instructing could be held more fluently and efficiently, in comparison to the stressful real working environment where a lot of distracting and dangerous elements exist, such as noise, sparks, flames and heat.

In retrospect, there are two major issues in the training system that needs further improvements, through the survey from the welder candidates. First, is enhancing the visual quality of the visual environment and actual work environment in 3D virtual space, it appears that user's expectations are higher than we thought in terms of visual realism. Another problem is the absence of haptic feedback on contacts between the torch tip and the mother material. Initially, an assumption was made in this training system that is there has to be a certain amount of gap maintained between the torch and base material in order to form the electric arc. Stick-out situation was considered as a failure in the training system. However, in practically, the common way that the welder starts welding appears to be contacting the torch tip on the material surface to form the electric arc before lifting it up to a certain level. Thus, it seems reasonable to include haptic feedbacks on stick-out situations.

8. Conclusions

Virtual Reality is an artificial environment created in software to give the impression of a real world situation and affords an effective means to rapidly prototype products. In addition, welding is a skill, and as such requires that its practitioners be trained to a standard; this kind of training requires time, money and talent. Modern welding with the integrated training program has the potential to reduce the training costs. However, cost savings is only beneficial if the result is a competent welder who is trained in a timely manner.

In the paper, the proposed virtual reality based training system with haptic feedback for metal active gas welding helps those welder candidates to efficiently learn complicate weld operations. The interface is intuitive and easy to use. However, realism needs to be improved to provide a more convincing virtual representation. Although there are 85% of the welder candidates support the system, but from the findings and feedback from them, the exits VR welding training system still cannot provide the accuracy training.

Currently, rendering of the material removal is not carried out in real time. The haptic forces representing the scaled vibratory, material welding resistance and welding force requires further development in order to enhance the virtual reality based training system for welding application.

In nutshell, the virtual reality based training system provides a reasonably realistic experience of the actual welding process wherein a user holds a real welding torch while seeing and hearing a virtual weld. This project needs a further development to refine the visual, audio, and haptic fidelity.

Recommendations

- Measure and include real world forces generated during welding.
- A framework would be useful allowing similar applications to be built with other graphical renderers, physics engines, acoustics feedback and effectiveness of tactile of welding material.
- Adoption of video playback and instant Computer Aided Instruction (CAI).

Abbreviation

Haptic library application programming interface (HLAPI), Haptic device application programming interface (HDAPI), Pulse-width modulation (PWM).

Appendix A

Questionnaire Form

UNIVERSITY OF MALAYA

ENGINEERING FACULTY

DEPARTMENT OF MECHANICAL ENGINEERING

Virtual Reality Based Training System for MAG Welding

We, Manufacturing Engineering students from University of Malaya, are currently running a final year project about the virtual reality (VR) based training system for Metal Active Gas (MAG) Welding with force feedback. This system it is targeted at familiarizing beginning welder candidates with the MAG welding techniques and best practices to become effective MAG welders. In addition, the motion tracking coordinates after the simulation can be used to train for robot welding by teach and playback or offline programming. Your valuable feedback will be appreciated.

Section A

Please tick 1 answer only

1 - Have you try any haptic device in any virtual simulator training system?

Yes No

2 - Do you think that the virtual reality based training system is necessary and convenient compared to conventional training program?

Questionnaire Form		
Yes	No	
Section B Post Experiment Questions		
1- Which display type did you prefer most?		
Head-Mounted Display (HMD)	Digital Video (DV)	
2- Which level of welding force feedback did you prefer most?		
Enabled	Disabled	
3- What did you not like about this virtual reality based training system? (Can choose many)		
Lack of the sense of reality		
Difficult to handle the device		
Lack of interactive teaching aid		
Lack of auditory feedback		
4- Does the user interface and control system easy to be used in the training?		
Poor	Medium	Good
5- Does the V.R. based welding give you the realism in practising of welding from the aspect of different torch orientation?		
Poor	Medium	Good
6- Does the V.R. based welding give you the realism in practising of welding from the aspect of different travel speed?		
Poor	Medium	Good
7- Does the V.R. based welding give you the realism in practising of welding in maintaining the proper electrode angle?		
Poor	Medium	Good
8- Does the V.R. based welding give you the realism in practising of welding in maintaining the proper welding speed?		
Poor	Medium	Good
9- Do you think V.R. based welding training system with force feedback improve your real-life welding skill and your welding gesture?		
Poor	Medium	Good
10- Do you agree welders should undergo the virtual training system before expose to the real welding?		
Poor	Medium	Good
11- Do you think that virtual reality based training system for MAG welding able to reduce the training cost compared to conventional welding training program?		
Yes	No	
12- Do you think that the playback video of your motion is necessary to review your performance?		
Yes	No	
13- Do you think that the instant Computer Aided Instruction (CAI) with haptics guidance should be included in this training system?		
Yes	No	
Thank you		

Appendix B

Factors of Poor Weld

Fault or Defect	Cause and Corrective Action
Porosity	- Scale or heavy dust on plate - Shielding problem (gas hose leaks) - Improper torch angle - Wire feed speed or voltage set too high - Welding over slag from covered electrode
Lack of penetration	- Weld joint too narrow - Welding current too low - Weld puddle rolling in front of the arc
Lack of fusion	- Welding current, voltage or travel speed too low - Welding over convex bead - Excessive oxide on plate - Torch oscillation too wide or too narrow
Undercutting	- Excessive travel speed, voltage or welding current - Insufficient dwell time at edge of weld bead
Cracking	- Incorrect wire chemistry - Weld beat too small - Poor quality of material being welded - Too much moisture - Excessive heat
Poor weld starts or wire stubbing	- Welding voltage too low - Wire extension too long - Poor work connection
Excessive spatter	- Use Ar-CO_2 instead of pure CO_2 - Gas flow rate or voltage too high
Burn through	- Travel speed too slow - Decrease width of root opening - Use Ar-CO_2 or Ar-O_2 instead of pure CO_2
Convex bead	- Welding voltage or current too low - Excessive electrode extension - Weld joint too narrow

Acknowledgements

A million thanks to the Department of Mechanical Engineering, Faculty of Engineering, University of Malaya, for providing the necessary facilities to support this study. This work was supported by the University of Malaya Research Collaborative Grant Scheme (PRP-UM-UMP), under Grant Number: CG006-2013.

Author details

Hwa Jen Yap[1*], Zahari Taha[2], Hui Kang Choo[1] and Chee Khean Kok[1]

*Address all correspondence to: hjyap737@um.edu.my

1 Department of Mechanical Engineering Faculty of Engineering, University of Malaya, Kuala Lumpur, Malaysia

2 Innovative Manufacturing, Mechatronics and Sports Lab, Faculty of Manufacturing Engineering, Universiti Malaysia Pahang, Pekan, Pahang, Malaysia

References

[1] Fletcher, C., Ritchie, J. M., & Lim, T. (2011). Virtual machining and expert knowledge capture. Paper presented at Digital Engagement 2011, Newcastle, United Kingdom.

[2] Mujber, T.S., T. Szecsi, Hashmi, M.S.J. (2004). Virtual reality applications in manufacturing process simulation. Journal of Materials Processing Technology, p. 1834-1838.

[3] Yap, H.J., Taha, Z., Lee, J.V. (2008). VR-based Robot Programming and Simulation System for an Industrial Robot. International Journal of Industrial Engineering – Theory, Application and Practice. 15(3) pp. 314-322.

[4] Leino, S., Lind, S., Poyade, M., Kiviranta, S., Multanen, P., Reyes-Lecuona, A., Mäkiranta, A., Muhammad, A. (2009). Enhanced Industrial Maintenance Work Task Planning by Using Virtual Engineering Tools and Haptic User Interfaces. Virtual and Mixed Reality-Lecture Notes in Computer Science. Vol 5622, pp 346-354.

[5] SensAble Technologies, Inc®. Retrieved May 9 2014, from http://www.vrlab.ctw.utwente.nl/eq/Documentation/PhantomOmni_Spec.pdf

[6] Motoji, M., Nishino, H., Kagawa, T., Utsumiya, K. (2010). A Haptic Parameter Exploration Method for Force Feedback Devices. In proceeding of the Fourth International Conference on Complex, Intelligent and Software Intensive Systems, Krakow, Poland, 15-18 February 2010, pp. 1158-1163.

[7] Wang, Y.Z., Yonghua Chen, Y., Nan, Z., Hu, Y. (2006). Study on Welder Training by Means of Haptic Guidance and Virtual Reality for Arc Welding. IEEE International Conference on Robotics and Biomimetics, 17-20 December 2006, pp. 954-958.

[8] Yang, U., Lee, G.A., Kim, Y., Jo, D., Choi, J.S., Kim, K. (2010). Virtual Reality based Welding Traning Simulator with 3D Multimodal Interaction. International Conference on Cyberworlds, 2010, pp.150-154.

[9] Kenneth, F., (2012). Virtual Welding. A Low Cost Virtual Reality Welder Training System. National Shipbuilding Research Program, 2012.

[10] Oz, C., Ayar, K., Serttas, S., Iyibilgin, O., Soy, U., Cit, G. (2012). A Performance Evaluation Application for Welder Candidate in Virtual Welding Simulator. Social and Behavioural Sciences, pp. 492-501.

[11] Kansai Bureau of Economy (2005). General outline about the research on transmission and skill training measures for the production, Japan. Retrieved from http://www.kansai.meti.go.jp/7kikaku/ginou/houkoku/tyousagaiyou_r.pdf

[12] Yasuhisa, O., Kouhei, M., Kentaro, H. & Masaki, S., (2011). E-Training System of Welding Work, copyright by the International Society of Offshore and Polar Engineers (ISOPE). In Proceeding of the Twenty-first International Society of Offshore and Polar Engineering Conference Maui, Hawaii, USA, June 19-24, 2011, pp. 174-179.

[13] Thurman, R. A., & Matoon, J. S. (1994). Virtual Reality: Toward fundamental improvements in simulation-based training. Educational Technology, Vol 34(5), pp. 56-64.

[14] Vora, J., Nair, S., Gramopadhye, A.K., Melloy, B.J., Meldin, E., Duchowski, A.T. & Kanki, B.G. (2001). Using virtual reality technology to improve aircraft inspection performance: Presence and performance measurement studies. In Proceedings of the Human Factors and Ergonomic Society 45th Annual Meeting, pp. 1867-1871.

Section 3

Industry Applications and Research

Virtual Robot Teaching for Humanoid Both-Hands Robots Using Multi-Fingered Haptic Interface

Haruhisa Kawasaki, Tetsuya Mouri and Satoshi Ueki

Additional information is available at the end of the chapter

http://dx.doi.org/10.5772/59189

1. Introduction

Humanoid robots are expected to support various human tasks, such as high-mix low-volume production and assembly tasks. Programming technologies such as robot language and teaching-playback [1] have been developed, but it is difficult to apply these technologies to multi-fingered robots because they require instruction for both motion and force at many points simultaneously.

Recently, several techniques have been proposed that use human motion measurements directly as robot teaching data for automatic programming: teaching by showing [2], assembly plan from observation [3-4], gesture-based programming [5], and robot learning [6-10]. Applications for dual arm robots [11] have also been presented. These are based on measurements of motions and forces generated in the real world. Task programming based on the observation of human operation is viable for humanoid robots because it is not necessary to describe motions and forces explicitly for the robot to accomplish a task.

Direct teaching that involves remote robot operation [12] presents two difficulties. The first is caused by the communication time lag that arises when the robot is distant from the operator, which can make the remote-robot system unstable. The second is the issue of constant operator stress when any mistake on the operator's part is immediately reflected in the robot motions and coudl result in a fatal accident. Robot teaching in a virtual reality (VR) environment can overcome these problems. We call this approach VR robot teaching. Several approaches to analyzing human intentions from human demonstrations have been presented [13-17]. Most of these studies, however, do not handle the virtual force generated in the VR environment as robot teaching data. Moreover, research on VR robot teaching for humanoid both-hands robots has not yet been presented.

Our group presented a concept of VR robot teaching for multi-fingered robots [18] in which the virtual forces at contact points were utilized to analyze human intention. We found that humans feel comfortable handling virtual hands based on a human hand model, but uneasy handling virtual hands based on a robot hand model, because the geometrical form and motional function of the robot hand is not the same as that of the human hand. To minimize the difference between human-robot fingertip position and orientation, mapping methods from human grasps to robot grasps have been studied [19-20]; these did not, however, take the manipulability of the robot hand into consideration. Hand manipulability is a key measure for stable and robust robot grasps [21]. Moreover, a segmentation method for processing human motion data, including plural tasks, whose segmentation tree is additive for any new primitive motion required for performing a new task, has been presented [22]. These studies did not, however, handle 3D forces at contact points because a force-feedback glove, consisting of a data glove and a force display mechanism using wire rope, were used as a haptic interface, which could only display one dimensional force to the fingertips. Hence, it was difficult to teach a task that included a contact with another object and a motion along a surface of the object. 3D forces at contact points are key information for human intention analysis. Moreover, an expansion of VR robot teaching is needed for humanoid both-hands robots.

This paper presents a VR robot teaching method [23] for a humanoid robot hand using a multi-fingered haptic interface capable of displaying 3D force at each fingertip of the operator. In this teaching, segmentation of motion, task recognition, and re-segmentation of motion are executed sequentially using 3D forces. That is, human motion data consisting of contact points, grasped force, hand and object positions, and the like are segmented into plural primitive motions based on a segmentation tree: the type of task is analyzed based on the acquired sequence of primitive motions, and re-segmentation of the motion is executed sequentially. We demonstrate how the segmentation tree is additive for new primitive motions as part of performing a new task using 3D forces. In this method, the position and orientation of the robot hand are determined so as to maximize its manipulability, on the condition that the robot grasps the object at its teaching contact point. This approach makes the virtual teaching system very user friendly. We present the experimental results of performing a task, which includes contacting another object and moving along the surface of the wall, using a humanoid robot hand named Gifu Hand III [24] and a multi-fingered haptic interface robot called the HIRO II [25]. Moreover, we extend the VR robot teaching to humanoid both-hands robots by adding primitive motions of human bimanual coordination, which consist of *Equal Grasp by both hands, Main Grasp by one hand, Pass from one hand to another,* etc., to the segmented tree. Type of task by both-hands is also analyzed based on the acquired sequence of primitive motions. This shows that the segmentation tree can also be additive for bimanual coordination tasks.

The proposed method will be useful in the efficient manufacturing of a wide variety of products in small quantities, and for teleportation with large time delay using humanoid hand robots.

http://dx.doi.org/10.5772/59189

2. Virtual robot teaching

2.1. Scheme of virtual robot teaching

A conceptual scheme of the VR robot teaching system is shown in Figure 1. The system consists of a VR robot teaching system and remotely located robot system. In the former, the human carries out various tasks in a VR environment, employing a virtual object by handling a multi-fingered haptic interface. From the series of human motions and 3D forces acting on the human's fingers, the motion intention of the human is analyzed. Based on the motion intention analysis, a series of robot commands, which include desired trajectories, grasping forces, and contact points, are generated for the object coordinate frame. The robot commands are tested in the robot simulation system and then sent to the remote robot system. In the robot system, the robot works according to the robot commands. The robot system can absorb a slight geometrical difference between the virtual space and real space, because the robot obeys commands relative to the object coordinate frame.

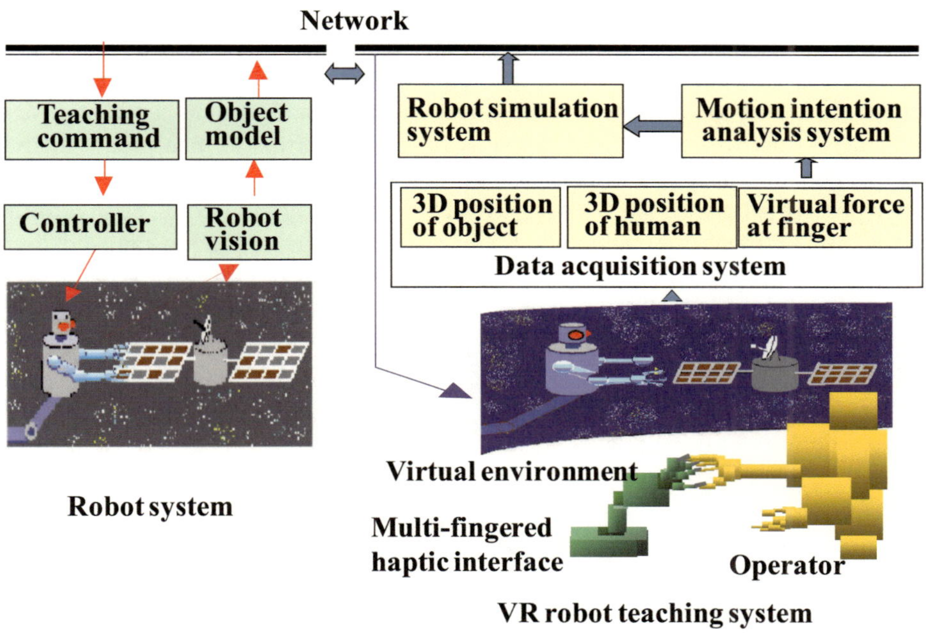

Figure 1. Conceptual figure of virtual robot teaching

This scheme has two advantages. The first is that communication time delay has no effect, since the robot commands are generated from the off-line motion analysis. The second is that the human is relieved of continual stress, since inadvertent human error can be compensated for.

2.2. Robot with Gifu Hand III

We consider a multi-fingered hand robot equipped with the Gifu Hand III developed by our group [24]. The shape and mechanism of the Gifu Hand III were designed to resemble those of the human hand. That is, it has a thumb and 4 fingers, the thumb has 4 joints with 4 degree of freedoms (DOF), and each finger has 4 joints with 3 DOF. All servomotors are mounted in the hand frame. A 6-axis force sensor can be attached to each fingertip, and a distributed tactile sensor with 859 detecting points can be mounted on the surfaces of the palm and fingers. Since the Gifu Hand III was designed so that not only the shape but also the mechanism were very similar to those of the human hand, as long as the shape of the object is simple and the size is manageable, most of the measured human motion data can be applied directly to the robot command.

2.3. Haptic interface robot HIRO II

The multi-fingered haptic interface HIRO II [25] shown in Figure 2 can present force and tactile feeling at the 5 fingertips of the human hand. The HIRO II design is completely safe. The mechanism of HIRO II consists of a 6-DOF arm and a 15-DOF hand with a thumb and 4 fingers. Each finger has 3 joints, allowing 3 DOF. The first joint, relative to the base of the hand, allows abduction/adduction. The second and third joints allow flexion/extension. The thumb is similar to the fingers except for the reduction gear ratio and the movable ranges of joints 1 and 2. In order to read the finger loading, a 6-axis force sensor is installed in the second link of each finger. The user must wear finger holders over his/her fingertips to manipulate the haptic interface. Each finger holder has a ball attached to a permanent magnet at the force sensor tip and forms a passive spherical joint. This passive spherical joint has two roles. First, differences between the human finger orientation and the haptic finger orientation are adjusted. Second, it allows operators to remove their fingers from the haptic interface in case of a malfunction. The suction force generated by the permanent magnet is 5 N. Humans can feel 3D force at each fingertip through the HIRO II.

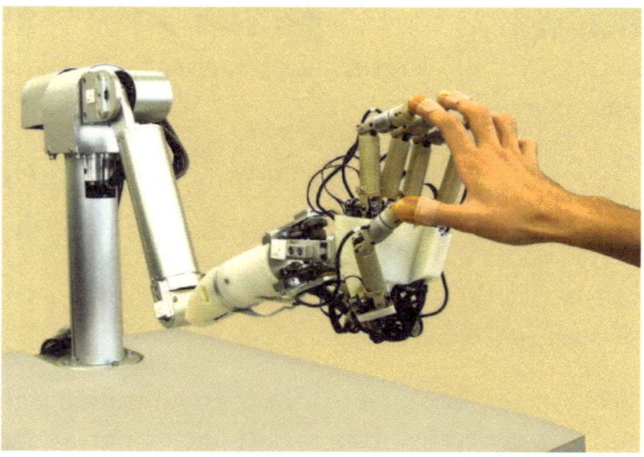

Figure 2. Multi-fingered haptic interface robot HIRO II

http://dx.doi.org/10.5772/59189

2.4. Motion segmentation

Assembly work consists of plural tasks, such as pick-and-place, peg-in-hole, peg-pullout-from-hole, and so on. Hence, the motion intention analysis system should have the ability to recognize the type of task from human motion data. A segmentation method [13] has been proposed to realize this function in which segmentation of motion, task recognition, and re-segmentation of motion are executed sequentially.

A flowchart of the segmentation of motion data is shown in Figure 3, which is a modified version of a previous one. In this segmentation tree, a pick-and-place task, peg-in-hole task, peg-pullout-from-hole task, turn-screw task, slide task, pick-and-press task, pick-and-follow task, trace task and press task are considered. The first 5 tasks can be performed without 3D force interface, but the last four cannot, because 3D contact force is required to present the human motion when the target object is in contact with multiple objects. We assumed that the human motion to execute these tasks consists of 14 primitive motions as follows: *Move, Approach, Grasp, Translate, Slide, Insert, Pullout, Release, Place, Turn, Press, Follow, Push,* and *Trace*. The last 4 primitive motions are added to segment the contact tasks when humans use the 3D force display. This means that the segmentation tree is additive for the potential use of 3D forces by a simple modification, indicated by the colored cells in Figure 3.

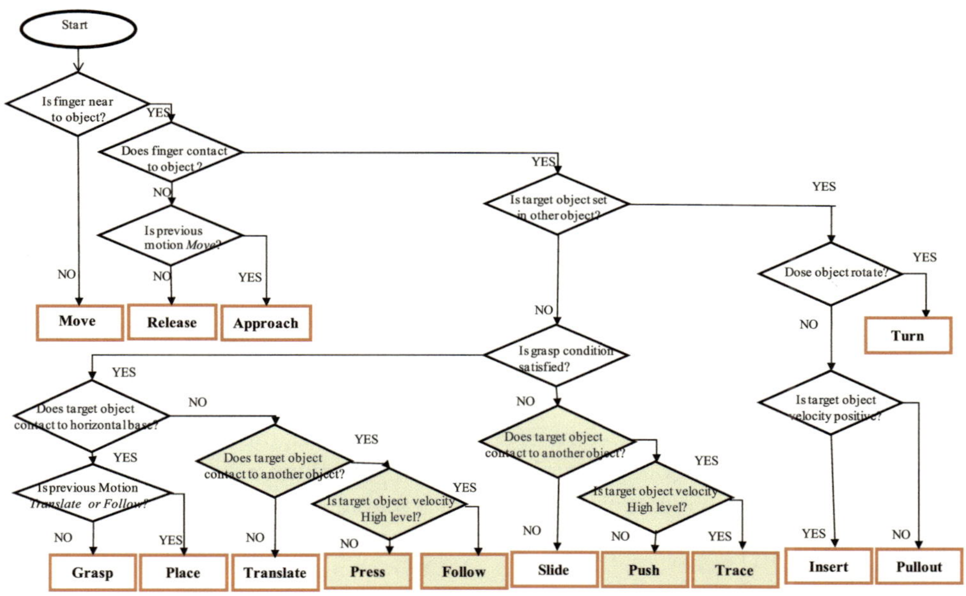

Figure 3. Flowchart of segmentation of motion data

The *Move* segment indicates only the operator's hand moving at a point distant from a virtual object; with *Approach,* the operator's fingertip is coming close to a virtual object, but does not touch it, and the previous motion is *Move*. With *Grasp,* the finger contacts an object located on a base or another object; the grasp condition is satisfied and the previous motion of the *Grasp* is not *Translate*. The grasp condition means that the virtual force generated by the interference between the finger and virtual object is greater than a specified value. This grasp is the precision grasp presented by Cutkosky [26]. In the *Translate* segment, the object moves with the hand and fingers as one unit; that is, the virtual object departs from the base or other object and the grasp condition is satisfied. In the *Place* segment, the object contacts the environment and the previous motion is *Translate*. In human operation, it is difficult to distinguish the *Translate* and *Place* segments exactly, and indeed the operator does not feel the distinction between them. We assumed that the starting point of the *Place* segment is the moment at which the virtual object first contacts the environment. In the *Release* segment, the fingertip leaves the object and the previous motion is not *Move*. Hence, the starting point of the *Release* segment is the moment at which one of the fingertips leaves the object. In the *Slide* segment, the object is touched by the hand satisfying the grasp condition and translated to a point. In *Insert*, a finger contacts a target object set inside another object, and the target object moves toward the other object; meanwhile in *Pullout*, a finger is in contact with a target object inside another object, and the target object moves away from the other object. In the *Turn* segment, the object is turned around an axis. In the *Press* section, the object in a satisfying grasp condition contacts another object, and in *Follow*, the object in a satisfying grasp condition moves along the surface of another object with contact force. In the *Push* segment, fingers touch an object and move it toward another object until they are in contact, but the grasp condition is not satisfied. In *Trace*, fingers touch an object and move it along the surface of another object with contact force, but again the grasp condition is not satisfied.

To segment the motion data, three coordinate frames are utilized: the reference coordinate frame, the origin of which is fixed in the task space; the object coordinate frame fixed in the object; and the hand coordinate frame fixed in the hand. The following 6 parameters are measured as the motion data: an object position with respect to the reference coordinate frame ${}^{ref}\boldsymbol{p}_{object}$, an i-th fingertip position with respect to the object coordinate frame ${}^{object}\boldsymbol{p}_{i\text{-}th\ finger}$, a virtual force at the i-th fingertip with respect to the reference coordinate frame ${}^{ref}\boldsymbol{f}_{i\text{-}th\ finger}$, and the object velocity ${}^{ref}\boldsymbol{v}_{object}$. Moreover, the index of the grasp space of hand ${}^{object}P_{finger}$ ($=\sum \| {}^{object}\boldsymbol{p}_{i-th\ \ finger} \|$), the sum of fingertip forces ${}^{ref}\boldsymbol{F}_{finger}$ ($=\sum {}^{ref}\boldsymbol{f}_{i-th\ \ finger}$) and the contact state flag, which indicates a contact state between the target object and the other object, are evaluated. By using these parameters, the distance between the hand and the object, the presence or absence of contact between a fingertip and the object, the contact relation between the target object and the other object, and the grasping condition are evaluated and used in the segmentation tree. As a result, the motion data is segmented into primitive motions.

2.5. Task analysis

Type of task is analyzed based on the sequence of the obtained primitive motions in the following manner. A sequence of primitive motions from *Move* to *Release* is 1 task because the hand must move to the target object to do something first, then release the object at the end of the task. When *Insert* is in the sequence of primitive motions, it is a peg-in-hole task. When the sequence of primitive motions includes *Pullout*, it is a peg-pullout-from-hole task. When *Turn* is in the sequence of primitive motions, it is a turn-screw task. When *Follow* is included in the

http://dx.doi.org/10.5772/59189

sequence of primitive motions, it is a pick-follow task. The inclusion of *Press* in the sequence of primitive motions indicates a pick-press task; *Follow* indicates a pick-and-follow task; and *Push* in the sequence of primitive motions, signifies a push task. When *Trace* and *Press* are both in the sequence of primitive motions, it is a trace task.

After task recognition, primitive motions are relabeled based on the recognized task. For example, if *Slide* is between *Place* and *Release*, it is combined into *Place*, because *Slide* is a fluctuation by the operator. Meanwhile, *Insert* and *Pullout* in a turn-screw task are combined as *Turn* because they happen at a low angular velocity to the target object. This modification process can be added as appropriate when a new primitive motion is added. After the relabeling based on the recognized task, the desired trajectories, contact points, and contact forces are analyzed within each segment.

2.6. Robot command

The geometrical form of the Gifu Hand III is similar to that of the human hand, but the two are not identical. In particular, the space between the thumb and opposing fingers is smaller in the Gifu Hand III because of a mechanical design limitation. In order to be able to map teaching data based on the human-hand model to teaching data for a robot hand, a virtual teaching method for multi-fingered robots based on a combination of scaling the virtual hand model to the size of the robot hand and hand manipulability has been developed. In this method, the position and orientation of the robot hand are determined so as to maximize the manipulability of the robot hand, on the condition that the robot grasps the object at the object's teaching contact point. More details can be found in [22].

3. Experiments

3.1. Experimental system

Figure 4(a) illustrates the experimental system. An operator manipulates virtual objects in the virtual environment through the multi-fingered haptic interface robot HIRO II. There are two objects in a box; both are cubic, 120 [mm] on each side, with a mass of 50 [g] and a friction surface coefficient of 0.4. Fingertip position is indicated by a small ball in the computer graphics (CG). Static and dynamic friction coefficients between fingertip and object are 1.0 and 0.5, respectively. The robot arm is controlled by the position PID control with a friction compensator. The robot hand is controlled by the impedance control, which consists of the position PD control and the force feedback control. The control sampling cycle is 1 ms.

3.2. Pick-and-follow task

A task in which a right-side object was translated to the right-side corner was executed. The operator executed the VR robot teaching in a virtual environment, as shown in Figure 4(b). First, the operator executed a pick-and-follow task, in which he moved his hand to the target object, grasped and picked it up on the base, translated the object to the wall along the x-axis

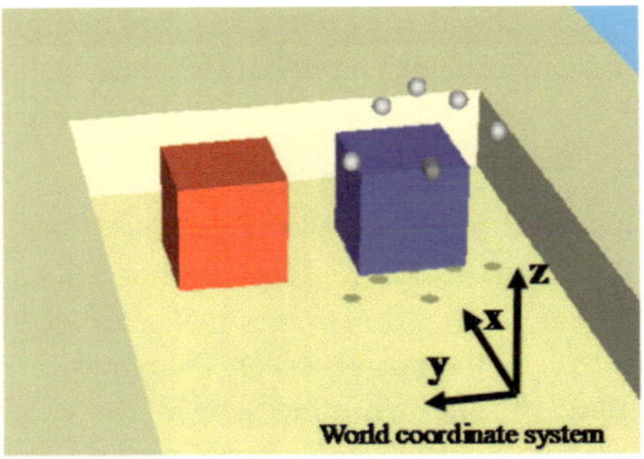

(a) Computer graphics

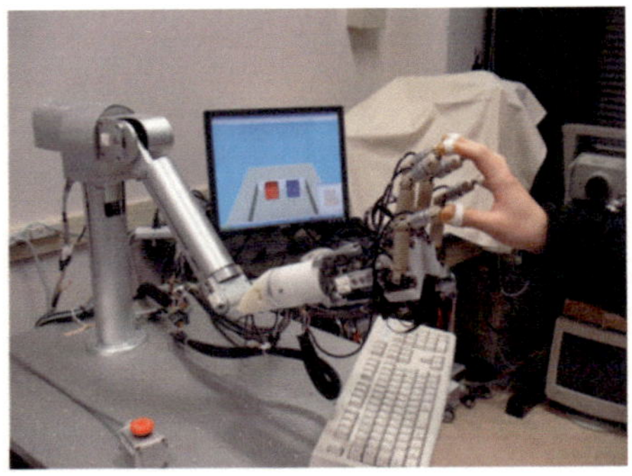

(b) VR environment

Figure 4. Experimental system

until contact, followed along the wall to the base while grasping the object and keeping contact between the object and the wall, and then released the object. The operator then executed a push-and-trace task without grasping the object, in which he pushed the object to the wall with two fingers, traced the wall to the corner keeping contact between the object and the wall, and then released the object. Figure 5 shows the measured parameters, primitive motions obtained by the proposed segmentation, and recognized tasks, which consisted of a pick-and-follow task and a push-and-trace task. Points on the curving parameter line show the timing to separate the primitive motions. For example, *Move* and *Approach* in the task are segmented by the magnitude of ${}^{object}P_{finger}$; *Grasp* is segmented by the gravitational direction element of ${}^{ref}\boldsymbol{F}_{finger}$; *Translate* is segmented by the gravitational direction element of ${}^{ref}\boldsymbol{p}_{object}$; *Follow* and *Release* are segmented by the norm of ${}^{ref}\boldsymbol{F}_{finger}$ and the contact flag.

After the segmentation of primitive motions, a motion sequence from *Move* to *Release* was grouped into a task, and a task type recognized. This showed that the segmentation of motion data and recognition of task were executed appropriately. After the recognition of task type, the primitive motions were relabeled based on the task understanding. For example, *Slide* between *Approach* and *Grasp* in the first pick-and-follow task was combined as *Grasp* because the *Slide* was a fluctuation by the operator. Similarly, the second *Push* between *Trace* and *Trace* in the second push-and-trace task was combined into *Trace*. After relabeling, robot finger trajectories were generated smoothly.

Desired position and force profiles were smoothed in order to reduce the vibration in robot hand motion. After performing an action, the position and orientation of the robot hand was determined to maximize the hand manipulability measure and robot commands were generated. The computer simulation was then executed to check the robot commands, as shown in Figure 6(a), in which the CG of primitive motions are presented. Finally, the tasks were executed experimentally by the 6-DOF robot arm with the Gifu Hand III, as shown in Figure 6(b). These images show that the proposed segmentation can be applied to robot teaching that includes performance of plural tasks.

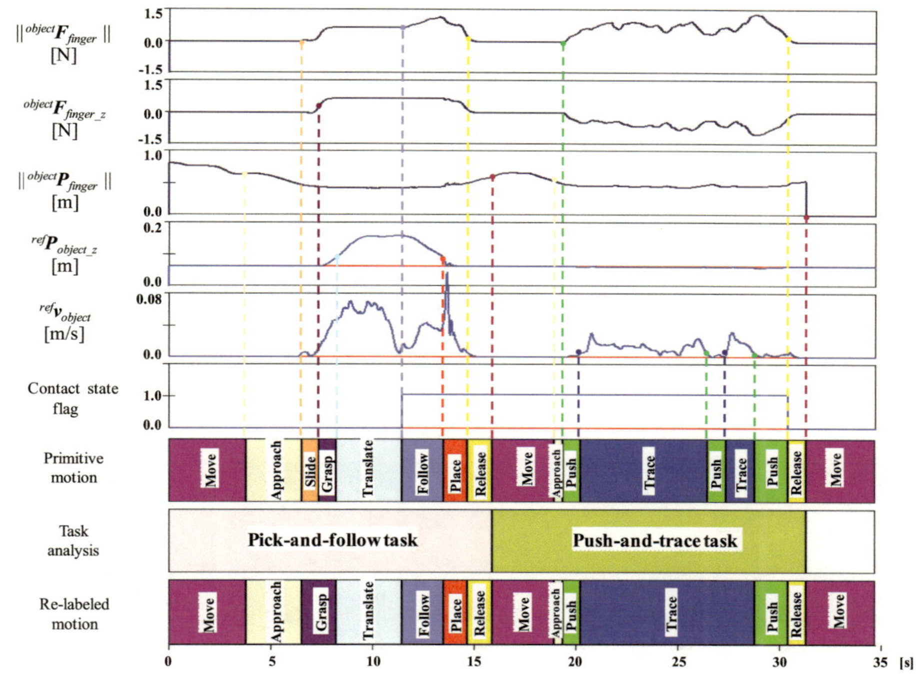

Figure 5. Segmentation of motion data and task analysis

The force profile at the thumb fingertip is shown in Figure 7. The x, y, and z elements of the force show the friction depending on contact force between the object and the wall, the normal contact force between the object and fingertip of the thumb, and the friction caused by gravitational force, respectively. The total force acting on the object is shown in Figure 8. These show the contact timings between finger and object, and object and wall. Experimental results almost follow the desired profiles. The robot could execute the task, and the operator could feel a realistic 3D force.

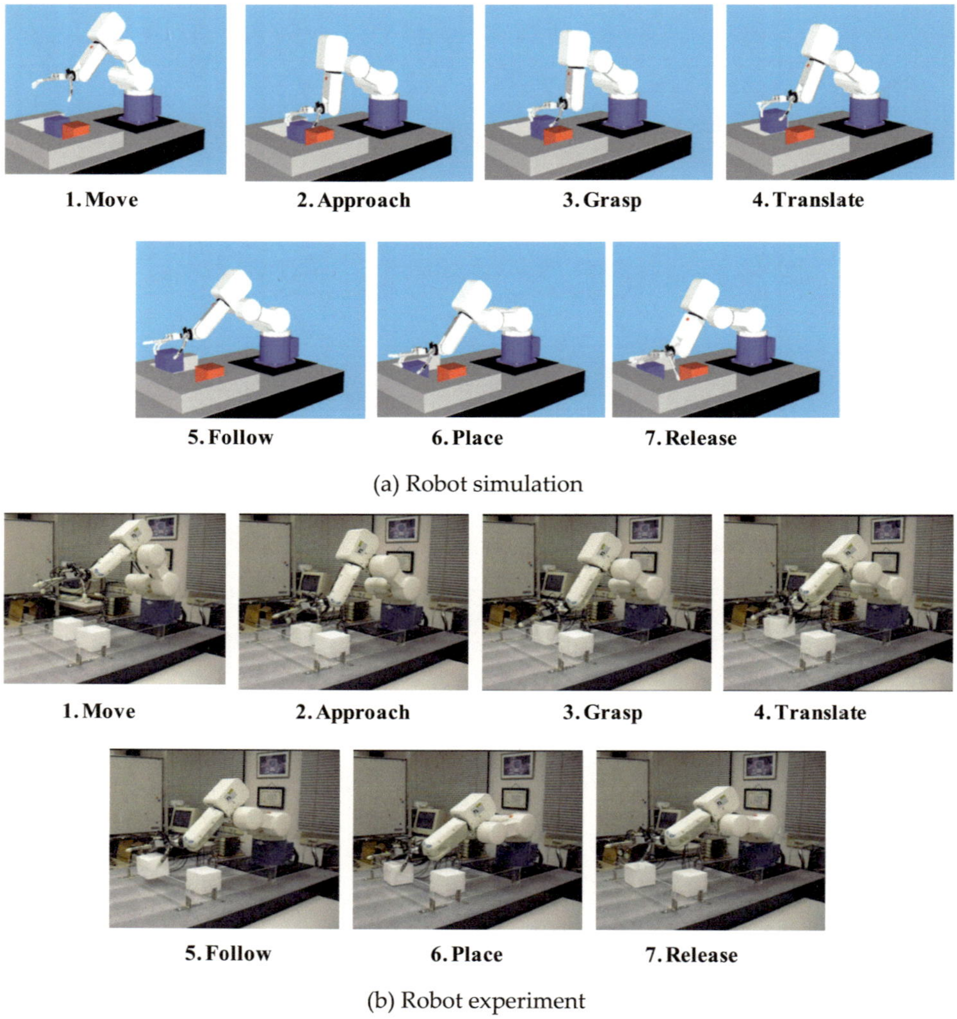

Figure 6. Robot simulation and experiment of the pick-and-follow

http://dx.doi.org/10.5772/59189

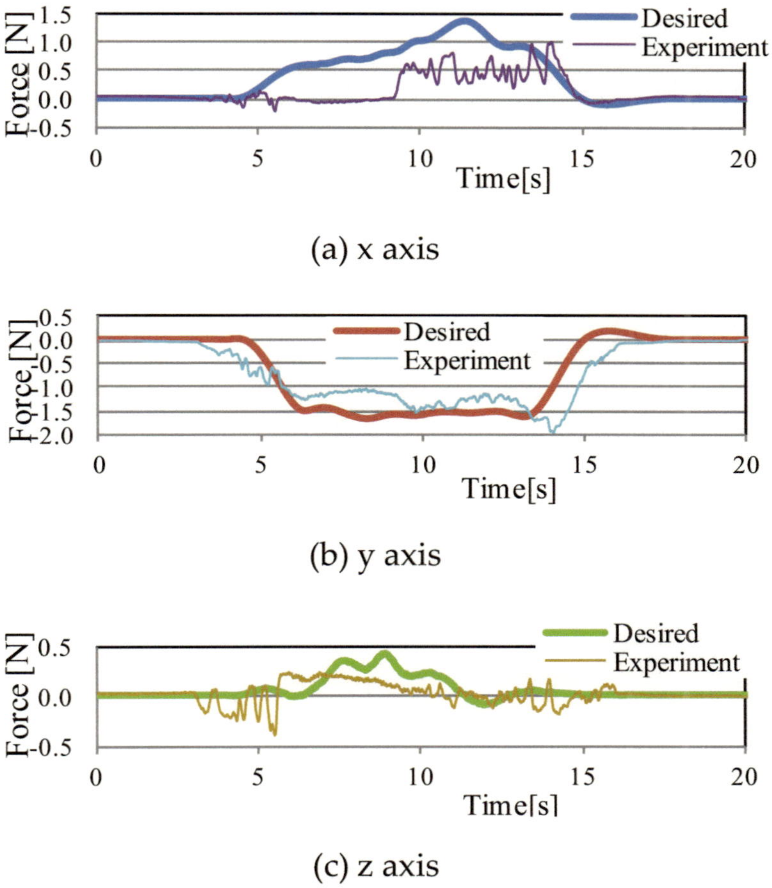

Figure 7. Thumb fingertip force

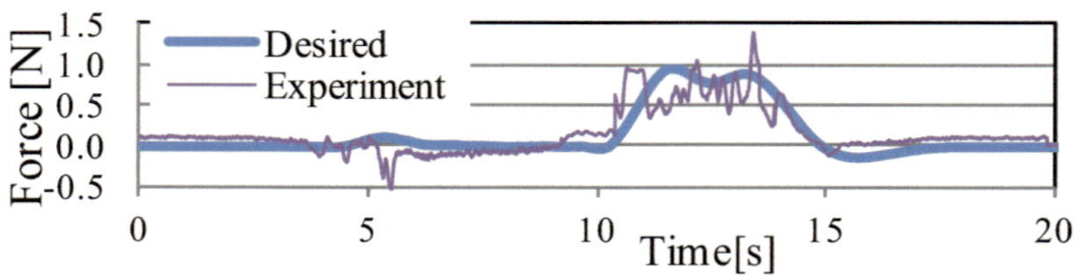

(a) x axis

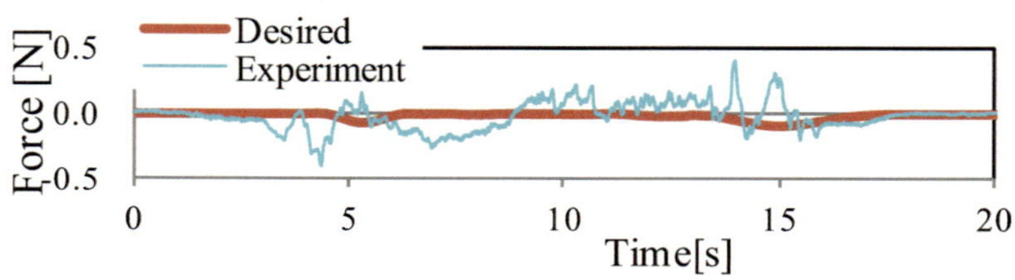

(b) y axis

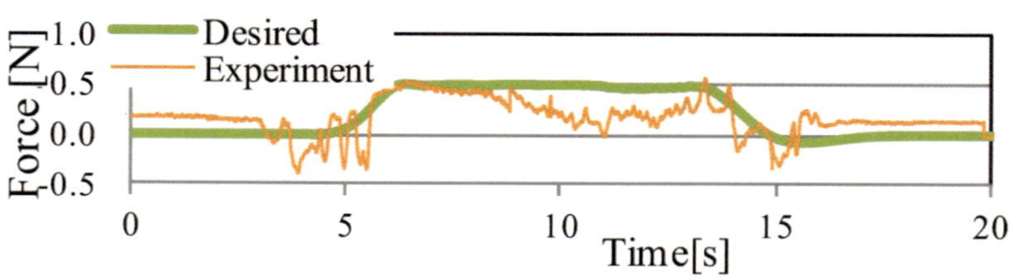

(c) z axis

Figure 8. Total force acting on the object

http://dx.doi.org/10.5772/59189

4. Virtual robot teaching for both-hand robots

Both-hands robots are expected to execute more varied and complicated tasks than single-hand robots, because both-hands robots can accomplish single-hand tasks with each hand independently, as well as both-hands coordinated tasks. We extended the VR robot teaching for single-hand robots in Section II to VR robot teaching for both-hands robots. The basic approach was to distinguish between single-hand task and both-hands coordinated tasks.

4.1. Work environment

The experimental system is shown in Figure 9. An operator manipulates virtual objects in CG through the bimanual multi-fingered haptic interface robot HIRO II. A peg-in-hole task in CG is shown in Figure 10 as an example of a work environment. The ten white spheres show the fingertip positions of the human measured by the HIRO II. The virtual objects are a circular ring and a cylinder with a pole. The VR system checks physical interference between the following geometrical relations: fingertip and the virtual object, the virtual object and environment, and one virtual object and the other. The position and orientation of virtual objects are transformed based on physical dynamics models.

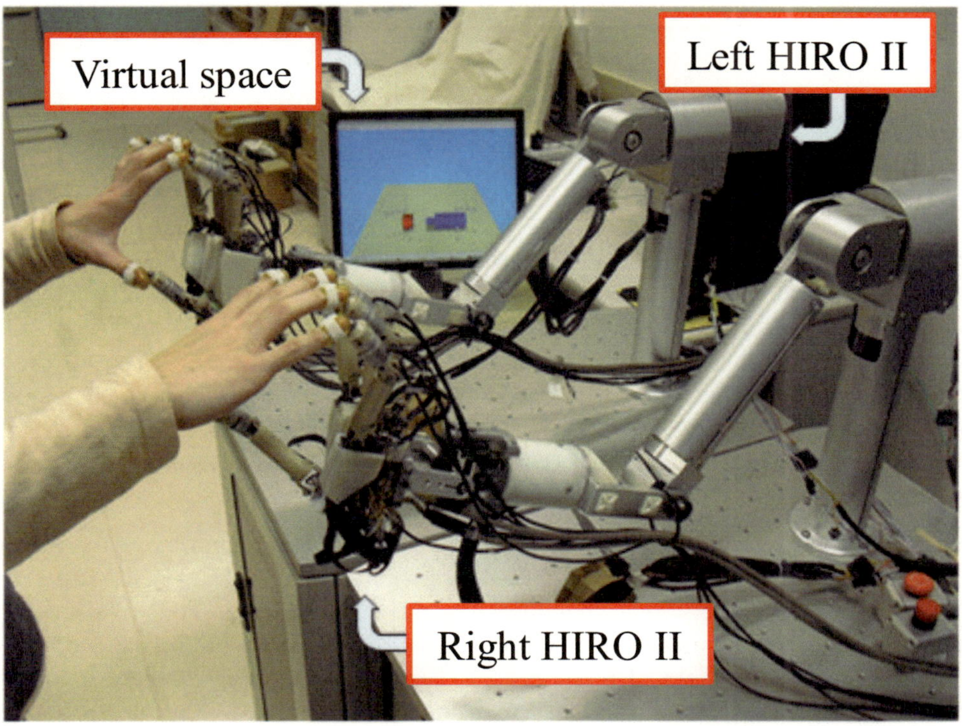

Figure 9. Bimanual multi-fingered haptic interface

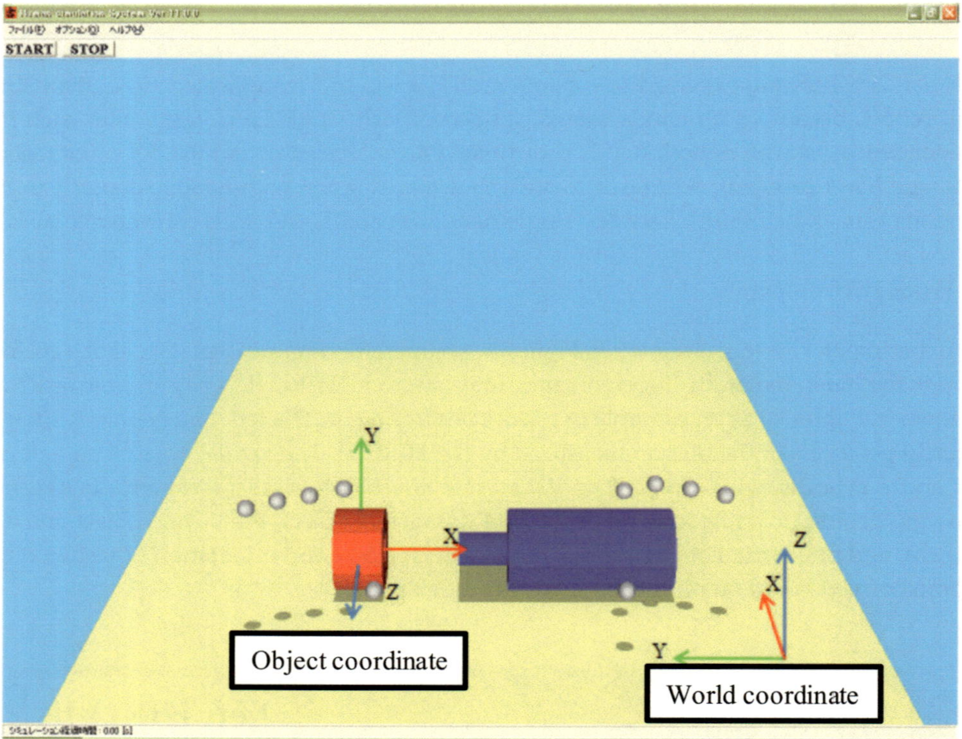

Figure 10. Virtual task environment

4.2. Segmentation and task analysis

The conceptual scheme of the VR robot teaching system was described in Section II. In this section, the system is extended to both-hands task. Both-hands task means bimanual coordination work, such as *Push-and-trace, Pick-and-follow, Peg-in-hole,* and *Pick-and-place,* etc. For example, the case in which an object is grasped in each hand and the two objects are brought into contact in air by the left and right hands would be considered a *Both-hand task*. Figure 11 is a decision flowchart for *Both-hand task*. In the figure, both *Left-hand task* and *Right-hand task* are related to the flow chart in Fig. 3. This part is an appended segmentation tree for both-hands tasks.

When humans translate an object using both hands, the sequence of motion of the work can be divided into plural primitive motions based on grasping state, work flow, and so on. These primitive motions include human intention. The robot should be controlled based on the human intention. We assume that both-hand tasks consist of the following 5 additional primitive motions: *Equal Grasp, Main Grasp, Pass, Fit,* and *Translate*. In the *Equal Grasp* segment, both hands grasp an object and translate it with equal contact force. In *Main Grasp,* the left or right hand has the main grasp on an object, and the other hand's grasp is ancillary. In *Pass,* one hand grasps an object and passes it to the other hand. The object is then translated to the

http://dx.doi.org/10.5772/59189

target position. In *Fit* the left and right hands translate two objects individually, then bring the two into contact. In *Translate,* the two objects are translated by the left and right hands individually, and do not interfere with each other. The segmentation tree for these primitive motions is shown in Figure 12. When new primitive motion is needed, the segmentation tree is additive by simple modification.

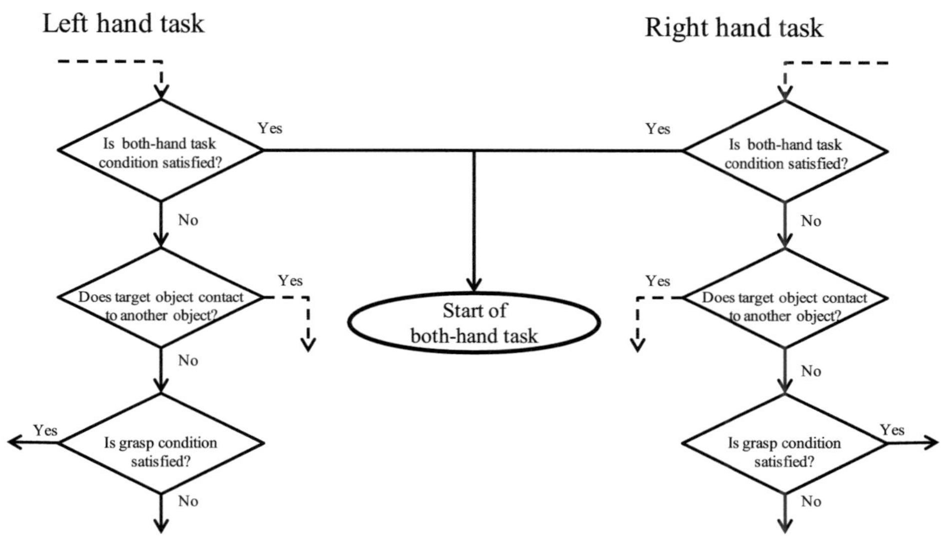

Figure 11. Flow chart of checking bimanual task

Task type is analyzed based on the sequence of the obtained primitive motions in the manner described in Section II-E. A sequence of primitive motions from *Move* to *Release* is considered to be one task, because the hand must move to the target object to accomplish something first, and must release the object at the end of the task. In task recognition, the task is recognized by a key primitive motion. For example, if *Insert* is in the sequence of primitive tasks, the task is a *Peg-in-hole task*; if the sequence of primitive tasks involves *Push,* the task is a *Push-and-trace task.*

After task recognition, primitive motions are relabeled based on the recognized task. For example, *Fit* between *Translate* and *Translate* is combined as *Translate* because *Fit* is a fluctuation by the operator. This modification process will be added as appropriate when a new primitive motion is added. After the relabeling based on the recognized task, the desired trajectories, contact points, and contact forces are analyzed within each segment.

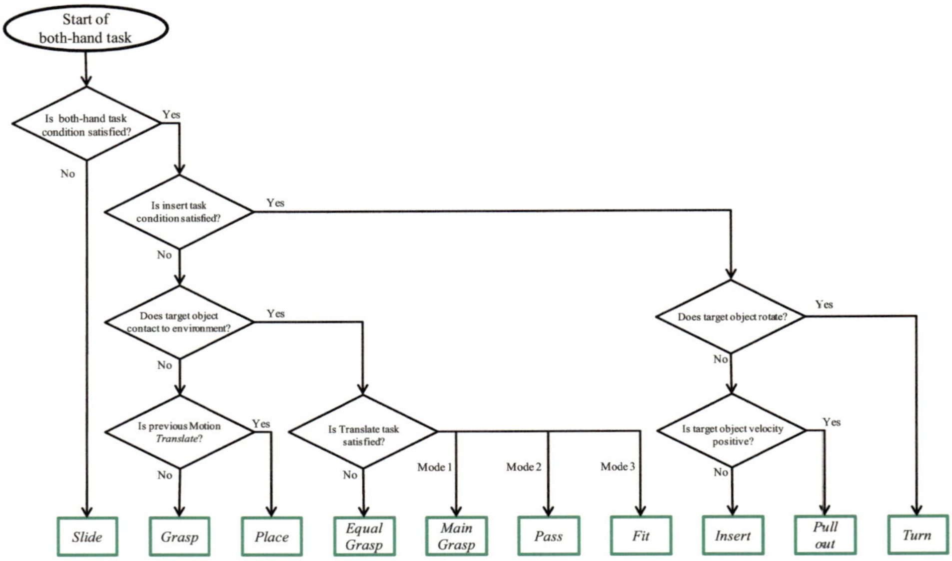

Figure 12. Flow chart of bimanual tasks

4.3. Experiment of Pick-and-Place Task

We executed VR robot teaching in a virtual environment through bimanual multi-fingered haptic interfaces, as shown in Figure 13. The operator executed a pick-and-place task, in which he moved his left hand to the target object, grasped and picked it up with the left hand, passed it to right hand, grasped it with the right hand, translated it to a target position, and released it. Figure 14 shows the measured parameters, primitive motions obtained by the proposed segmentation, and the recognized task, which consisted of two pick-and-place tasks. Points on the curving parameter line show the timing to separate the primitive motions as explained in Section II-B. For example, in bimanual operation, *Main Grasp* and *Equal Grasp* are segmented by the norm of ${}^{ref}\boldsymbol{F}_{finger}$ and the contact flag.

After the segmentation of primitive motions, a motion sequence from *Move* to *Release* was grouped into a task, and a task type recognized. This showed that the segmentation of motion data and recognition of task were executed appropriately. Once the task type was recognized, the primitive motions were relabeled based on the task understanding. For example, in bimanual operation, the sequence *Main Grasp* by left hand, *Equal Grasp,* and *Main Grasp* by right hand were combined into *Pass.* After relabeling, robot finger trajectories were generated smoothly.

Desired position and force profiles were smoothed to reduce the vibration in robot hand motion. After performing a task, the position and orientation of the robot hand was decided to maximize the hand manipulability measure [21] and robot commands were generated. The computer simulation was then executed to check the robot commands, as shown in Figure 15, in which the CG of primitive motions is presented.

http://dx.doi.org/10.5772/59189

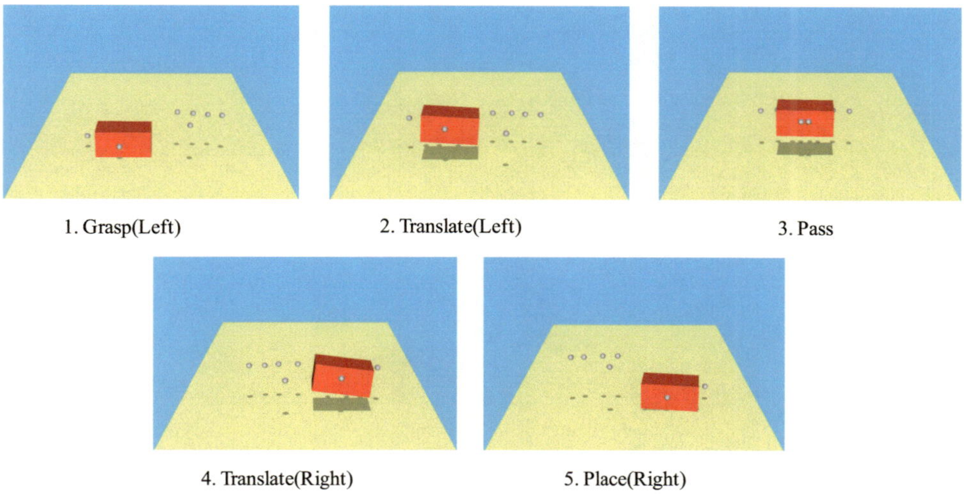

Figure 13. Human simulation

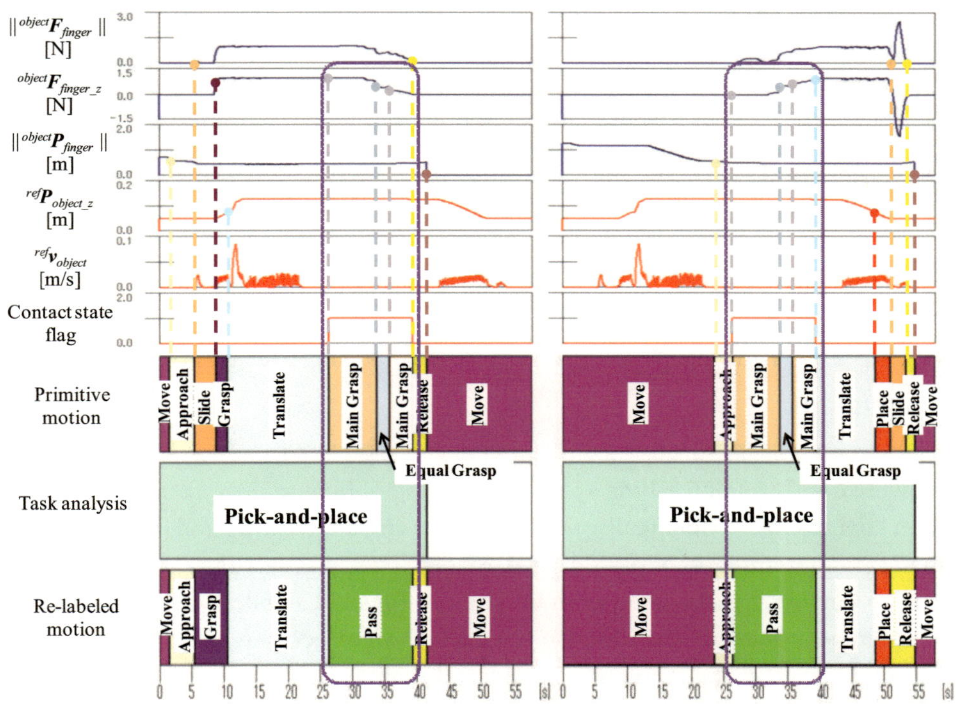

Figure 14. Segmentation of motion data and task analysis

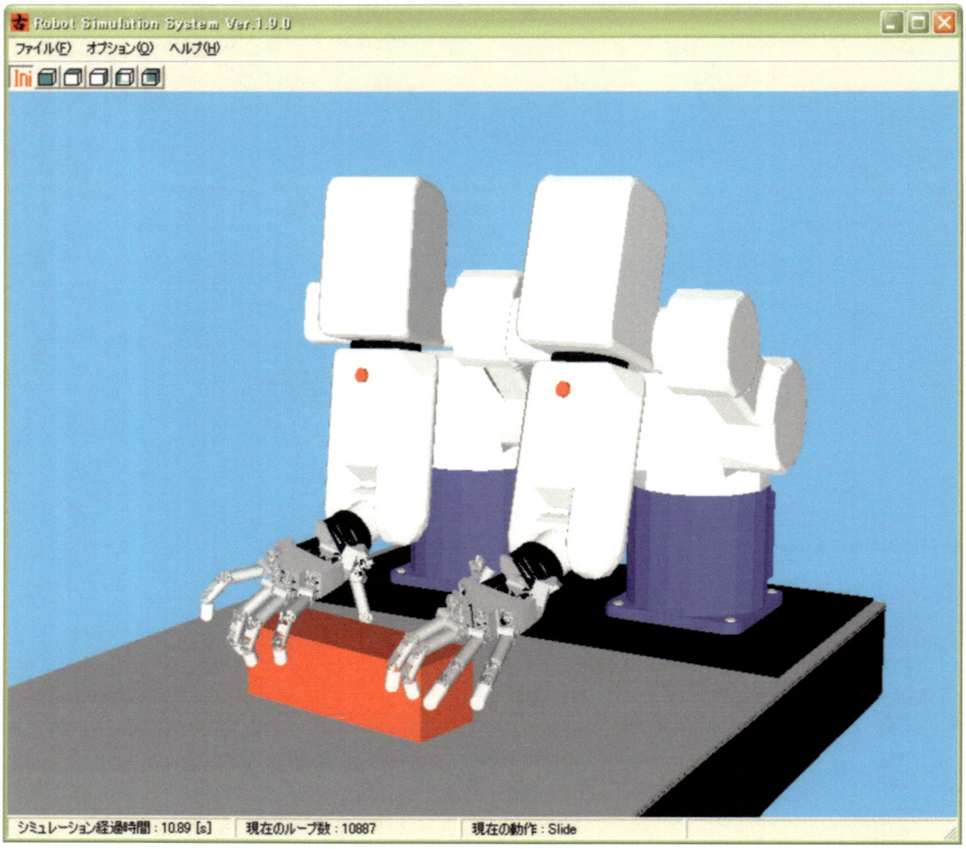

Figure 15. Robot simulation

5. Conclusions

We presented a VR robot teaching system, consisting of human demonstration and motion-intention analysis in a virtual reality environment using a multi-fingered haptic interface for automatic programming of multi-fingered robots. This approach has extended VR robot teaching to bimanual tasks using both-hand multi-fingered haptic interfaces. By using 3D forces at contact points between human fingers and an object, new tasks, including contact with multiple objects, can be learned in a virtual reality environment. The segmentation is executed according to the proposed segmentation tree, which is additive for new primitive motions. Task type is analyzed based on the obtained sequence of primitive motions, and the primitive motions are relabeled based on the recognized task. This method permits us to demonstrate plural tasks sequentially in a virtual reality environment.

http://dx.doi.org/10.5772/59189

This approach makes the virtual teaching system user-friendly. Our experimental results for performing an assembly task using a humanoid robot hand named Gifu Hand III and a multi-fingered haptic interface robot HIRO II demonstrate the effectiveness of the proposed method. Furthermore, we demonstrated that the VR robot teaching method can be extended to both-hands robot teaching.

Acknowledgements

This paper was supported in part by SCOPE (No. 121806001), by the Ministry of Internal Affairs and Communications, and by a Grant-in-Aid for Scientific Research from JSPS, Japan ((A) No. 26249063). The authors would like to thank the members of our laboratory, and in particular, Mr. Syunsuke Nanmo for his cooperation with the experiments.

Author details

Haruhisa Kawasaki[1*], Tetsuya Mouri[1] and Satoshi Ueki[2]

*Address all correspondence to: h_kawasa@gifu-u.ac.jp

1 Department of Mechanical Engineering, Gifu University, Gifu, Japan

2 Department of Mechanical Engineering, Toyota National Colleges of Technology, Toyota, Japan

References

[1] H. Asada, Y. Asari The Direct Teaching of Tool Manipulation Skills via the Impedance Identification of Human Motion, In Proceedings IEEE International Conference Robotics and Automation, pp. 1269-1274, 1988.

[2] T. Kuniyoshi, M. Inaba, H. Inoue, Teaching by Showing: Generating Robot Programs by Visual Observation of Human Performance, In Proceedings 20th International Symposium Industrial Rrobots, pp. 119-126, 1989.

[3] K. Ikeuchi, T. Suehiro, Toward an Assembly Plan from Observation – Part 1: Task Recognition with Polyhedral Objects, IEEE Transactions on Robotics and Automation, Vol. 10, No. 3, pp. 368-385, 1994.

[4] S.B. Kang, K. Ikeuchi, Toward Automatic Robot Instruction from Perception-Temporal Segmentation of Tasks from Human Hand Motion, IEEE Transactions on Robotics and Automation, Vol. 11, No. 5, pp. 670-681, 1995.

[5] R. M. Voyles, J. D. Morrow, P. K. Khosla, Gesture-Based Programming for Robotics: Human-Augumented Software Adaptation, IEEE Intelligent Systems, November/ December, pp. 22-29, 1999.

[6] J. Kulick, M. Toussaint, T. Lang and M. Lopes, Active Learning for Teaching a Robot Grounded Relational Symbols, Proceedings of the Twenty-Third International Joint Conference on Artificial Intelligence, pp. 1451-1457, 2013

[7] S. Calinon and A. Billard, Active Teaching in Robot Programming by Demonstration, 16th IEEE International Conference on Robot & Human Interactive Communication, pp. 702-707, 2007.

[8] L. Peternel and J. Babiˇc, Humanoid Robot Posture-Control Learning in Real-Time Based on Human Sensorimotor Learning Ability, IEEE International Conference on Robotics and Automation (ICRA), pp. 5329-5334, 2013

[9] H. Kitagawa, T. Terai, P. Minyong, and K. Terashima, Application of Neural Network to Teaching of Massage using Muti-fingered Robot Hand, Journal of Robotics and Mechatronics, Vol. 14, no.2, pp.162-169, 2002

[10] L. Rozo, P. Jiménez and C. Torras, Learning Force-Based Robot Skills from Haptic Demonstration, Proceedings of International Conference on Applied Bionics and Biomechanics, 2010

[11] J.-G. Ge, Programming by Demonstration by Optical Tracking System for Dual Arm Robot, Proc. of 44th International Symposium On Robotics (ISR2013), pp. 1-7, 2013

[12] S. Lee, M. Kim band C.-W. Lee, Human-robot integrated teleoperation, Advanced Robotics, Vol. 13, No. 4, pp. 437-449, 1999

[13] H. Lee1 aand J. Kim, A survey on Robot Teaching: Categorization and Brief Review, Applied Mechanics and Materials Vol. 330 (2013) pp 648-656, Trans Tech Publications, pp.648-656, 2013

[14] M. Kaiser, R. Dillmann, Building Elementary Robot Skills from Human Demonstration, in Proceedings IEEE International Conference Robotics and Automation, pp. 2700-2705, 1996.

[15] T. Sato, Y. Nishida, J. Ichikawa, Y. Hatamura, H. Mizoguchi, Active Understanding of Human Intention by a Robot through Monitoring of Human Behavior, Transactions of JRSJ, No. 4, Vol. 13, pp. 545-552, 1995 (in Japanese).

[16] M. Tsuda, H. Ogata, Y. Nanjo, Programming Groups of Local Models from Human Demonstration to Create a Model for Robotic Assembly, in Proceedings ICRA, pp. 530-537, 1998.

[17] H. Onda, T. Suehiro and K. Kitagaki, Teaching by Demonstration of Assembly Motion in VR-Non-deterministic Search-type Motion in the Teaching Stage-, Proceed-

http://dx.doi.org/10.5772/59189

ings of the IEEE/RSJ International Conference on Intelligent Robots and Systems, pp. 3066-3072, 2002

[18] H. Kawasaki, K. Nakayama, G. Parker, Robot Teaching Based on Intention of Human Motion In Virtual Reality Environment, TVRSJ Vol. 5, No. 2, pp. 899-906, 2000. (in Japanese).

[19] S. B. Kang, K. Ikeuchi, Toward Automatic Robot Instruction from Perception-Mapping from Human Grasps to Manipulator Grasps, IEEE Transactions on Robotics and Automation, Vol. 13, No. 1, 1997.

[20] R. N. Rohling, J. M. Hollerbach, Optimized Fingertip Mapping for Teleoperation of Dexterous Robot Hand, in Proceedings IEEE International Conference on Robotics and Automation, pp. 769-775, 1993.

[21] H. Kawasaki, K. Nakayama, T. Mouri, S. Ito, Virtual Teaching Based on Hand Manipulability for Multi-Fingered Robots, In Proceedings of IEEE International Conference on Robotics and Automation, pp. 1388-1393, 2001.

[22] H. Kawasaki, T. Furukawa, S. Ueki, T. Mouri, Virtual Robot Teaching Based on Motion Analysis and Hand Manipulability for Multi-Fingered Robot, Journal of Advanced Mechanical Design, Systems, and Manufacturing, Vol. 3, No. 1, pp. 1-12, 2009.

[23] H. Kawasaki, S. Nanmo, T. Mouri, S. Ueki, Virtual Robot Teaching for Humanoid Hand Robot Using Muti-Fingered Haptic Interface, Proceedings of 2011 IEEE International Conference on Communications, Computing and Control Applications (CCCA'11), pp. 1-6, 2011

[24] T. Mouri, H. Kawasaki, K. Yoshikawa, J. Takai, S. Ito, Anthropomorphic Robot Hand: Gifu Hand III, In Proceedings of International Conference ICCAS2002, pp. 1288-1293, 2002.

[25] H. Kawasaki, T. Mouri, Design and Control of Five-Fingered Haptic Interface Opposite to Human Hand, IEEE Transaction on Robotics, Vol. 23, No.5, pp. 909-918, 2007.

[26] M. R. Cutkosky, On Grasp Choice, Grasp Models, and the Design of Hands for Manufacturing Tasks, IEEE Transactions on Robotics and Automation, vol. 5, No.3, pp. 269-279, 1989.

Chapter 7

Neural Network Modelling and Virtual Reality

Igor Belič

Additional information is available at the end of the chapter

http://dx.doi.org/10.5772/59310

1. Introduction

Virtual reality [VR] is generally understood as the simulated, therefore not real, environment that can resemble the physical world. In most cases virtual reality refers to the human versus environment interaction and the creation of sensory experiences. Technical limitations, the computing power, as well as the basic understanding of the concept of reality, are the limiting factors that still hold back the progress. Virtual reality is also used to describe a wide variety of applications commonly associated with the 3D environments.

Human beings depend on 3D visualization since it allows us to see patterns and relationships that would otherwise remain hidden or at least wrongly interpreted. New VR technologies provide tremendous breakthroughs in visualization of any scenarios from any perspective. There are trends to join two completely different environments such as real and virtual into one merged reality.

VR is mainly centered to the human perception, with the final goal being the complete deception of human senses in a way that the users should not be able to detect that they are taking part in a virtual reality system. This is the so called VR Touring test. [1, 2]

In our case this is not a mandatory condition, VR contribution to the modelling of the materials is entirely different. VR models should provide the accurate ground for deeper understanding and finally for the reliable prediction of material properties. VR technology must be used to support the modelling of extremely complex environments (such as complex polycrystalline materials) to the level never possible before.

Neural networks are systems that actually create the virtual reality. Their performance depends on the dataset called the training set used to train the neural network and define its behaviour. Once trained, the bond between the real and virtual established through the training set remains, while everything outside this set, that is almost the complete model of reality, is virtual. Neural networks produce models that may be very close to the reality (which is the ultimate goal) but nevertheless they will always remain virtual.

Neural networks are used to perform the modelling of the real data. Most often the measured data points are, due to the practical limitations, scarce but we need the information on the observed system in the complete data sub-space. Models are then often used to perform various optimization or system control tasks. No matter what the purpose of modelling is, it always produces virtual reality. Modelling actually simulates-recreates the reality.

The organization of the chapter is following:

The sub-chapter "VR and modelling" starts with an explanation of why the VR is so important for the modelling of the material microstructures (or as the matter of fact at any other modelling).

Follows a brief description on how the data on metallic material microstructure is obtained providing the entry point and the connection to VR.

The fourth sub-chapter covers the modelling steps that produce the building blocks of virtual material. The sub-chapter concludes at the point where VRM (Virtual Reality Material) is ready to be fine-tuned according to the data gathered on real material to produce the VRM as close as possible to represent the reality. The presented approach is the non-mesh based representation of the material. The core idea is to generate randomly shaped grains, where each grain represents a stand-alone object existing as separate object bound to its' surrounding, just like it is the case at real polycrystalline materials.

In fifth sub-chapter the metrics to assess the real and virtual building blocks of material is presented. The established metrics gives us the means to compare the shapes of material's building blocks. In order to make a realistic model of the observed material, the shape of the grains represented by the neural network must come as close as possible to the observed material. The virtual grains are first generated. Separately the microstructural properties of the observed material are gathered and the process of grain-shape optimization is used to modify the shape of virtual grains to come as close as possible to the observed real sample.

The sixth sub-chapter explains how the virtual grain boundary can be changed in order to come closer to reality.

The seventh sub-chapter provides the evidence on how the VR approach provides additional information not accessible before.

At the end conclusions summarize the covered topic.

It is important to note that all the described methods are provided in 2D in order to give as clear picture as possible. Using the 3D space only complicates the explanation. All the graphics need to be put in perspective, which even further blurs the concept.

2. VR and modelling

There are many reasons that speak in favour of using VR and modelling together. VR and modelling are separate fields that live their own life, where VR tends to be popular and modelling remains narrow in serving only narrow purposes. VR itself must have the underlying model that defines the behaviour, but the model as such has no other purpose as to provide the ground for the VR to live. On the other hand modelling of materials did not show any tendency to go into the domain of VR, i.e. into the 3D visualisation. The existence of such modelling is justified by providing the information useful for the engineers needing the data on material's lifetime expectancy, durability, mechanical, electrical, thermal, and other properties. The use of VR brings the totally new perspective to the modelling of materials since it provides additional information and therefore provides the insights that were not possible before. Material properties like lifetime expectancy cannot be predicted without knowing the 3D structure. Cracking of material is another phenomenon that can only be properly studied and explained in 3D. The diffusion process is also the phenomenon that can be studied on completely different level using 3D VR environment.

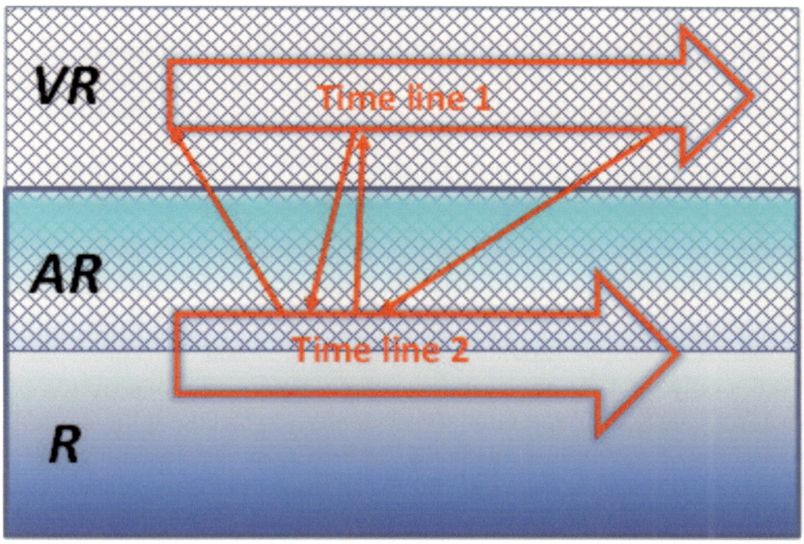

Figure 1. For the VR to be used at modelling of materials, three "levels of reality" can be discerned: R – the reality; AR – the augmented reality; VR – the virtual reality. The time space in VR is completely separated while the R and VR share the same time space. The interactions between the VR and R spaces are schematically shown.

The process of creation and exploitation of VR model (Fig. 1) takes several steps:

1. In geometric sense the only reliable information on the material can be gathered from the 2D samples. The variety of shapes, composition, and different phenomena detected in the real material is tremendous. Actually it can never again be repeated in the same composition as it is on the observed sample. Despite the fact that natural laws always govern the

observed material, the tremendous number of material's constituent elements that took part in the process of material fabrication, result in completely chaotic structures. Therefore no 2D sample can provide the representative information on the observed material to the extent that would suffice for the prediction of material's behaviour and properties.

2. On the basis of the description of the real world the virtual material is created. It is the virtual reality in every sense. Although the visualization of the virtual material is not the goal of the virtualization it adds the value to the system since never before the exploration of 3D material structures was possible with such ease and clarity. The virtual material is built on information gathered from the probed sample. Despite the fact that the information was gathered from the 2D samples, the virtual material exists in 3D.

3. VR model is being used to predict the important material's properties. Along the way the discrepancies between the VR and R are detected, new facts are being revealed and the VR model is being corrected in order to provide better results.

3. Gathering the information on material

The characterization of microstructure plays a central role in material science and engineering. Significant effort was invested in the development of new characterization and analysis techniques. There are several approaches to the characterization of materials such as:

- Chemical composition characterization mainly involves the determination of the composition and the distribution of the chemical components through the material.
- Crystallography.
- Structural morphology [3].

Stereology (optic microscopy) provides information on grain size, grain boundary, etc., although it relies only on a 2D observation. A three-dimensional description of the microstructural features, such as grain-boundary geometry, crystallographic grain orientations, compositional variations, and experimentally derived microstructural models, are used to predict the material's temporal behavior [4]. For the polycrystalline metallic materials, the basic constituent element is grain. The generation of a virtual microstructure therefore depends on obtaining a reasonably reliable spatial arrangement of grains, along with their crystallographic orientation [5]. In order to build more realistic VR microstructures the information on morphology of the grains is needed (the data on crystallographic grain orientation and grain-boundary properties). The source of such information is the electron backscatter diffraction (EBSD) technique, which has proven useful for the characterization of the crystallographic aspects of the microstructure. EBSD is used to perform quantitative microstructure analysis in the scanning electron microscope (SEM) on a millimeter to nanometer scale. EBSD has significantly improved the process of characterization of materials by linking the microstructure and the crystallographic texture. The potential of EBSD to obtain mapping orientation and crystal type for various materials in SEM makes it a powerful tool for a reliable information

http://dx.doi.org/10.5772/59310

gathering used to build the VR model of the material [6]. To further characterize the microstructure, Jinghui et al. proposed a new procedure using EBSD pattern imaging. The image quality enhancement procedure combined with EBSD analysis was considered to quantify the complex microstructures. Moreover, this application is important to relate the microstructural and mechanical properties of the observed material [7].

SEM equipped by EBSD was extended to a three-dimensional analytical technique. A focused ion beam (FIB) is used to remove layers of material (slices) from the sample. After the removal of each slice EBSD is used to collect the data from the newly uncovered surface. High-resolution two-dimensional cross-sectional images are then joined and interpolated into 3D space to visualize the structure of the material [8]. When surface topography is of interest, SEM has been demonstrated to be successful for both characterization and geometry measurements. The computer imaging tools are used for the stereoscopic matching (2D to 3D), for calculation of the surface elevation and for the data interpolation. The spectroscopic matching algorithm produces quite accurate three-dimensional image of the material [9].

The objective of metallography/stereology is to describe the geometrical characteristics of the 2D microstructural shapes such as the amount, number, size of grains, etc. A material's microstructure is chaotic in nature. The variety of grain shapes is tremendous (size, morphology, orientation, etc.)[10].

The material's sample surface is mainly represented in a 2D image (Fig. 2).

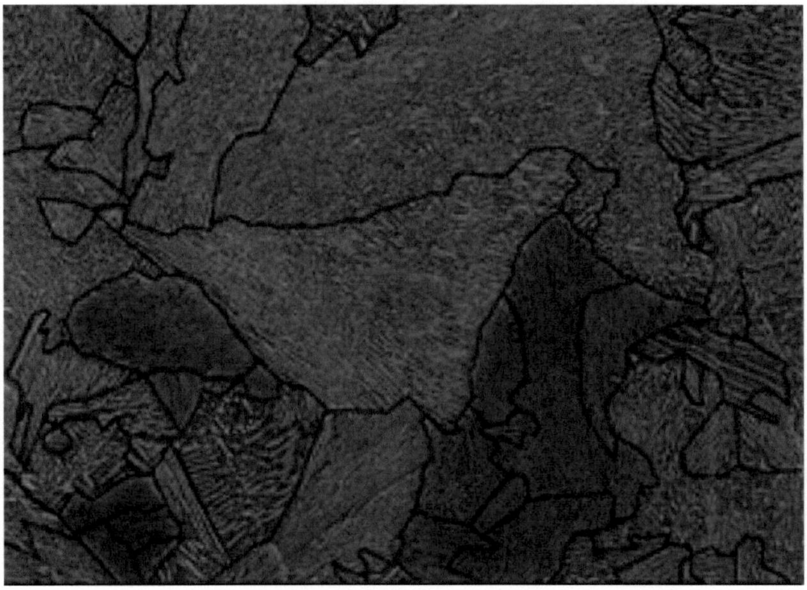

Figure 2. An example of the SEM image of the probed material microstructure (2D).

From the microscopy image (Fig. 2) the grain (or domain) boundaries must be detected. The result of the boundary detection is shown in Fig. 3.

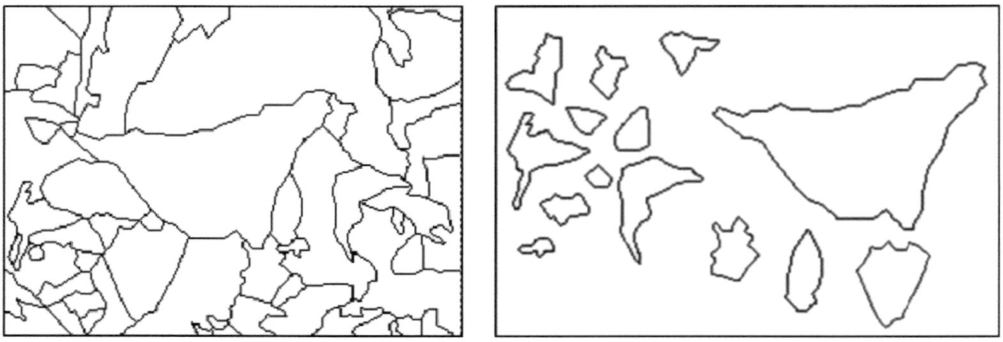

Figure 3. The grain (domain) boundaries are detected and finally separate shapes for grains (domains) are formed.

Fig. 3 illustrates the detection of grain (domain) borders, and separation of closed contour objects that define separate objects – grains.

It is important to note that the term grain is used throughout the chapter. It is not always clear whether the shape is actually describing the grain or it is describing the domain of some prevailing property.

Separate grains are the core elements where real and virtual materials meet. According to the information gathered from the separate grain shapes, the VR model is created and fine-tuned.

4. The neural network model of material

The goal is to create the virtual environment composed of a vast number of basic building blocks – virtual grains. We want to recreate the microstructure of the polycrystalline materials with a special emphasis on metallic materials. The literature provides the basic understanding of the so far used modelling principles and techniques leading to more or less practically useful models. Many researchers are trying to build models which will finally provide the reasonably reliable reconstruction of real materials and thus enable to provide insight into the micro to macro properties of the modelled materials which has for quite some time proven to be the unreachable goal.

The chapter describes a somewhat different approach to the same problem. The microstructure of the material is the consequence of a very complex evolutionary process, where the microstructure represents the unique state of the material. The state of the material can be registered in 2D with a reasonable accuracy using the relatively accessible equipment. The microstructure of the material can be understood as the geometric manifestation of the complex chaotic process that actually produced it.

Currently we do not know the process that would satisfactorily describe the 3D properties of polycrystalline materials. Since in reality we cannot easily observe the material in 3D, we use simplified methods for microstructure assessment (i.e. line intercept method …). Current

http://dx.doi.org/10.5772/59310

methods used to describe the real materials microstructure do not suffice to build the adequate virtual model usable for material performance modelling.

The software installed on the optical or scanning electron microscopes provides the grain size distribution by one of the standardized line intercept method. We have shown that no reasonable correlation exists between the measured linear grain size distribution and 2D cross-section size distribution. Far more complicated is the case between the 2D cross-section grain size distribution and the 3D grain volume distribution. From the linear assessment of grain size distribution we know far too little regarding the actual grain size distribution of the observed material. This is one of the elementary reasons why the modelling of micro to macro properties did not bring good results.

The main building block of the material microstructure is a grain which is also understood to be the main building block of its' virtual counterpart. In the virtual environment such grain represents an object described by the main properties such as: border area defining the shape, orientation, etc. From the computational point of view the grain object has its' own processes such as: random generation of the grain, volume calculation, cross-section area, determination whether the given point belongs to the grain surroundings or to the grain itself, grain re-shaping procedures etc.

The neural network was introduced for the generation of virtual grain. It makes the grain manipulation easier and the representation of grain very compact. The virtual grain generation is only the first step in the process of building the fully 3D polycrystalline material model.

4.1. The random grain geometry

The randomly generated grain is the main building block of the virtual material. It must fulfil the following conditions:

- The shape of each grain must be the consequence of the random process.
- Each grain is uniquely shaped object.
- It must resemble the shape of the grains met in the modelled material – the grain shape must be random but with the control of important properties (size distribution, grain roughness, etc.).
- The representation must be as compact as possible.
- The shape must be easily transformed.
- The position, orientation and movement in the coordinate system must be simply controllable.

In our work we have used two steps to generate the virtual grains, the first is geometric, the second uses the neural networks. The geometric generation of grains is just an intermittent phase used to provide means to present grain shapes to the neural networks. Once neural network is trained the grain shape is completely represented by the neural network parameters and the formal geometric representation is no longer needed.

The process of the random grain generation starts within the polar coordinate system (Fig. 4) and is conducted through four steps.

Step 1.Generation of corner points

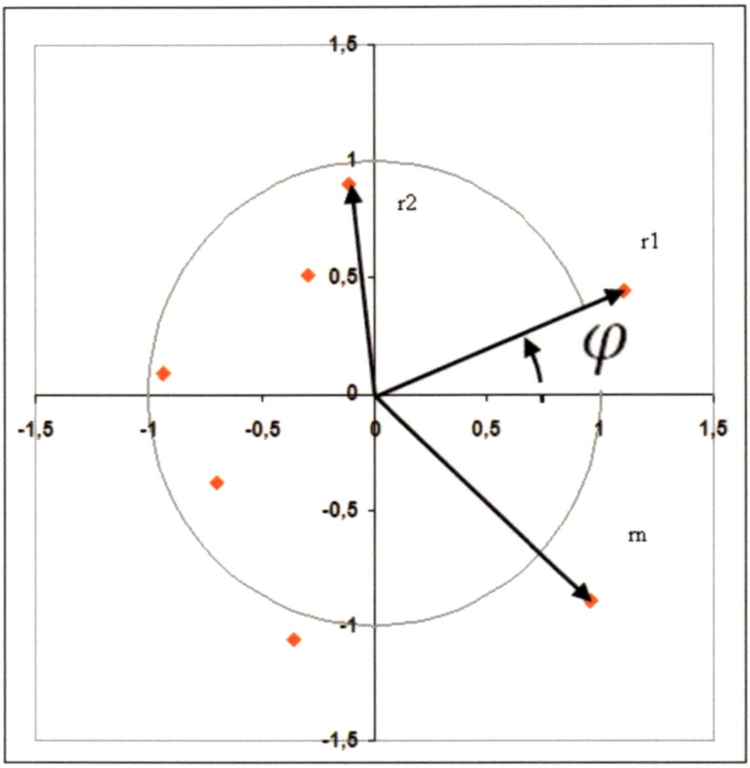

Figure 4. The random generation of the 2D grain shape – 1st step the corner points.

For each consecutive corner point the pairs $\mathbf{r}_i$ and φ_i are randomly generated. For both elements constrains are introduced in terms of max and min value. The generation process is stopped when the sum of consecutively generated angles φ exceeds $\mathbf{2\pi}$ (360°).

Step 2.Finding the carrier lines for the generated corner points

The 2nd step is conducted in Cartesian coordinate system. For the neighbouring corner points the grain border carrier lines are calculated and denoted by two parameters – the slope and the y-intercept (Fig. 5).

Step 3.Finding the valid border line sections

In step 2 the general linear equations for the grain border lines were defined. In order to conclude the grain boundary generation, the valid line sections (those parts that really represent the boundary) must be found (Fig. 6).

http://dx.doi.org/10.5772/59310

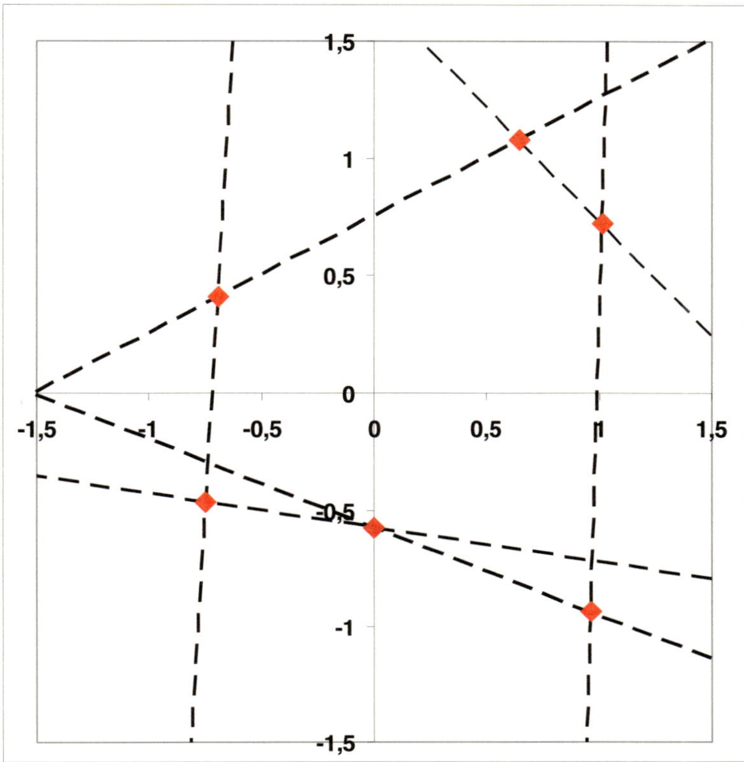

Figure 5. 2nd step: finding the grain boundary carrier lines.

Step 4.Defining the grain boundary by the number of border points

The analytical part of the grain generation process ends with the number of representative points in the R/Angle coordinate system (Fig. 7 left). The function depicted in Fig.7 right forms the training set used for the neural networks to learn the grain boundary.

4.2. Neural networks

One of the common uses of neural networks is the multi-dimensional function approximation usually referred to as modelling [11-14].

Neural networks are model-less approximators, meaning they are capable of modelling regardless of any relational knowledge of the nature of the modelled system.

In our work we are using the feedforward neural networks with supervised training scheme.

The basic building element of any neural network is an artificial neural network cell (Fig. 8 top).

Artificial neural network consists of a number of inputs (synapses) that are connected to the summing junction. The values of inputs are multiplied by adequate weights w (synaptic

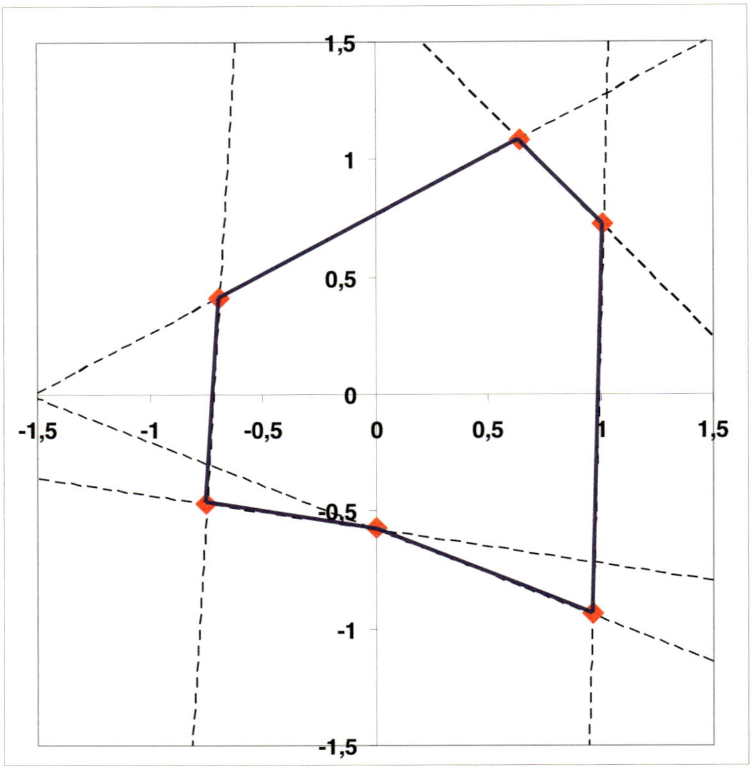

Figure 6. 3rd step: to form the grain boundary it is necessary to find the valid sections of the border lines.

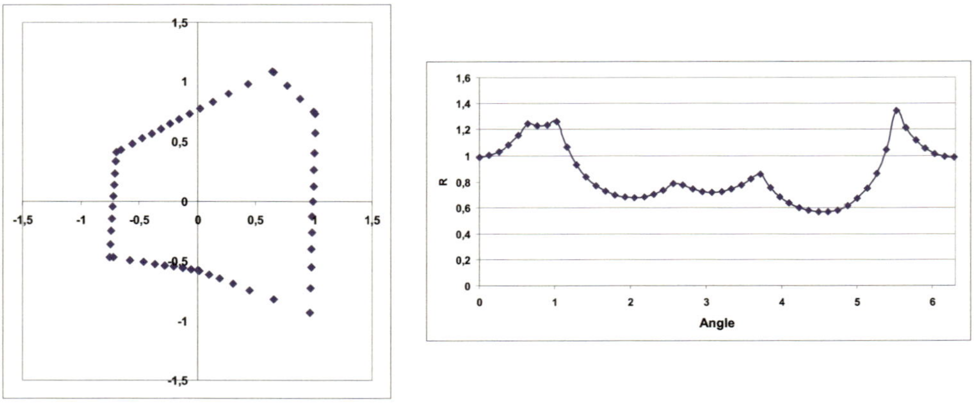

Figure 7. 4th step: defining the grain boundary by the border points – left in Cartesian coordinate system, right in R/ Angle coordinate system.

weights) and summed with other inputs. The training process changes the values of connection weights. The value of summed and weighted inputs is the argument of an activation function

http://dx.doi.org/10.5772/59310

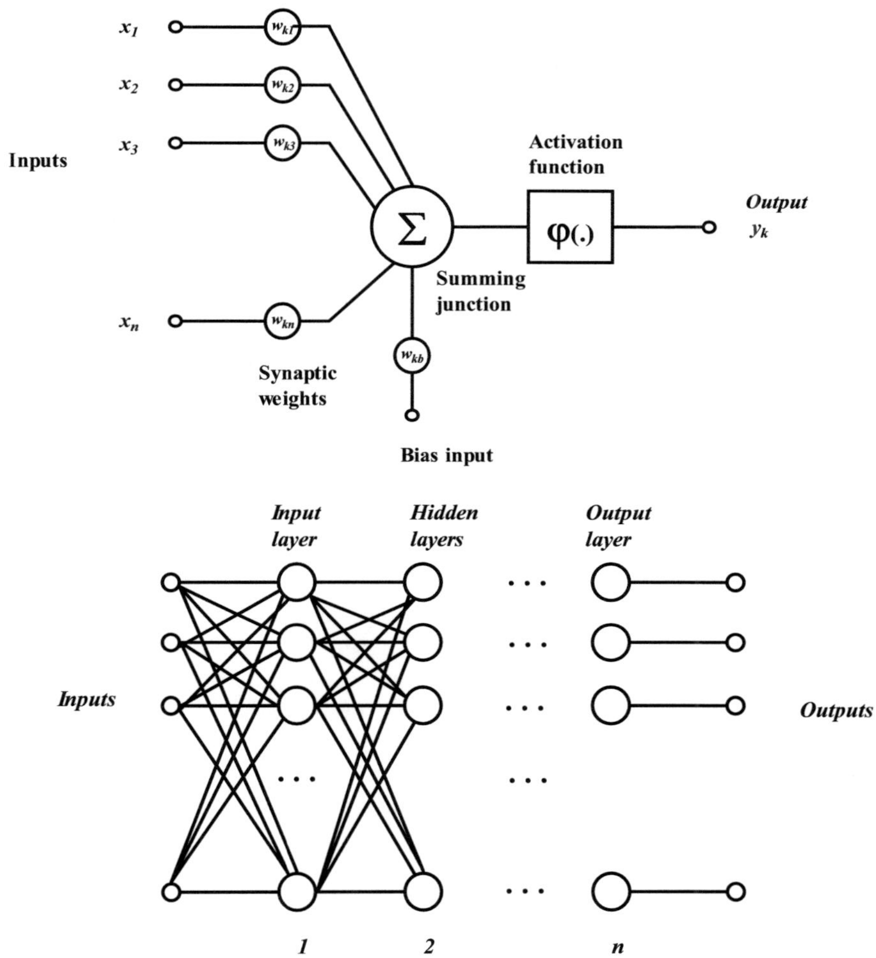

Figure 8. The artificial neural network cell (top) and the general neural network system (bottom).

which produces the final output of an artificial neural cell. In most cases, the activation function is of sigmoidal type $\phi(x) = 1 / (1 + e^{-x})$.

Artificial neural network cells are combined in the neural network architecture which is by default composed at least of two layers that provide communication with outer world (Fig. 8 bottom). Those layers are referred to as the input and output layer respectively. Between the two, there are hidden layers which transform the signal from the input layer to the output layer. The hidden layers are called hidden for they are not directly visible to the input or output of the neural network system. These hidden layers contribute significantly to the adaptive formation of the non-linear neural network input-output transfer function and thus to the characteristics of the system.

The process of adaptation of a neural network weights is called training or learning. During supervised training, the input – output pairs are presented to the neural network i.e. for each presented input value the desired output value (target value) is also known for they are both part of the training set. The training algorithm iteratively changes the weights of the neural network in order to get closer to the presented output values.

The data points are consecutively presented to the neural network. For each data point, the neural network produces an output value which normally differs from the target value. The difference between the two is the approximation error in the particular data point. The error is then propagated back through the neural network towards the input, and the correction of the connection weights is made to lower the output error. There are numerous methods for correction of the connection weight. The most frequently used algorithm is called the error backpropagation algorithm.

The training process continues from the first data point included in the training set to the very last, while the queue order is not important.

When the training achieves the desired accuracy, it is stopped. From here on, the model can reproduce the given data points with a prescribed precision for all data points.

In our case the training set was composed of 50 points representing the grain boundary (Fig 9). The number of 50 points was experimentally chosen. With the neural network it is only possible to model unique functions. The grain boundary represented in Cartesian coordinate system (Fig. 7 left) does not fulfil the condition of uniqueness, while the same boundary represented in the polar coordinate system (Fig. 7 Right) is unique. Once trained the complete grain boundary is represented by the neural network weights (Fig. 9). For the selected neural network architecture (1-10-10-1) 141 weights are needed (Fig. 9 left). For the grain boundary definition no further calculation is needed, the grain is fully described.

In the computational sense the grain is an object combining data and methods. Grain data is included in the neural network weights, methods (processes) are:

- Random generation of the grain,
- Volume calculation,
- Cross-section area calculation,
- Determination whether the given point belongs to the grain surroundings or to the grain itself,
- Grain re-shaping procedures,
- Grain scaling,
- etc.

From Fig. 9 one can observe that the grain shape has no sharp edges as it is the case at geometric shape (Fig. 7). The roughness of the grain boundary is within the neural network representation quite easily adjustable.

http://dx.doi.org/10.5772/59310

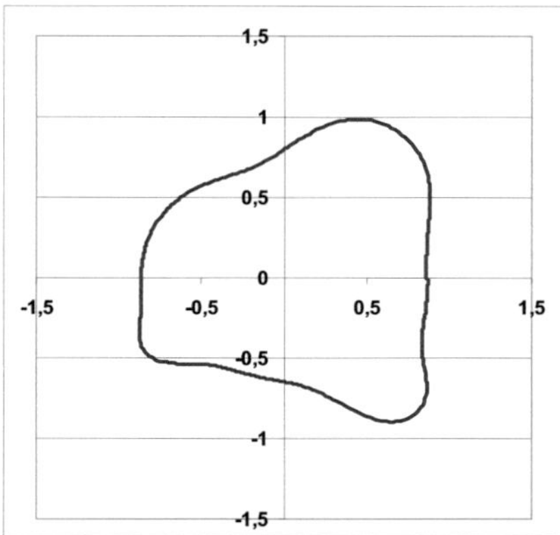

Network configuration	
	Nr. of neurons
Input layer	1
Hidden layer 1	10
Hidden layer 2	10
Output layer	1

Network Weights							
-20,1394	16,57829	-12,0663	11,02814	10,81368	-5,22849	17,48975	-2,32303
-2,75313	0,381123	15,50267	-7,96601	15,02321	-1,37285	-4,6597	2,366897
-12,8173	6,883308	-6,84222	4,327835	14,4265	5,380355	-4,35451	-3,83106
0,879532	-4,9429	-2,06009	1,665017	3,613425	2,669609	-0,44858	-11,9671
-9,20121	7,757444	3,872915	-0,29155	1,975464	4,291922	-0,29747	-0,54338
0,005008	-0,64556	-1,70808	-1,36996	-0,40923	-1,78735	-0,69336	-1,10473
-0,04648	0,016847	-0,46383	-0,24586	-1,24302	1,652688	2,240653	0,687929
-7,37926	-0,03256	-4,58703	-5,36011	0,109945	3,986874	1,591683	2,110393
-1,11288	-0,32804	0,318889	0,491652	0,364788	1,467655	-0,07764	0,038729
-0,72084	0,190075	-0,49006	-0,45105	-0,13426	5,917402	0,861509	-1,69872
8,317055	-0,89562	-3,55831	-7,61664	-5,07454	-1,80703	2,69317	2,159475
-5,43323	-3,18402	1,483116	-7,42498	-2,03566	3,760095	7,516295	4,539834
0,587503	-9,43768	-9,97553	2,256574	-0,77394	-2,04102	1,433845	-0,16736
-0,54284	-2,13196	-2,83951	0,710255	2,811366	3,844169	-4,80431	-10,3132
1,657332	-5,90994	-9,44306	2,677164	4,821523	4,009794	1,099531	-0,01844
0,642114	-0,94388	-5,2084	0,968387	-2,11834	-6,0353	1,841588	-0,0824
0,315456	-1,83389	6,474098	7,724677	0,467653	-7,44827	-1,74718	-2,15884
-1,71998	6,988257	6,975227	6,205049	-3,31152			

Figure 9. The grain boundary represented by the neural network. It was modelled by the neural network of the size 1-10-10-1 (upper table). The lower table represents the network weights.

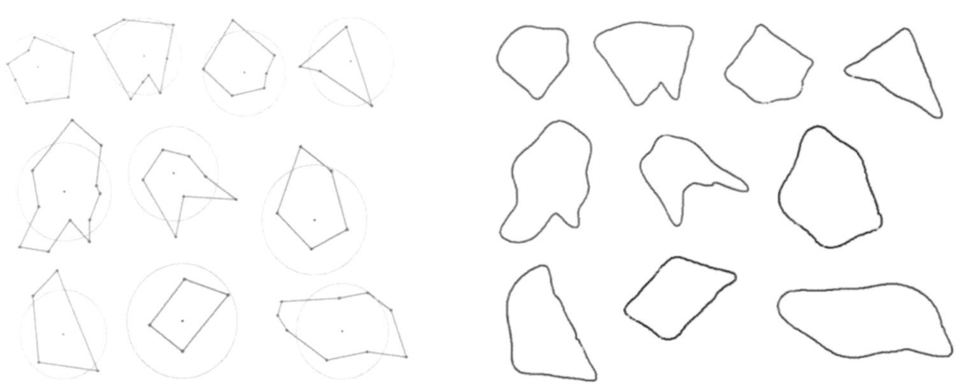

Figure 10. Randomly generated grains – left: the geometric representation: right: the neural network representation.

By implementation of the described steps we can generate a vast number of random virtual grains. The shape of each grain is unique and from the practical aspect it is not likely ever to be repeated. This is exactly the case we encounter at real materials. As we can observe from Fig. 10 right the neural network representation is smoother and closer to the reality as its' geometric counterpart.

5. The grain similarity metrics

Many existing methods attempt to describe the roughness of grains in 2D and 3D, but none of them is capable of uniquely describing this parameter. A common way to describe the angularity of different particles is to use a numerical parameter called the spike parameter. In this case the particle abrasivity is related to the size and sharpness of triangles. Maximum and minimum circumscribed circles can also be used, but they have certain limitations. Many other methods were developed to describe the particle boundary, such as: shape factor, aspect ratio, roundness, etc. [15]. Since there are no solutions that would suit our needs, the new assessment method that takes into consideration many details of the grain boundary was developed.

5.1. Roughness histogram method

For each generated grain, the roughness histogram is obtained. In general, for the grains generated by the neural network 300 points are used to describe the grain boundary. The roughness histogram method measures the grain boundary's departure from an ideally round object (circle).

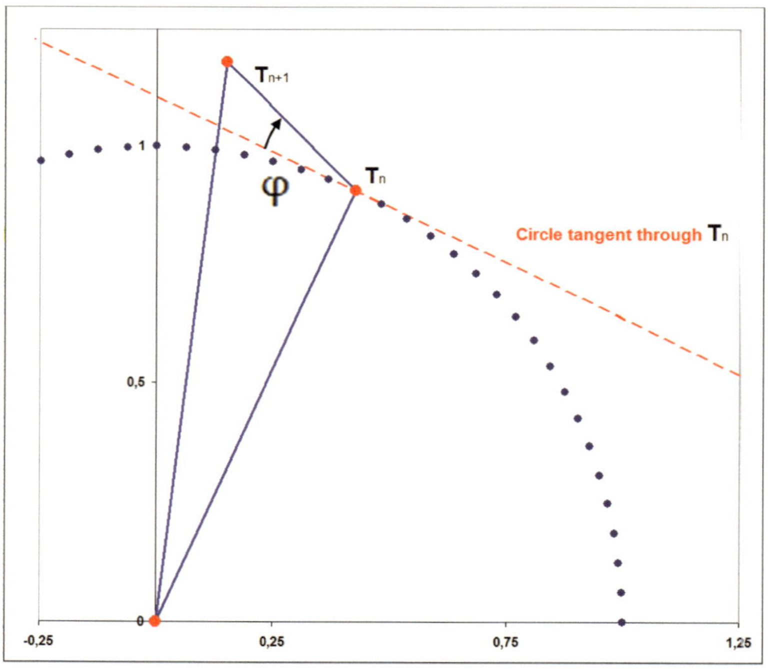

Figure 11. The angle φ represents a measure of the grain surface departure from the ideally round shape observed at the point T_n. The observed section of the grain is represented by the line connecting the two adjacent points T_n and T_{n+1} of the grain boundary.

The tangent on the circle takes the angle of **π/2** to the radial line. Since the adjacent grain-boundary points are ideally not placed on the circle, but anywhere else, the line connecting the two adjacent boundary points takes an angle to the tangent. The angle between the two represents the departure of the grain boundary from the circular shape (Fig. 11).

The angle φ representing the measure of the departure of the grain boundary from the round shape in the point T_n is obtained. The results of the calculation are given in the histogram in Fig. 12. The histogram consists of 18 (+1 for error detection) classes therefore it can be treated as a vector in 18 dimensional space. To calculate the distance ***d*** between two vectors (histograms) $\vec{F}$ and $\vec{E}$ the most commonly used approach is to use the Euclidean distance which is calculated by the formula

$$d = \sqrt{\sum_{i=1}^{18} (f_i - e_i)^2}. \tag{1}$$

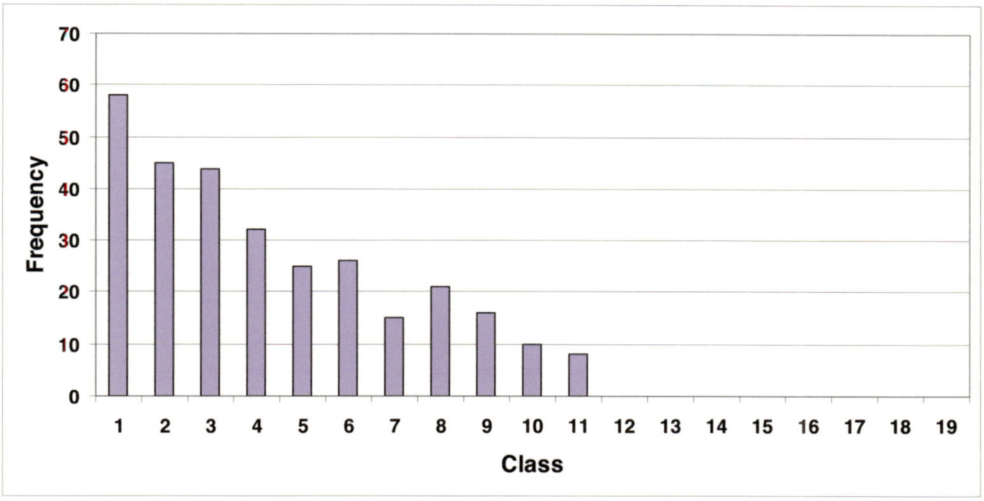

Figure 12. An example of a grain-roughness histogram.

The coordinate system for each generated grain must be put into the grain's centre of gravity (Fig. 13).

The grain-centring process takes the following steps: grain is sectioned in a series of triangles defined by the coordinate centre and the two adjacent grain-boundary points. In the case of the two-dimensional shape the intersection of all the straight lines that divide the shape into two parts of equal momentum about the line defines the centre of gravity. It is the average (arithmetic mean) of all the points composing the shape [16].

The grain coordinate system origin is moved to the gravity centre of the grain.

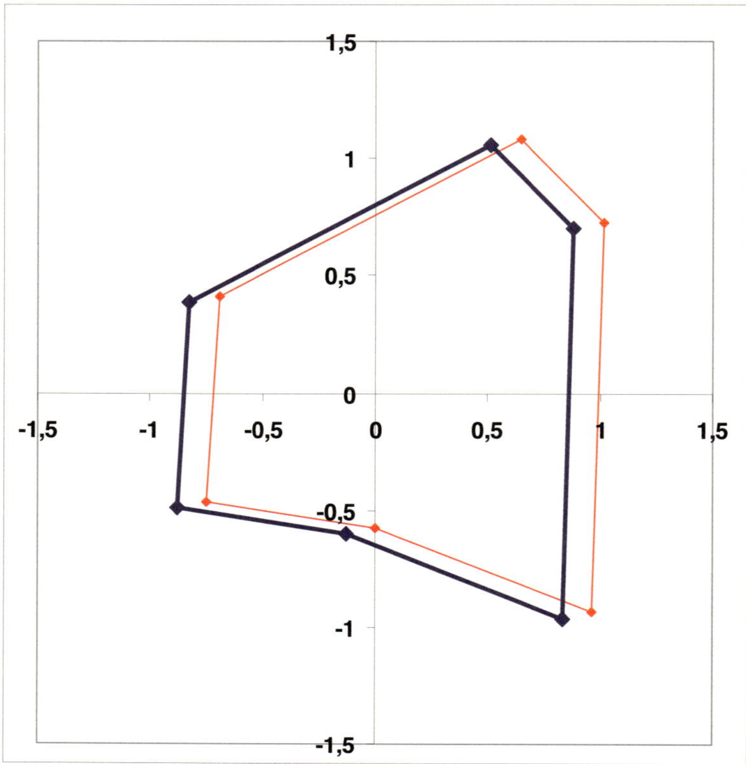

Figure 13. Randomly generated grain centred in the coordinate system (bold line). The centring process is completed prior to the neural network training.

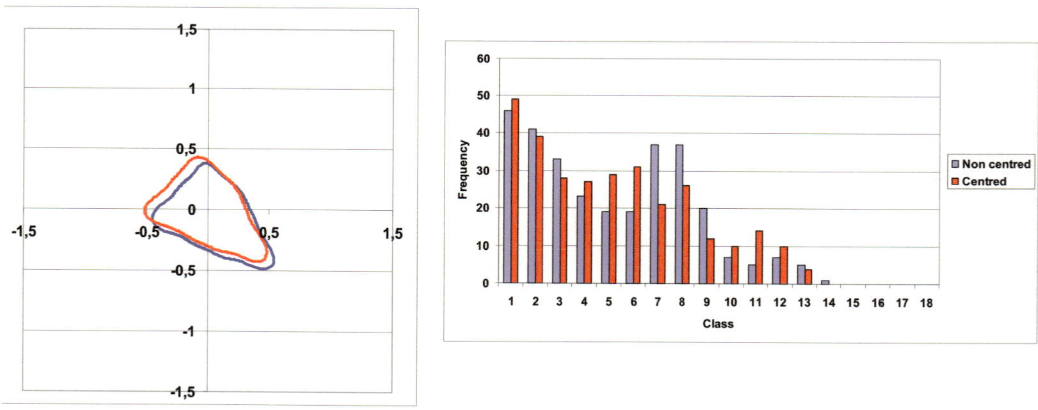

Figure 14. (left) Two instances of the same grain (not-centred and centred, (right) Roughness histograms of non-centred (blue) and centred (red) grains.

The roughness histogram method only gives comparable results when used on centred grains. In Fig. 14 there are two instances of the same grain. The first one is not centred, and the second one is placed in its gravity centre.

Many tests show that the method used is fast, stable, and can represent the roughness, regardless of the size, rotation, and mirror image of the grains in the coordinate system.

6. Joining the properties of real and virtual material

The basic virtual grain shape is provided by the neural network. The desired (achieved by the analysis of real material) grain-roughness histogram normally differs from the currently observed virtual grains. The main goal of the procedures that perform the grain-shape optimization is to obtain the virtual grain-roughness that is as close as possible to the desired one. We know that the match between the targeting grain-roughness and the achieved one should not be too strict since the basic shape of the grains influence the grain-roughness histogram significantly and our goal is not to reproduce the grain shape as well.

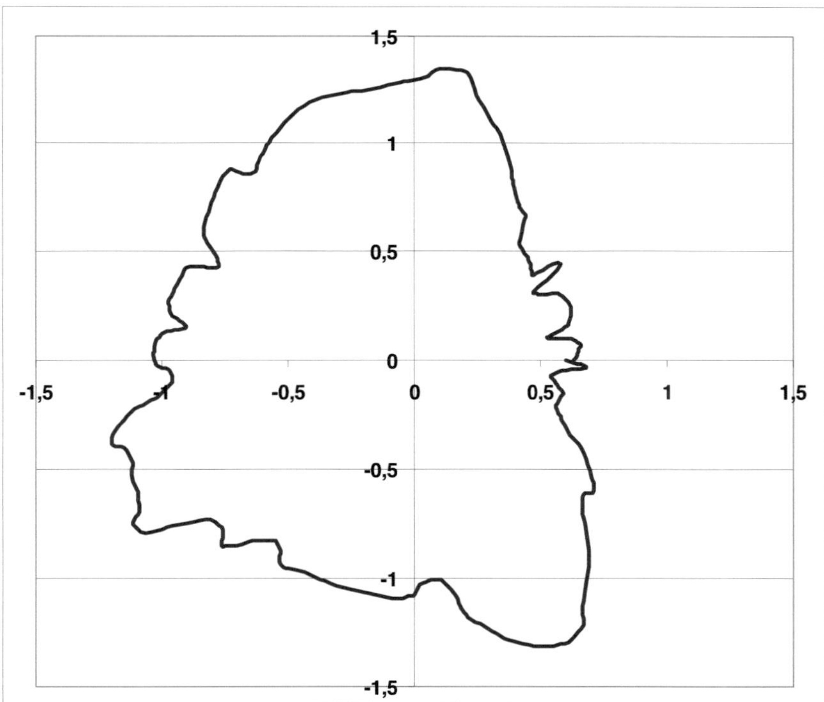

Figure 15. The result of the grain boundary modification.

The grain-shape optimization process must fulfill the following conditions:

- It must not alter the starting grain shape significantly.
- The main influence must affect the grain boundary.
- It must be a controllable and convergent process.

Let us assume that the neural network produces the grain-boundary function denoted by $B(\phi)$. The random grain-boundary modification must fulfill the condition that the point at the angle $\varphi=0$ remains the same as at the angle $\varphi=2\pi$. The modification of the grain-boundary function must provide the rougher boundary, while at the same time it must be random in shape. Equation (2) describes the circumstances.

$$B_M(\varphi) = B(\varphi) + R(\varphi) \tag{2}$$

where $B_M(\phi)$ represents the modified boundary function, $B(\phi)$represents the original grain-boundary function provided by the neural network, and $R(\phi)$ represents the random function that actually modifies the grain boundary. An example of the modified virtual grain is shown in Fig. 15.

The complete random process of the grain-boundary modification is controlled by only three parameters.

7. The grain size distribution — The first overlooked detail in classic modeling

Basically three ASTM (American Society for Testing and Materials) methods are used for the evaluation of the grain-size distribution [17]:

- Comparison method,
- Line-intercept method,
- Planimetric method.

The existing methods provide the size distribution of grains only in 2D. However, many attempts were made to describe the grain-size distribution in 3D from the data obtained in 2D. Due to the computational complexity researchers replaced the realistic grains with spheres, which eventually lead to a grave systematic error. More complex grain model proposed by Zhao [18] uses polyhedral grains for the grain-size assessment. The results have shown that this model is more efficient in calculating the 3D grain-size distribution from 1D and 2D distributions.

However, comparing the 2D and 3D grain size distribution in a cellular material shows similar results. The areal distributions of planar sections taken for various polyhedral shapes demonstrated a good agreement between the expected and the calculated areal curves for an assumed complex polyhedral symmetry [19]. When a sectioning plane intersects the features

http://dx.doi.org/10.5772/59310

in the microstructure, the image obtained reveals features that are reduced in dimension by one [20], as follows:

- Volumes (three-dimensional) are described by areas,
- Surfaces (two-dimensional) by lines,
- Curves (one-dimensional) by points.

The shape of the grains can be relatively simply quantified by measurements made on grain structure. The ratio of the grain's longest chord and its perimeter to the equivalent diameter can be analysed using image analysers [21]. However, among others, particle shape angularity and roughness are the most difficult parameters to define. The development of new methods to characterize particle properties has been motivated by the need to improve particle modelling. A new technique was proposed by Sukumaran et al. [22] to quantify particle shape and angularity using an image analyser. The true shape of the particle is approximated by an equivalent polygon and a new shape factor is defined as the deviation of the global particle outline from a circle. Most techniques developed so far tend to reduce a shape into a simpler shape representation. The common criteria cited by researchers while evaluating the shape representation are: scope, uniqueness, stability, sensitivity, efficiency, etc. [23]. The problem associated with particle surface characterization is that they provide statistical functions and parameters that are not unique for a particular particle surface [24]. Very popular methods for the roughness characterization of particles in general are fractals. However, the methods used to calculate the fractal dimension can be effective when applied under some limiting conditions.

Using the described modelling the line intercept method [25, 26] was tested for its' validity. For this purpose we have generated a virtual material with an area of 1 mm^2. The goal of the test was to analyse the differences between the grain size distribution obtained by the line intercept method and the exactly known grain size distribution of the modelled virtual material. At the line intercept method the line crosses the underlying grains at arbitrary position (from the grains perspective). Since the grain shapes are very non-uniform the representative crossing of the grain that would correlate with its' actual size does not exist.

If we take into examination one single virtual grain and perform its' slicing then one single grain can produce the size distribution. Furthermore, depending on the angle at which the slicing is performed, the distributions for one grain are very different (Fig. 16). From the experiment it is clear that line intercept method, where the line crosses the grain at arbitrary position, cannot represent the adequate information regarding the involved grain size.

It is generally accepted that the large number of involved grains eventually statistically correct the errors made at each grain by the line crossing. 1 mm^2 of the virtual material was generated and the line intercept method covered 1mm of it. The process was repeated several times and the results are presented in Fig. 17 where only two experiments are shown.

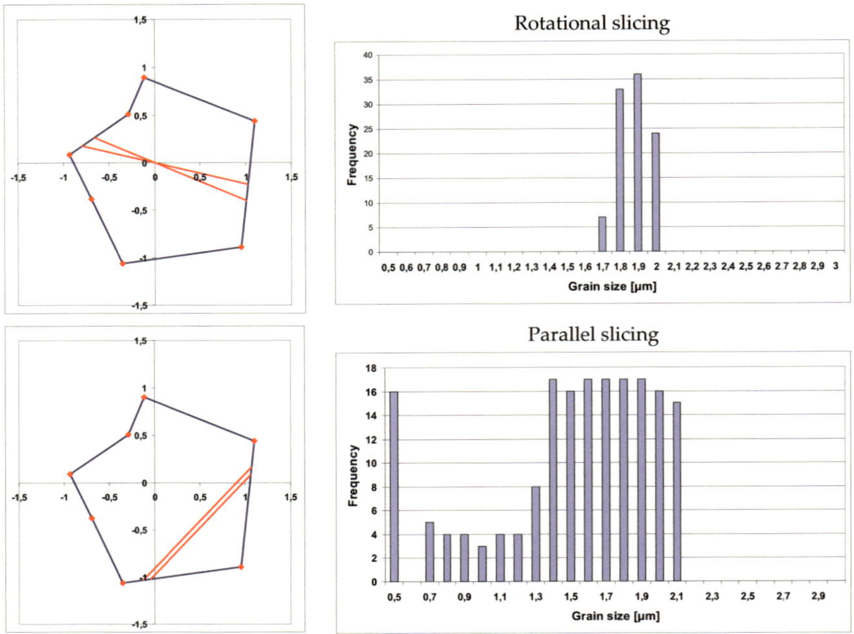

Figure 16. Single grain slicing – "size distribution" for rotational and parallel slicing.

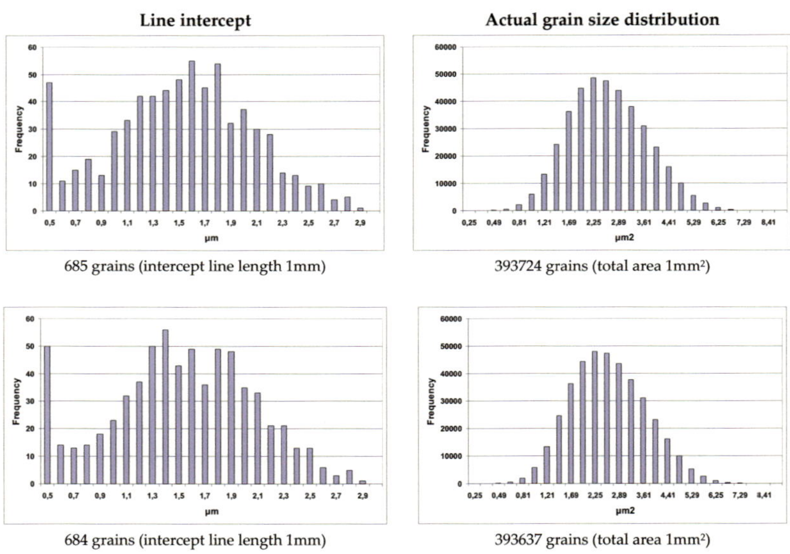

Figure 17. Comparison of line intercept method (left) and the actual area size distribution (right) determined for two virtual materials.

http://dx.doi.org/10.5772/59310

From Fig. 17 it is evident that there are substantial differences between the line intercept distribution and the real grain size distribution. It is also evident that the random grain generation process produces the virtual material of almost normally distributed grain sizes. It has to be noted that the random generation process was not influenced by any means to produce such a distribution. The real distribution is very stable and was almost the same for all experiments. On the other hand the distributions obtained by the line intercept method vary significantly. The lower parts of the size distributions falsely indicate that there is a large amount of small particles in the sample. This anomaly is due to the fact that a large amount of grains is always crossed at the grain sections having low crossing length.

8. Conclusions

VR technologies that provide the enhancement of modelling will provide significantly deeper understanding of real materials. This is also true for the nano-structures where the geometry plays a central role.

The entry point to the VR is the information gathered through the various techniques. Generally main geometric properties are gathered through the various microscopies. Preparation of samples for the microscopy is critical since errors at sample preparation stage are directly integrated in the model.

From the microscopy images the separate grains (domains) are extracted. This is a second critical process since it adds additional errors to the model supporting the VR. Extracting the closed contours from the digital image that contain grains (domains) is not a trivial task. For some microstructures this task is next to impossible.

Once the grain shapes are extracted, their boundary roughness histogram is calculated and averaged over the grains. The boundary roughness histogram is the one that model is taking as target, so the modelled material will exhibit almost the same histogram. From the extracted grains their size distribution is determined. Boundary roughness histogram and grain size distribution are used to create the model.

The main building block of the virtual microstructure is the random grain. Virtual grain is first generated and described by geometric means. The second step is training the neural network to hold the grain boundary. Once trained the geometric form can be discarded, grains are completely represented by separate sets of neural network weights, no complex computations are needed to provide the grain volume, grain cross-section area, grain reshaping in order to get it closer to the reality, etc. The grain is an object. It joins its own data as well as methods such as:

- Random generation of the grain,
- Volume calculation,
- Cross-section area,

- Determination whether the given point belongs to the grain surroundings or to the grain itself,
- Grain re-shaping procedures,
- Grain scaling,
- Etc.

By using the generated virtual material of 1mm^2 area it was shown that commonly used line intercept method cannot represent the real size distribution of the material although it is generally used under ASTM (American Society for Testing and Materials) standardization.

The finding is the first and direct consequence of using VR to support modelling.

Acknowledgements

The research was financially supported by the Slovenian Research Agency program group P2-0132 (Institute of Metals and Technology, Ljubljana, Slovenia)

Author details

Igor Belič*

Address all correspondence to: igor.belic@imt.si

Institute of Metals and Technology, Slovenia

References

[1] Saggio G., Ferrari, M. (2012). New Trends in Virtual Reality Visualization of 3D Scenarios, Virtual Reality-Human Computer Interaction, Dr. Tang Xinxing (Ed.), ISBN: 978-953-51-0721-7, InTech, DOI: 10.5772/46407. Available from: http://www.intechopen.com/books/virtual-reality-human-computer-interaction/new-trends-in-virtual-reality-visualization-of-3d-scenarios

[2] Gilson S., Glennerster, A.(2012). High Fidelity Immersive Virtual Reality, Virtual Reality-Human Computer Interaction, Dr. Tang Xinxing (Ed.), ISBN: 978-953-51-0721-7, InTech, DOI: 10.5772/50655. Available from: http://www.intechopen.com/books/virtual-reality-human-computer-interaction/high-fidelity-immersive-virtual-reality

[3] Brandon, D.; Kaplan, D. W. Microstructural Characterization of Materials. 5–20, British Library, Sussex, 2008.

[4] Lewis, A. C.; Bingert, J. F.; Rowenhorst, D. J.; Gupta, A.; Geltmacher, A. B.; Spanos, G. Two and three-dimensional microstructural characterization of a super-austenitic stainless steel. Materials Science and Engineering 418, 11–18, 2006.

[5] Rollett, A. D.; Lee, S. B.; Campman, R.; Rohrer, G. S. Three dimensional characterization of microstructure by electron back-scatter diffraction. Annual Review of Materials Research 37, 627–658, 2007.

[6] Wilkinson, A. J.; Britton, T. B. Strains, planes, and EBSD in materials science. Materials Today 15, 366–376, 2012.

[7] Jinghui, W. U.; Peter, J. W.; Garcia, C. I.; Hua, M.; Deardo, A. J. Image quality analysis: A new method of characterizing microstructures. ISIJ International 45, 254–262, 2005.

[8] Bansal, R. K.; Kubis, A.; Hull, R.; Fitz-Gerald, J. M. High-resolution three-dimensional reconstruction: A combined scanning electron microscope and focused ion-beam approach. Journal of Vacuum Science and Technology 24, 554–562, 2006.

[9] Podsiadlo, P.; Stachowiak, G. W. Characterization of surface topography of wear particles by SEM stereoscopy. Wear 206, 39–52, 1997.

[10] Gokhale, A. M. Quantitative characterization and representation of global microstructural geometry. Metallography and Microstructures 9, 428–447 (2004).

[11] AitGougam L, Tribeche M, Mekideche-Chafa F. A systematic investigation of a neural network for function approximation. Neural Networks 8(21), 1311-1317, 2008.

[12] Tikk D, Kóczy LT, Gedeon TD. A survey on universal approximation and its limits in soft computing techniques. International Journal of Approximate Reasoning 33(2), 185-202, 2003.

[13] Wang J, Xub Z. New study on neural networks: The essential order of approximation. Neural Networks 23, 618-624, 2010.

[14] Igor Belič (2012). Neural Networks and Static Modelling, Recurrent Neural Networks and Soft Computing, Dr. Mahmoud ElHefnawi (Ed.), ISBN: 978-953-51-0409-4, InTech, DOI: 10.5772/35923. Available from: http://www.intechopen.com/books/recurrent-neural-networks-and-soft-computing/neural-networks-and-static-modelling

[15] Podsiadlo, P.; Kuster, M.; Stachowiak, G. W. Numerical analysis of wear particles from non-arthritic and osteoarthritic human knee joints. Wear 210, 318–325, 1997.

[16] Yun, B. J.; Yi, J. W.; Kim, S. D. A new vertex coding scheme using the centre of the gravity center of a triangle. http://www.eurasip.org. (accessed: May 2012).

[17] Schuman, M.; Haas, T.; Perez, T. O.; Riepe, S. Grain-size distribution of multicrystalline silicon for structure characterization of silicon wafers. In: Proceedings of the European PV Solar Energy Conference and Exhibition. 5–9 (Fraunhofer Publica, Hamburg, 2001).

[18] Zhao, X. B. Measurement and calculation of three-dimensional grain sizes and size distribution functions. Microscopy and Microanalysis 4, 420–427, 1998.

[19] White, P. L.; Vlack, L. H. V. A comparison of two and three dimensional size distributions in a cellular material. Metallography 3, 241–258, 1970.

[20] Russ, J. C.; Dehoff, R. T. Practical Stereology, 2nd Edition. 3–34 (Plenum Press, New York, 1999).

[21] Wejrzanowski, T.; Sphychalski, W. L.; Rozniatowski, K.; Kurzydlowski, K. J. Image based analysis of complex microstructures of engineering materials. International Journal of Applied Mathematics and Computer Science 18, 33–39, 2008.

[22] Sukumaran, B.; Ashmawy, A. K. Quantitative characterization of the geometry of discrete particles. Geotechnique 51, 1–9, 2001.

[23] Iyer, N.; Jayanti, S.; Lou, K.; Kalyanaraman, Y.; Ramani, K. Three-dimensional shape searching: State-of-the-art review and future trends. Computer-Aided Design 37, 509–530, 2004.

[24] Stachowiak, G. W.; Podsiadlo, P. Surface characterization of wear particles. Wear 229, 1171–1185, 1999.

[25] Metallography and Microstructures. Vol. 9, ASM Handbook, ASM International, Materials Park, OH, 2005.

[26] VanderVoort GF. Metallography: Principles and Practice. ASM International. Materials Park, OH, 1999.

Chapter 8

Mobile Virtual Reality — An Approach for Safety Management

Dong Zhao

Additional information is available at the end of the chapter

http://dx.doi.org/10.5772/59227

1. Introduction

Workplace safety is paramount for all production sectors throughout the world. However, every year the number of occupational injuries attracts concerns on the safety management for every industry. Existing studies have endeavored great efforts on injury causations and found that more than half of workplace accidents are due to human errors.

For most human errors, professional training is believed to be an effective safety enhancement and management approach. Active and interactive training is often of higher level of comprehension while the passive methods of learning are not as effective, especially for adult learners. Most current electrical safety training programs in terms of video tape, paper-based handouts or slide shows can hardly present the electrical hazards vividly to trainees and, on the other hand, the trainees are not provided enough opportunity to participate in these activities. In fact, it is believed that an active and interactive training program can lead to a better comprehension of training material [1]. Such participatory training brings a real life aspect into the training in an "it can happen to you" scenario and allows the trainees to relate to conditions and regulations in real life situations and with a life or death importance. The best scenario is when people do not have to consciously think about following safety procedures because it is second nature to them.

Safety training as safety management means has been existing for years, however what type of training can be the effective approach remains a question. Rooney, et al. [2] suggested that effective training should comprise of both the initial skill training and further refreshing training to reduce human mistakes. The initial skill training is generally conducted in the classroom and supplemented with on-the-job experience. It prepares workers for experiences they will routinely encounter and those they will infrequently encounter. If training does not include the infrequent events or situations, the likelihood of successfully handling such situations will depend solely on the problem solving and decision making skills of the worker. In addition to initial training, refresher training on non-routine or modified tasks will minimize worker mistakes and reduce the potential for a worker's skills to deteriorate. A refresher training program is needed to assist workers in developing and maintaining a high skill level. Such a program will address a worker's loss of skills and enhance skills beyond the initial training level.

Following the same logic, virtual reality (VR) technology becomes an innovative method to promote the training effectiveness. VR-based training has been used with varied successes in many industries such as fire-fighter training, mine safety training, safe procedure in surgical training, security in refineries, safe equipment operation, and civil engineering education. Specifically within the construction industry, VR technology has been used for constructability analysis of precast concrete structural analysis application development [3], electrical design and installation [4], construction prototyping.

Mobile virtual reality (MVR) is an adoption of VR simulation on mobile/portable devices connected to cloud technology for end users. Besides the inclusion of features from VR, another important characteristic of the MVR-supported training programs is the flexibility (in terms of time and location) that they offer to the user. In traditional classroom-based training/ instruction, availability of the training provider and trainees need to be coordinated to schedule the training session. MVR, especially when designed for use with a mobile device, allows for convenience of location and time. The user can participate in the training in a job trailer, office, or conceivably the back of a truck with a smart phone. There is no limitation to classroom or training schedules. Tracking the user performance can be built into the applications, which reduces the need for direct trainee observation. Taking mining as a MVR example, users are able to explore sights and sounds of a virtual mine shaft where the screen of the iPad or iPhone is a window into the mine and interact with the environment via the touchscreen. Based on their activities, the trainee is sent messages and questions, and the mine shaft environment changes to match the response criteria.

Current training modes do not count for all learning style and result in information transfer losses (see gaps in Figure 1a). In terms of safety training, information transfer losses include the loss between the information to be expressed and the expressed information (gap 1) and the loss between the expressed information and delivered information (gap 2). Current static two-dimensioned training modes limit the types of safety information and the pool of information receivers, leading to gap 1. Some dangerous tasks and safety issues cannot be allowed for trainees to rehearsal and practice in real life, leading to gap 2. On the contrary, MVR increases a third dimension and mobility, expands the portions of both expressed and delivered information, and eventually helps to deduce the gaps of information losses (see Figure 1b).

The effectiveness of information perceiving is also confined to traditional training modes. As stated before, for adult trainees, interactive and active training methods instead of passive methods can lead to a better comprehension of training material. Such participatory training brings a real life aspect into the training in an "it can happen to you" scenario and allows the trainees to relate conditions and regulations with real life situations and a life or death

http://dx.doi.org/10.5772/59227

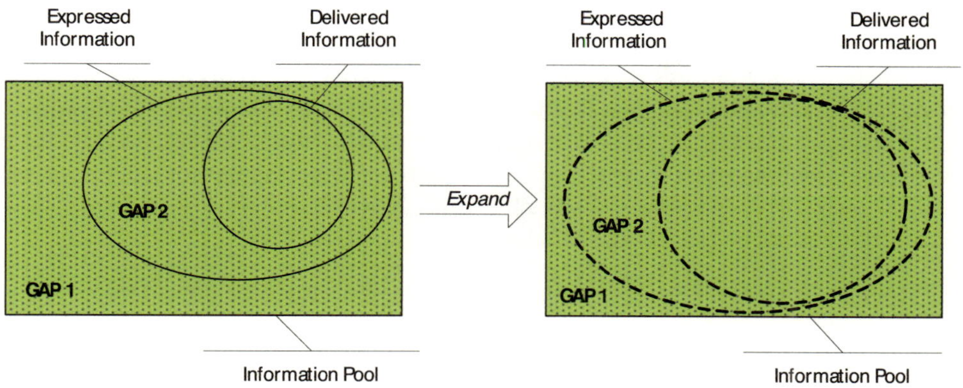

Figure 1. Information transfer in traditional training (L) and MVR-supported training (R)

importance. The best scenario is when people do not have to consciously think about following safety procedures because it is second nature to them. However, current electrical safety training programs in terms of video tape, paper-based handouts or slide shows can hardly present the electrical hazards vividly to trainees and, on the other side, the trainees are not provided enough opportunity to participate in.

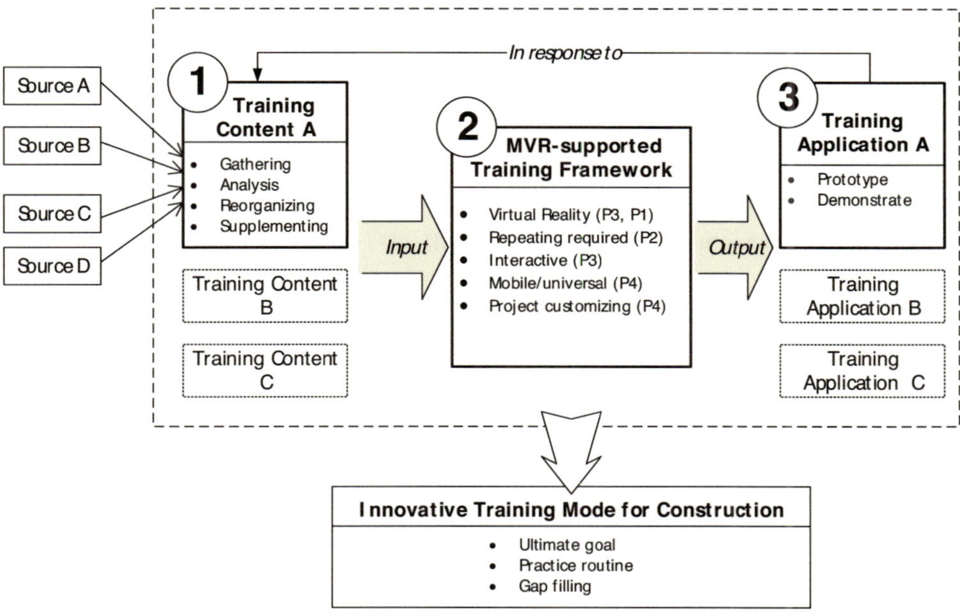

Figure 2. Program development framework

This chapter introduces such comprehensive approach that incorporates real-world safety concerns into virtual-world simulations. The approach includes three steps: (1) real-world data collection and coding using a text analysis method; (2) scenarios determination using latent class clustering; and (3) simulation in a virtual environment. The whole process enables to transfer existing safety failures reflected in injuries into training points in a 3D virtual environment for users to practices. This chapter will also provide an example to demonstrate the approach using electrical fatality data from the U.S. construction industry. Mostly, the data and programs demonstrated in this chapter are selected from the author's previous works (Zhao and Lucas, 2014; Zhao et al., 2014b; Zhao et al., 2014c). Fig. 2 gives the framework of the demonstration case of electrical safety in the construction industry.

2. Real-world data collection

This section introduces a systems method to collect real-world accident cases and extract information for building the virtual program. Here, the author takes an example from the electrical safety in the construction industry to demonstrate the data collection process.

2.1. Factor background

As Figure 3 shows, the ideal solution for integrating construction safety innovation in electrical contracting (EC) needs to fit: 1) the technical and cultural nature of the industry in terms of innovation, 2) the needs of small construction firms and 3) the nature of hazards for ECs. This solution needs to be safer, affordable, accessible, participatory and context/task-specific while integrating technology innovations into practical routines to achieve higher effectiveness and better human habitus in construction. Also, this solution needs to respect human learning behavior and human cognitive rules. As a result, an innovative training approach such as the MVR appears to be a viable solution.

Relevant factors need to be distilled to represent the cases. A fishbone (or Ishikawa) diagram is a helpful tool to complete this step. Based on events and causal factors thinking, the fishbone diagram provides a systematic way of breaking down a complicated problem and identifying areas for data collection. Figure 4 illustrates fishbone diagram to generate factors which are used in the electrical safety example in the next section.

2.2. Data collection example

The example choose the data from U.S. electrocution investigation reports. These reports provide an historical perspective from 1989 to 2012. This period of time was also deemed appropriate, as it contains data during many of the years previously reported with alarming statistics on electrical incidents in US construction.

The fishbone mapping tool also provides an accessible process for distilling complex reporting structures into salient categories of data for study. As a result, (previously shown in Figure 4), 13 factors were categorized using five categories which included: when, who, where, what and how. Under each category, 13 related factors were created based on the information gathered from FACE reports as well as from extended literature reviews. Therefore, using these factors, information from narrative text can be coded into an information table (shown in Figure 5).

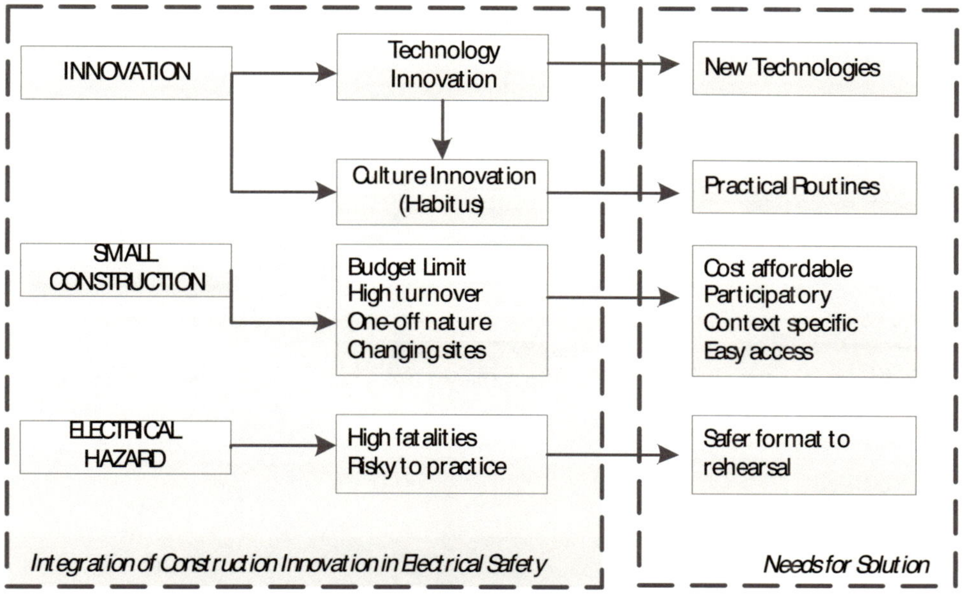

Figure 3. Needs for construction innovation in electrical safety

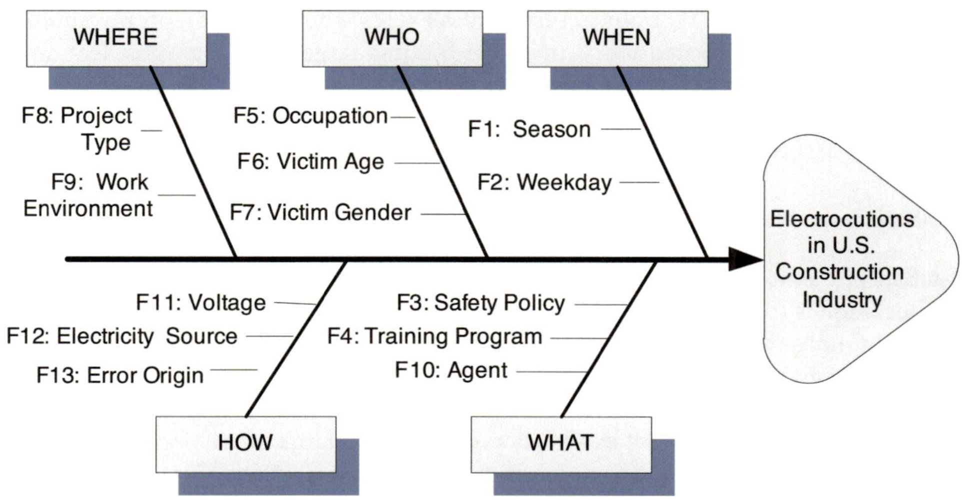

Figure 4. An example of fishbone diagram

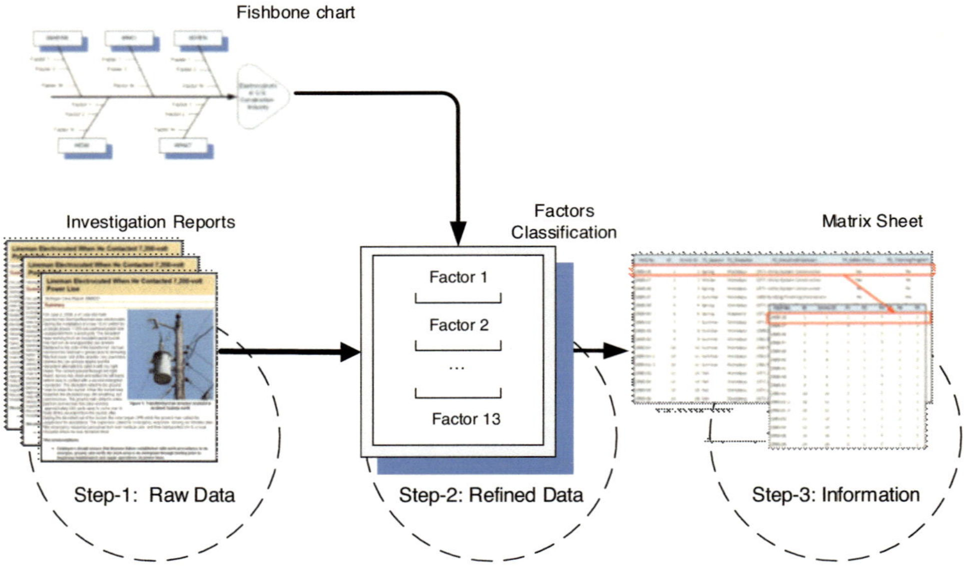

Figure 5. Coding process diagram

3. Scenarios identification

This section elaborates a statistical method to build the connection between real-world data and virtual elements. Typical elements in a scenario comprise characters, scenes and events. The characters, including the trainee, represent all roles who participate in the simulation. Here, characters can be created based upon the training target's demographic features. The scenes depict necessary circumstances such as time, place and properties, which are created in accordance with the factor values of a hazardous pattern. The events refer to all the training tasks, hazards associated with the tasks and the respective safety procedures.

3.1. Statistical analysis

The statistical method is the Latent class analysis (LCA). LCA has some merits over other similar techniques (de Oña et al., 2013): (1) being able to use different type of variables; (2) being able to choose different type of statistical criteria; and (3) being able to using subsequent membership probabilities with maximum likelihood method. Latent classes are unobservable subgroups or segments. Cases are homogeneous within the same latent class while distinctive from each other in different latent classes, depending on certain criteria (Vermunt, 2008). The latent class analysis is a technique to identify the smallest number of latent subgroups or clusters that are sufficient to explain all the associations among manifest variables in a sample group. As shown in Figure 6, a latent class is represented by *N* distinct categories/values of a nominal latent variable.

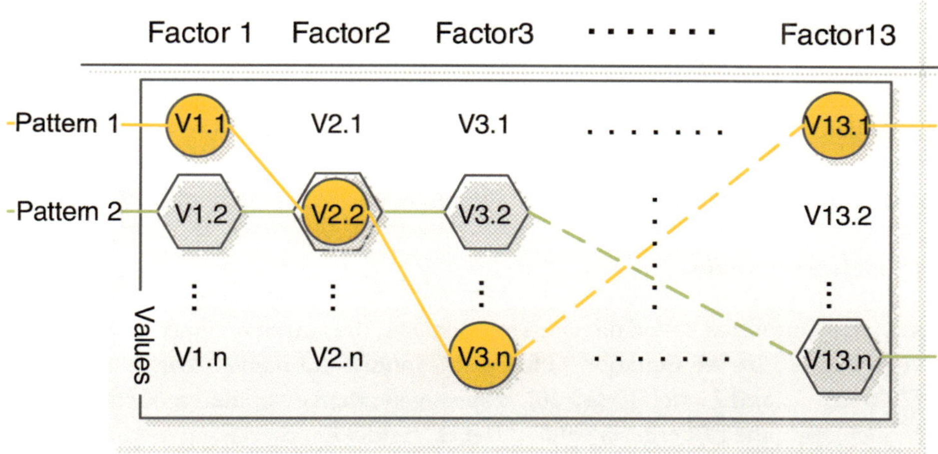

Figure 6. Coding process diagram

Recently, LCA is able to include mixed-scale-type variables and covariates, and thus has been adopted in a wide-range of research areas including accident analysis (Collins and Lanza, 2010; Depaire et al., 2008). Given X representing the latent variable with value Y, and suppose M be the LC number and N be the variable number. A particular LC is enumerated by the index x, $x=1, 2, \ldots, M$, with value set Y $(y_1, y_2, \ldots, y_n)$. The aim of LCA is to determine the vector notation Y, referring to a complete injury system pattern, by computing the conditional multivariate probabilities P $(Y=y)$, as:

$$P(Y=y)=\sum_{x=1}^{M}\left[P(X=x)\prod_{n=1}^{N}P(Y_n=y_n\mid X=x)\right] \tag{1}$$

where $P(X=x)$ denotes the proportion of injury cases belonging to LC x.

The most widely used LC fitting criterion is the likelihood ratio chi-squared statistic L^2. L^2 builds on the likelihood of the data under the null hypothesis relative to the maximum likelihood, as:

$$L^2=2\sum_{i=1}^{I}\left[C_i\times\ln\frac{C_i}{C\times P(Y=y_i)}\right] \tag{2}$$

where C denotes the total injury case size; C_i denotes the observed frequency of pattern i; $P(Y=y_i)$ denotes the probability of having the pattern i; and I denotes the total number of possible patterns in the N-dimensional frequency table, as:

$$I=\prod_{n=1}^{N} n \tag{3}$$

L^2 statistic is advanced on calculations especially for a large number of variables as it enables a decomposition of them into smaller components. Further, this work also incorporates other popular criteria to evaluate the LC model's goodness-of-fit for the sake of research reliability. They are the L^2 based Akaike's information criterion (AIC), the Bayesian information criterion (BIC), and the consistent AIC (CAIC). These statistical criteria measure LC's parsimony. A lower criteria value means a higher parsimony, which indicates a better model fitting. An LC model with a lower BIC value is preferred rather than one with a higher BIC value.

3.2. Data analysis example

After previously imported coded data into this analysis, the author assigned LC number from 1 to 10 (M=1, 2, …, 10, see Equation 1) to the LC model and named them model#1 (M=1), model#2 (M=2), …, and model#10 (M=10), respectively; then evaluated model#1 to model#2 through calculating their fit criteria values. The LC model fit criteria applied in this example included the likelihood ratio chi-squared statistic L^2, BIC(L^2), AIC(L^2) and CAIC(L^2), and usually a lower value of which indicated a better model fitting. The results of model fit evaluation are demonstrated in Figure 2, which indicates that the model#3 (3 LCs, M=3) has better performance (lower BIC, CAIC) than other models. In addition, model #3's *p-value* of 0.056 (good when greater than 0.05) and *Npar* value of 50 (the number of parameters) also indicate a good separation between latent classes.

According to the results, Model 3 with 3 segments provided LC-dependent univariate distributions for each variable, allowing each later class to represent a typical electrocution system pattern. The overall probabilities of falling into LC #1, LC #2, and LC #3 are 41%, 36%, and 23%, respectively. To identify the characteristics of each pattern, the researchers examined values' loadings for each LC. The loading indicates the degree of correlation between the variable values and the designated LC. In multivariate statistical analysis, some research (Stevens, 2002) preferred a cut-off of 0.4 for important loading while some other (Kline, 1994) suggested 0.3 as an acceptable threshold, irrespective of sample size. Here, this work chooses the loading of 0.37 or greater to determine a closer correlation between the variable value and the corresponding LC of model #3. In this way, the significantly related values to each of the three scenarios are identified, alphabetically listed as following three groups:

- **Scenario A**: younger (age<40) male non-electrical workers die due to indirectly contacting high-voltage power lines or powered machines/tools, usually in Summer or Winter at outdoor workplaces. The employers do not have written safety policies nor provide safety training programs. This pattern is particularly related to the residential building construction projects.

- **Scenario B**: middle-aged (age 40-64) male electrical workers die due to directly contacting high-voltage power lines or electrical components, usually in Spring, Fall or Winter weekends at outdoor workplaces. The employers have written safety policies and provide safety training programs. This pattern is particularly related to the heavy and civil construction projects.

- **Scenario C**: adolescent (age<20) male workers died due to directly contacting low-voltage electrical components or powered machines/tools at an indoor workplace. Whether the employer has written safety policies or provides safety training programs is uncertain. This pattern is particularly related to the non-residential building construction projects.

As a result, three scenarios are identified from real-world contexts. Three construction types are coincidently allocated into the three scenarios. It implies that Scenario A is highly correlated to the residential building construction projects; Scenario B is highly correlated to the heavy and civil engineering construction projects; and Scenario C is highly correlated to the non-residential building construction projects. The results can be interpreted in a tri-plot diagram (see Figure 7), showing each scenario's characteristics in a more visual manner. In the diagram, the three angels indicate the three scenarios while the distance between any two points reflects their relationship (the shorter, the closer).

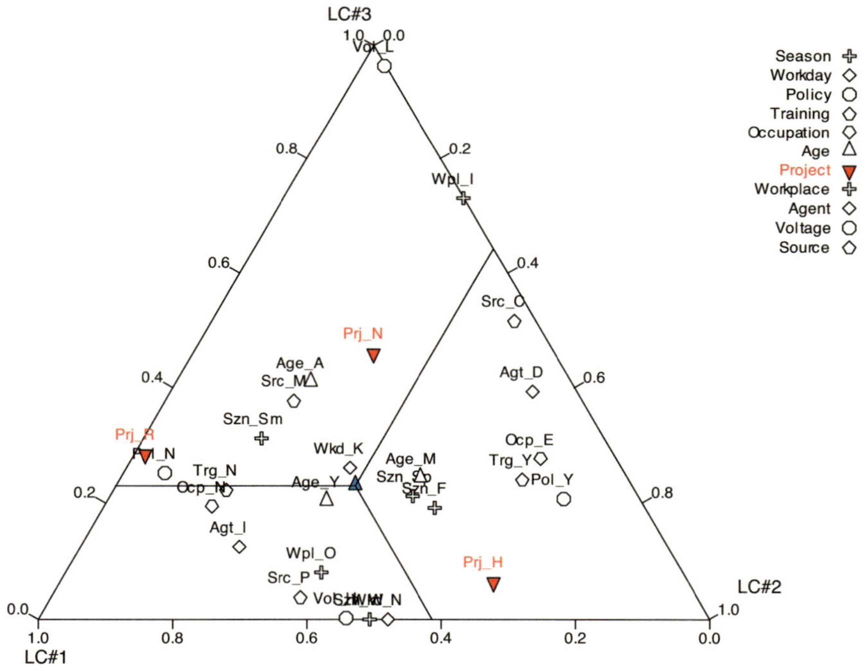

Figure 7. LC analysis triangle

4. Program development

This section introduces the program development using mobile virtual reality technology. The example for demonstration is the previously identified scenario B. Given the identification of typical workplace scenario, six training-critical points are created: the potential electrical hazardous awareness; the safe approach distance; the work condition clearance; the lockout and tag out; the suitable personal protective equipment (PPE); and the effective communication. These training points were required by OSHA regulations, National Fire Prevention Association codes (NFPA 70) and FACE report recommendations(Zhao et al., 2012). Based on the prototype simulation, a training point is linked to an event which consists of triggers and outcome animations. Taking the training point of work condition clearance for example, barriers such as waterlogging or storage boxes were added into the scenario. Users can only access the panel safely until they clear these barriers by touching them. If this training point is not completed, an electrical accident such as a shock may be triggered later and the outcome of an electrical shock will be represented via an animation (Zhao and Ye, 2012).

4.1. Design and modelling

The modeling process includes two separate parts: the 3D object modeling and 3D environment modeling. The 3D objects include buildings, machines, equipment, tools, materials, electrical components, background settings and worker actors. Most of these models were created using Autodesk's 3ds Max, such as a mobile crane and electricity transmission tower. 3D environment modeling includes designs of area terrain, sky clouds, sun point, wind, rain (if necessary), light layout, landscape as well as relative sounds. Prior complete 3D models are imported into the completed 3D working environment, the whole of which resulted in a training scenario. Each electrical hazard and its responding tasks were simulated as interactive events through coding scripts. Scenarios and events were linked by animations. The training scenarios, including 3D objects and 3D environments, and integrated training events are together comprised of a training Module. 3D characters and properties are modeled in Autodesk's 3ds Max. Scenes are designed and compiled in Torque 3D game engine. For mobility, the output is published as an Android application.

4.2. User interface design

The User Interface (UI) is designed to connect all previously developed 3D objects and the 3D environment, which can be customized for specific project. The function of UI is to display a distinct set of scenarios, which are further broken down into a series of tasks, such as:

- load the 3D environment and facility model to the user scene;
- receive user input of the 3D character with relevant behavior for the user control in the preset environment;
- load the scenarios, display 3D elements, and activate the storybook;
- track the activities that are performed during the scenario, and response timely.

4.3. Development example

The training content of this example demonstrates one of construction scenarios in which electrical accidents often occur. The designated scenario is based on the previously identified

http://dx.doi.org/10.5772/59227

scenario B: middle-aged male electrical workers die due to directly contacting high-voltage power lines or electrical components at an outdoor highway construction jobsite in September. The example scenario assumes energized indoor electrical components as the hazard. In the way, the storybook is compiled as:

- Character (or avatar): a young male electrician is modeled as the character;
- Time: Sunny day with the heavy sunshine and sun glares;
- Place: an unexposed highway construction surrounded with high-voltage distribution towers;
- Properties: comprise protective equipment, heavy machines like boomed cranes, road roller, and trucks.
- Task: lifting construction materials from truck to pave the road surface.

The prototype incorporated these features into one scenario which was a road construction site with overhead power lines surrounded The scenario development included two major aspects: environment modeling and storybook coding. The environment modeling simulates construction-related objects and characters while the storybook coding linked these objects and characters with hidden electrical hazards. The modeling and coding was completed using Autodesk 3DS max (see Figure 8) and Torque 3D package.

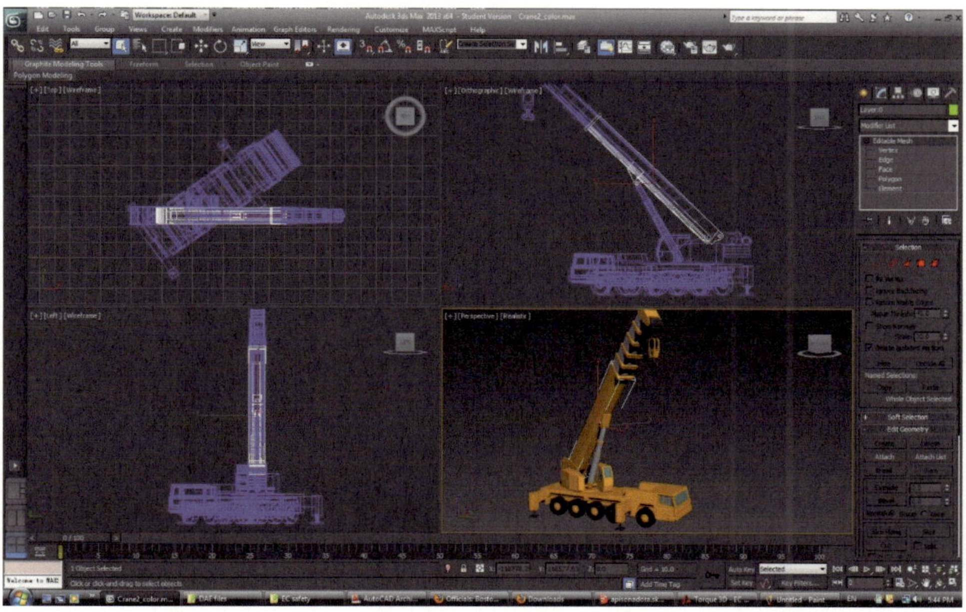

Figure 8. Elements Modelling

Simulation is processed on a module basis. Training elements are respectively simulated into virtual reality modules. Each module represents a major hazardous environment that could lead to electrocution. The working conditions, electrical hazards that workers are exposed to, and related work tasks are simulated in modules. The MVR simulations allow the users to recognize the hazards, identify them and intervene in a simulated virtual world. Trainees may participate in the safety working tasks, feel the hazards as well as its crucial outcome of failures (e.g., getting electrocuted), and hopefully transfer this experience to their real life working environment. Also, users are allowed to choose the specific module that is related to their daily work to get trained. This provides users the opportunities to choose which scenarios they would like to complete and allows them to be trained for designated working tasks or work environments.

Figure 9. User Interface Testing

The simulation storybook is presented through a thread of independent interactive events. These events are triggered by various approaches depending on the desired reaction. When the user walks through the scenario following instructions, a variety of hazard triggers will be touched and then the pre-programed reactions will be activated as responses. For examples, a touch approach is used to trigger the training event for safety emergency responses on "contact power line" when the user touches a power line. When the user goes close to the 10-feet distance line indicating the distance from the overhead power lines' upright projection allowed by safety regulations, the training element of "safe working distance and clearance" will be triggered and instructions will appear in the text panel explaining this safety regulation. These events are a mixture of animations and text used to present training contents to the user. All information expressing methods used in the scenario are aimed at increasing the learning efficiency and enhancing the training effectiveness. The learning efficiency and training effectiveness will be studied through evaluation processes in future research.

http://dx.doi.org/10.5772/59227

5. Merits of MVR

There are several ways to make learning more active and engaging. Training methods like on-the-job training, full scale training mock-ups, and the use of VR simulation offer more engagement. However, due to the dangerous characteristics of electricity, the on-the-job training and mock-ups can hardly allow trainees to fully rehearse electricity-related tasks, access all electrical hazards and experience possible consequences in real life. As a result, the effectiveness of these training methods might be limited. In contrast, a MVR-based training method is not constrained by these limits and instead can provide trainees full participatory experience without the safety risk from electricity.

MVR is advanced contributed to its adoptability. MVR technology provides a new perspective of safety training for dangerous hazards. A MVR-based training program has the ability to create a problem-based learning exercise in an environment that replicates the trainees' actual working environment (McAlpine and Stothard, 2003). It offers an interactive, active, and cognitive learning-by-doing experience for users (Stanney and Zyda, 2002) but without the concern for "real-world repercussions" (Eschenbrenner et al., 2008).

MVR is also advanced ascribed to the flexibility. MVR technology overcomes the training limitations on time and location and facilitates the mandatory and effective rehearsals in the virtual world. As a result, it will help establish the concepts of safety risk mitigation as habitus in workers' minds and place habitus into the context of real world practices.

Combing cloud technology, the safety training scenarios are used to be simulated in 3D interactions and on mobile devices, such as an iPad or a smartphone. The VR simulations allow the user to be exposed to the hazards within the simulated 3D environment so they can recognize those hazards, strengthen proper working memory and transfer the relative experiences into real life work or experience. Meanwhile, the cloud technology allows the user to access the training everywhere, and at any time, using any device (Chen et al., 2014). User data will be stored on remote servers and be automatically synchronized in real time with any authorized delivery devices. In this manner, users are no longer locked to a single device and do not have to transfer their data manually when switching devices.

Outside of the technology, MVR may contribute to the knowledge of safety management in terms of safety culture fostering. Literature suggests that unsafe procedures and violations by workers, such as forgetfulness, negligence and recklessness, are the primary causes leading to OSH injuries (Kletz, 2001). There is opportunity to reduce unsafe behaviors through appropriate and effective training, though, even if they cannot be eliminated completely. Goldenhar et al. (2001) highlighted that the most direct way to change statistics in human mistakes was through effective worker training. Neville (1998) suggested that effective training programs could help save large costs by preventing accidents. Effective training not only saves lives but also eliminates the extra indirect costs associated with accident investigations, insurance rates, equipment downtime and repair and productivity losses.

The MVR application may help to establish the safety culture transferring trainees' safe practices in a virtual world into their routines in real situations. In this perspective, culture is not considered a set of beliefs and values but the "whole way of life" which includes practices and routines(Zhao et al., 2014a) (Manseau and Shields, 2005). Bourdieu (2003) referred to this set of predispositions which guide improvisations in daily routines as the habitus or practical knowledge as repeated routines. One strength in understanding culture as habitus is that routines can be observed and documented, whereas values and beliefs must be inferred, making them less amenable to research. As a result, rather than formulating risk control as a break in habitus, it may prove more useful to conceive of OSH risk mitigation as a process. This process will allow people to show their own propensity toward adoption (decision-adoption process) in an appropriate way, especially when problems are encountered. Therefore, the habitus, a set of practical routines and dispositions towards certain ways of solving problems, is suggested as an innovative approach to the safety-culture-integrated OSH risk management. Combining risk mitigation as a continuous process of controls, rather than a group of static checkpoints of control, with a habitus-based process of safety training could not only mitigate OSH risk but also complement sustainable productivity and growth for the firm.

6. Conclusions

Workplace safety is paramount for all production sectors throughout the world. However, every year the number of occupational injuries attracts concerns on the safety management for every industry. Existing studies have endeavored great efforts on injury causations and found that more than half of workplace accidents are due to human errors. This chapter introduces an innovative safety management approach and the development process of such MVR-integrated application.

MVR is an adoption of virtual reality (VR) simulation on mobile/portable devices which are connected to cloud technology for end users. It allows safe simulation of real-life events in a digital environment that might otherwise be too dangerous or expensive to create (Haller et al., 1999). VR is described as a 3-dimensional world seen from a first-person view that is under real-time control of the user (Bowman et al., 2005). It also has the ability to create a problem-based learning exercise in an environment that replicates the trainee's actual working environment (McAlpine and Stothard, 2003). Training programs via VR offers an interactive, active, and cognitive learning experience for the user (Munro et al., 2002; Stanney and Zyda, 2002). As a result, they are often used in place of on-the-job training or full size simulation. Applied to the construction industry, MVR overcomes time and location barriers for workers and provides them more flexibility to access.

MVR also benefits trainees with a participatory training environment. Such participatory training brings a real life aspect into the training in an "it can happen to you" scenario and allows the trainees to relate conditions and regulations with real life situations and a life-or-death importance (Zhao et al., 2009). The best scenario is when people do not have to consciously think about following safety procedures because it is second nature to them (Trybus, 2008). Moreover, MVR provide trainees with the ability to experiment without concern for

http://dx.doi.org/10.5772/59227

"real-world repercussions" and the ability to "learn by doing." With a MVR program, the user controls the objects and couples this with information and later task-based testing, thus, an interactive and active-learning experience is created.

Most importantly, MVR simulation may contribute to building safety culture in terms of safe practical routines. Through this technology, training programs might allow construction workers to be familiar with common hazards, including dangerous electrical hazards, and to mock up relevant prevention practices without real injury repercussions. It may not only improve trainees' awareness of potential risks in a reality-based working environment, but also unconsciously influence routine behaviors as second nature, which will largely lead to the safety culture. Trainees are expected to be prepared for their future electrical tasks by rehearsing in a virtual environment. The goal of repeated rehearsal is not only to enhance trainees' professional skills but also, more importantly, to help build up their habitus for safe practices. Training goals are achieved when users complete the task repeatedly and with success. As a result, proper safety procedures and responses in the specific scenario are aimed to be enhanced and embedded in trainees' minds.

Author details

Dong Zhao*

Address all correspondence to: dongz@vt.edu

Department of Building Construction, Virginia Polytechnic Institute and State University, Blacksburg, VA, USA

References

[1] Kowalski KM, Vaught C. Principles of adult learning: Application for mine trainers US CDC: US Department of Health and Human Services; 2002:1-1

[2] Rooney JJ, Vanden Heuvel LN, Lorenzo DK, Stoecklein M, Christensen M. Reduce human error. Quality Progress. 2002;35(9):27-36.

[3] Setareh M, Bowman D, Kalita A. Development of a Virtual Reality Structural Analysis System. Journal of Architectural Engineering. 2005;11(4):156-64.

[4] Barrett M, Blackledge J, and Coyle E. Using Virtual Reality to Enhance Electrical Safety and Design in the Built Environment. ISAST Transactions on Computers and Intelligent Systems. 2011(3):1-9.

[5] Zhao D, Thabet W, McCoy A, Kleiner B. Electrical Deaths in the U.S. Construction: An Analysis of Fatality Investigations. International Journal of Injury Control and Safety Promotion. 2014;21(3):278-88.

[6] Zhao D, McCoy A, Kleiner B, Feng Y. Integrating Safety Culture into OSH Risk Mitigation: A Pilot Study on the Electrical Safety. Journal of Civil Engineering and Management. 2014:1-10.

[7] Zhao D, Lucas J. Virtual Reality Simulation for Construction Safety Promotion. International Journal of Injury Control and Safety Promotion. 2014:1-11.

[8] de Oña J, López G, Mujalli R, Calvo FJ. Analysis of traffic accidents on rural highways using Latent Class Clustering and Bayesian Networks. Accident Analysis & Prevention. 2013;51(0):1-10.

[9] Vermunt JK. Latent class and finite mixture models for multilevel data sets. Statistical Methods in Medical Research. 2008;17(1):33-51.

[10] Collins LM, Lanza ST. Latent Class and Latent Transition Analysis: With Applications in the Social, Behavioral, and Health Sciences: Wiley; 2010:1-330

[11] Depaire B, Wets G, Vanhoof K. Traffic accident segmentation by means of latent class clustering. Accident Analysis & Prevention. 2008;40(4):1257-66.

[12] Stevens JP. Applied Multivariate Statistics for the Social Sciences. 5th ed. New York, NY, USA: Routledge; 2002:1-699.

[13] Kline P. An Easy Guide to Factor Analysis: Routledge; 1994:1-194.

[14] Zhao D, Thabet W, McCoy A, Kleiner B. Managing electrocution hazards in the US construction industry using VR simulation and cloud technology. Ework and Ebusiness in Architecture, Engineering and Construction. 2012:759-64.

[15] Zhao D, Ye Y. Using virtual environments simulation to improve construction safety: An application of 3D online-game based training. Future Control and Automation. Lecture Notes in Electrical Engineering. 172 LNEE. VOL. 1 ed. Takamatsu, Japan: Springer Verlag; 2012: 269-77.

[16] McAlpine I, Stothard P, editors. Using multimedia technologies to support PBL for a course in 3D modeling for mining engineers. World Conference on Educational Multimedia, Hypermedia and Telecommunications 2003; 2003; Honolulu, Hawaii, USA: AACE: 2449-2455.

[17] Chen A., Golparvar-Fard M., Kleiner B., 2014. Saves: An Augmented Virtuality Strategy for Training Construction Hazard Recognition, Construction Research Congress 2014. ASCE:2345-2354.

[18] Eschenbrenner B, Nah FF-H, Siau K. 3-D Virtual Worlds in Education: Applications, Benefits, Issues, and Opportunities. Journal of Database Management. 2008;19(4): 91-110.

[19] Kletz TA. Learning from accidents. Oxford ; Boston: Gulf Professional Pub.; 2001:1-345

[20] Goldenhar LM, Moran SK, Colligan M. Health and safety training in a sample of open-shop construction companies. Journal of Safety Research. 2001;32(2):237-52.

[21] Neville H. Workplace accidents: they cost more than you might think. Industrial Management. 1998;40(1):7-9.

[22] Zhao D, Feng Y, Ye Y, Suh M. Integrating Safety Culture into OSH Risk Mitigation via Information Technologies. In: Xu J, Fry JA, Lev B, Hajiyev A, editors. Proceedings of the Seventh International Conference on Management Science and Engineering Management. Lecture Notes in Electrical Engineering. 241. Philadelphia, PA: Springer Berlin Heidelberg; 2014: 335-44.

[23] Manseau A, Shields R. Building Tomorrow: Innovation In Construction And Engineering. Burlington, VT: Ashgate; 2005:120-32.

[24] Bourdieu P. Outline of a Theory of Practice. New York, NY: Cambridge University Press; 2003:1-63.

[25] Haller M, Kurka G, Volkert J, Wagner R. omVR-A Safety Training System for a Virtual Refinery. ISMCR '99, Topical Workshop on Virtrual Reality and Advanced Human-Robot Systems; June 10-11; Tokyo, Japan1999: 24-8.

[26] Bowman DA, Kruijff E, Laviola JJ. 3D User Interfaces: Theory and Practice. Boston, MA: Pearson Education; 2005:6-7.

[27] Munro A, Breaux R, Patrey J, Sheldon B. Cognitive Aspects of Virtual Evironments Design. In: Stanney K, editor. Handbook of Virtual Environments: Design, Implementation, and Applications. Mahwah, NJ: Lawrence Erlbaum Associates; 2002: 415-34.

[28] Zhao D, Lucas J, Thabet W. Using Virtual Environments to Support Electrical Safety Awareness in Construction. Proceedings of the 2009 Winter Simulation Conference; Austin, TX: IEEE; 2009: 2679-90.

[29] Trybus J. Making Safety Second Nature: Using Simulation Tools to Practice Safety. Professional Safety. 2008;12(0):54-5.